On the Nature
of Things

On the Nature of Things

By

LUCRETIUS

*A new translation
by Charles E. Bennett*

Published for the Classics Club ® by

WALTER J. BLACK, INC. · ROSLYN, N. Y.

CONTENTS

FOREWORD

THE QUEST—never more desperate than now—for a way of life is the passion of all great poetry. Sometimes it is a conscious seeking, and men speak directly of what they seek, and of what, in their seeking, they have found. More often, in poetry, the quest is not a conscious one, being but imperfectly realized, and that after the fact; and the results are communicated indirectly, by image and story. But the passion is the same, and the results contribute to the same high end.

It would appear that the quest is more earnest and more passionate—more desperate—at some times than at others. The shock of circumstances hurls men into predicaments where they can no longer support their lives except they find a new way of thinking about life which can no longer be lived on the old terms. In such a predicament, men have behaved, historically, in two ways: they have sent their dreams into a Utopia, safe from the actualities which were crushing their bones within them; or they have looked these actualities in the eye, wrestled with them, nor would let them go till they were blest by them.

The historian of the future will see more clearly than ourselves how strongly the last three decades have been marked by this quest for a way of life. He will see, more clearly than we, that near the beginning of the present century we reached the end of our way. There was no going on in that way; the wreckage of a whole civilization was piled there. And much of the apparently unrelated phenomena of life and thought and art are the projected shapes of man's troubled need for a way of thinking about life.

Of the two possible responses to this predicament, we chose the more honest and the more painful. We did so, even with some ostentation, scorning in a curiously bitter literature the narcotics of Utopia—and with a vehemence that testified to the sweetness of the temptation and the acrid sourness of the fruits we chose to eat, instead.

I will not labor the point, but clearly here is a moment in man's tragedy and a mode of thought shaped for the cyclic return of the *De Rerum Natura*. It is customary to speak of the modernity of Lucretius' conceptions in natural science, his anticipation of the atomic theory, the nebular hypothesis, the chemical cycle of birth, death, and birth. And this is interesting, by the way. But the dynamic —I had almost said religious—reality for us today is the need that pressed upon his mind, the attitude which that mind assumed in consequence, and the character, rather than the results, of its procedure. As in our own situation, he was under the necessity of separating reality from chimaera; his temper, like our own, was to handle hard facts with bare hands; as with us, he found false domes and spires across his path, to be moved only with great labor and at some cost of reviling from the superstitious and the crafty. And, beyond all, like ourselves, he wanted to know.

This attitude and character and procedure define him as a large projection of our own mind moving toward us

from what we had supposed were the serenities of antiq-
uity. Men were troubled then, as now—very curiously like
as now. However it was with other men, Lucretius re-
sponded much as we should have done—much as we are
doing. He comes to us in this new translation by Pro-
fessor Bennett with a large understanding of our predicament and an ancient and heartening authentication of our
response to that predicament, in attitude and temper and
procedure. He should be very welcome in our house; and
his voice, with its curious and curiously sweet mingling
of science and sensibility, will be very like our own voice
speaking.

DAVID MORTON

INTRODUCTION

To ESCAPE the confines of blind tradition and of igno rance has ever been the goal of thoughtful men. Along the road toward the complete emancipation of the human mind the achievement of Titus Lucretius Carus stands as a landmark for all time. From a world in which fear and superstition were rampant, Lucretius emerges in his *De Rerum Natura* as an apostle of freedom—the freedom to be realized by substituting the light of an intelligent understanding of the world and its meaning for the darkness of fear and doubt. The message of intellectual freedom which is the inspiration behind the work of Lucretius takes second place only to the manner in which that message is presented. The powers of the philosopher are enhanced by the genius of the poet; the product of their combined skill is indeed magnificent.

De Rerum Natura is an exposition, in immortal verse, of a Greek system of philosophy applied specifically and practically to the Roman world of the first century before Christ. To appreciate fully the significance of the poem, it may be well to consider briefly the man whose work it is and the setting in which it was written.

Any account of the life of Lucretius must be based very largely upon conjecture and upon conclusions derived from the reading of his work. The almost complete absence of contemporary biographical information about the poet or commentary on his work may be ascribed to the fact that both the literary and the scientific achievements of Lucretius were generally either disregarded or discredited by the Roman world of the later Republic and the Empire. A single brief statement—cryptic, incoherent, and entirely unsatisfactory—included in the works of St. Jerome, and based on a lost work of Suetonius, written two centuries after the death of Lucretius, tells us that Lucretius lived during the period from 95 to 52 B. C., that he was driven mad as a consequence of a love philter, that his great work was accomplished in the lucid intervals of insanity, that he ended his own life, and, finally, that his work was "emended" by Cicero. Every point in this one brief narrative has with good reason been open to question, particularly in view of the fact that its author was guilty in other instances of careless inaccuracy in the use of his sources. In treating the life of Lucretius, moreover, it is natural that St. Jerome should feel the antagonism of a churchman for an iconoclast who seemingly denied all religion.

From evidence provided by the poet himself in *De Rerum Natura* and from the absence of contradictory information we may logically infer that Lucretius was of urban Roman origin. That he belonged to a family of the aristocracy seems apparent from the tone of his dedication of his work to Memmius, a Senatorian, probably unworthy in character and temperament of the tribute paid him by the poet. There is reason to assume, further, that his life dates should be given as 99 (or 98) B. C. to 55 B. C., rather than the dates mentioned by Jerome. In a life of Vergil by Donatus, based as is Jerome's work on the lost

work of Suetonius, we are told that Lucretius' death—and
there is no indication here that it was self-inflicted—occurred on the same day on which the younger poet
reached manhood, that is, on Vergil's seventeenth birthday, which would fix that date as 55 B. C. For the stories of
insanity and suicide there is no substantial evidence, unless we adopt the view that insanity may be only an intensification of the sort of genius and mental preoccupa-
tion which concerns itself vividly and imaginatively with
the workings of the universe, and consider the obviously
unfinished condition of the poem as sufficient basis for the
theory of a sudden conclusion to the poet's life.

Whatever may have been the factual details of the life
of the man, they could in no way diminish the value of
his work, and have little real significance. From the nature
of the work itself certain conclusions may be drawn concerning the character of the author. Only a man whose
life, in its later years, at least, was devoted in large measure
to contemplation and to observation of nature could have
produced the thoughtful and pertinent illustrative passages which are perhaps the greatest charm of *De Rerum
Natura;* only a true scholar would be familiar with the
variety of ancient philosophical concepts which Lucretius
expounds or refutes in developing his own argument, and
with the works of the many writers, both Greek and
Roman, whose influence is clear in the materials and in the
mode of expression of Lucretius; yet only a man of broad
understanding could exhibit the kindly sympathy for
humanity which is revealed throughout Lucretius' poem.

De Rerum Natura was known throughout the period of
the Roman Empire and the Middle Ages, but, because of

its challenge to the tenets of the established religion, first pagan, then Christian, the poem was held in scorn by the contemporaries of Lucretius and by the Church Fathers who dominated the thought of the early centuries of the Christian era. It was only when the theology of the schoolmen began to yield to scientific inquiry during the Renaissance that the Epicurean philosophy of Lucretius came into its own and through its influence on the studies of seventeenth century science took its place in the history of thought.

Although it expounds a Greek system of philosophy, *De Rerum Natura* is thoroughly Roman in its tone and in its import. The indomitable energy of the Roman of the best period of the Republic, his reverence for law, his passion for order, his power of impressing his authority on the minds of men—all are there in large measure. And yet those same qualities and that same message have a timelessness and a universality that are the stuff of greatness. The Roman note on which the poem is keyed is introduced at the very beginning in the invocation of the goddess Venus. While it might seem at first to be inconsistent with Lucretius' flat denial of the efficacy of divine power in the world, this invocation may be logically interpreted as a poetic device to symbolize the world of nature which is Lucretius' subject and to establish its relation to the immediate world of his audience.

In view, then, of the essentially Roman character of the poem, we must conclude that its author, despite his apparent philosophic detachment, was in a very real sense a product of his age. Lucretius, to be sure, makes few definite allusions to the events and conditions of his day, and he makes no pretense of extolling Rome's greatness, past or present. But the circumstances which inspired him to undertake the work were inherent in the disturbed condition of the period, and in the background of the poem is a succession of pictures of a society demoralized by greed and ambition, by knavery and love of pleasure. The times of Lucretius were times of war and civil strife, of conspiracy and massacre. While Caesar and Pompey were making their imperial conquests abroad the republican system at home was breaking down. The government was characterized by corruption and venality, by the inefficiency and injustice of the ruling classes, and the consequent intensification of discontent and party strife.

Lucretius shows little direct concern with the political causes and evidences of Rome's decay, and never commits himself to a consistent philosophy of affairs of state. Torn between an instinctive sympathy for the ills of the downtrodden and the ties and responsibilities of his own social and intellectual position, Lucretius found his wisest, or easiest course in avoiding political controversy. In the rottenness and superficiality of the state religion, however, Lucretius saw the chief evidence of the disintegration of Roman society, and of the source of most human ills. On that subject he did not hesitate to express himself in very definite terms.

Belief in the gods was, to be sure, general and in its way genuine among all classes at Rome, but it was a belief permeated by superstition and fear, a fact of which advantage was frequently taken by priests and soothsayers who assumed the right to meddle in every phase of the affairs of men. Acceptance of the principle of divine interference resulted in unreasoning reliance upon the practice of divination to insure favorable omens for public and private undertakings. It had, further, the result of rendering any scientific approach to the study of natural phenomena quite impossible, since any seeming abnormality of nature—a thunderstorm, an earthquake, a volcanic eruption—was regarded as evidence of the wrath of invisible powers somehow offended by men. Again, the religion of Rome, as practiced in Lucretius' time, led men to live in lifelong fear of eternal torment after death, brought about by some offense, perhaps trivial and perhaps unknowingly committed, against the whims of the inscrutable gods. The emancipation of men's minds from these two fears—the fear of the arbitrary interference of gods in the affairs of men, and the fear of death—was the mission which Lucretius sought to accomplish.

In the philosophy of the Greek, Epicurus, Lucretius found refuge from the disquieting conditions of his time, and, far more significantly, a comprehensive answer with which to counter the arguments of the supporters of the Roman religious system. Epicureanism, as we find it in Lucretius, is Epicureanism at its best. It is not the hedonistic philosophy which many of the poet's contemporaries adopted as a cloak for sensualism and self-indulgence, but rather a philosophic peace of mind, free from pain and trouble. Because freedom from demoralizing fear is essential to the achievement of such mental poise, Lucretius' primary purpose, taken directly from the teachings of Epicurus, is the undermining of the superstitious concepts of the religion he knew and the supplanting of them with a semi-scientific explanation of the creation and functioning of the universe. If men could understand that natural phenomena could be explained by natural laws, there would be no need to rely on superstitious explanations.

Epicurean science is not primarily a probing search for absolute truth, but rather the most effective means conceivable for releasing men from the grip of fear of the consequences, either immediate or final, of giving offense to the deities who govern the world. Thus the Epicureans developed a theory of natural laws to explain all questions of existence and hence to remove all necessity for belief in the interfering action of the traditional gods. Epicureanism, as Lucretius presents it, has also its ethical side, following logically upon its scientific teachings; for it advocates along with peace of mind, and as a prerequisite for achieving it, a simple life, free of excesses of all kinds and of political entanglements, which Lucretius ascribes ultimately to the fear of death and of eternal punishment.

Lucretius' poem contains the best exposition we have of the philosophic system of Epicurus, whose own writings are preserved only in fragmentary form and show carelessness and lack of skill in composition. In so far as it is possible to determine, Lucretius follows closely the teachings of Epicurus, making few, if any, original additions to the system itself. But in leaving for posterity a systematic and comprehensive record of Epicureanism, Lucretius made a distinct and positive contribution to the development of that philosophy.

As he wrote *De Rerum Natura* Lucretius kept always in mind his purpose of freeing men's minds from the bonds of superstition, and it is from that point of view that the entire scientific system is presented. That he hoped to achieve renown because of the importance of his subject and for the artistic merit of his verse he makes clear in his introduction, but in the mind of the poet both subject and verse seem to be subordinated to the task to which he dedicates himself.

At the core of the Epicurean philosophy of nature is a theory of atoms, which in its main features the Epicureans borrowed from Democritus. According to the tenets of this atomic philosophy, nothing has ever been created from nothing by divine power, nor can matter ever be completely annihilated. Proof enough to satisfy Lucretius as to the truth of this hypothesis is to be found in the order and regularity apparent everywhere in the world of nature. All existing things are made up of tiny atoms, infinite in number, indestructible and indivisible, though themselves composed of parts, moving about in infinite space and causing constant change and renewal of life. The atoms fall into a large—but finite—number of classes according to size, shape, and texture. Some are smooth and round, others jagged or hooked, and it is these physical differences among the atoms, as well as the varying proportions of atomic matter to space in created bodies, which are responsible for all variety in nature. The atoms, in their uncompounded state, are impelled straight downward, presumably by their own weight, in an eternal parallel motion, at a constant and rapid rate, which does not, as Lucretius rightly concluded, vary with their respective weights. From this downward motion, at uncertain intervals and apparently without reason, individual atoms deviate slightly, thus coming into sudden contact with other atoms. The impact of their collision sends the atoms rebounding in different directions, bringing them to meet still other atoms. When like or harmonious atoms finally come together, by some inexplicable process, they combine with one another, still in motion, to form material substance. It is the causation of the first slight swerve of the atoms which Lucretius fails to explain and which presents the most perplexing difficulty in following his reasoning.

With the atomic swerve as a hypothesis it is a relatively simple matter for Lucretius to develop a logical explanation of the creation of the world, its elements and its creatures, and of the ever-evolving new worlds which he assumed to be coming into existence and which he believed to be inhabited. Thus earth, air, and ether were formed, followed by the sea, the stars, the sun and the moon, and the walls of the world. Once these parts of the universe were formed, life appeared on the earth, likewise by a process of atomic combination. Recognizing something approaching the Darwinian theories of evolution and of the survival of the fittest, Lucretius tells of the existence of monstrous creatures which lived relatively early in the span of earth's history and which eventually proved to be unsuited to their changing environment and consequently disappeared. The poet pictures all living creatures, including mankind, as springing originally from the earth, which by his own time he believed to have grown old and to have passed her age of greatest fertility.

Since Lucretius assumes that the atoms are indestructible and indivisible—and it is only the scientists of our own generation who have disproved his assumption—it is clear to him that the sum of things, regardless of change and the transformation of one thing into another, remains constant. New things come into existence only with the disappearance of other things. The physical world, created by intricate and numberless combinations of atoms which are themselves indestructible, is yet a world of change, and is subject to ultimate disintegration. Evidences of decay and regeneration are to be seen everywhere and are represented by Lucretius as being the result of violently opposing motions. Only so long as a balance of the two forces, constructive and destructive, can be maintained, can the world continue to exist in its present form.

Natural causes, according to Lucretius, explain not only the origin of the world and of the life therein, but also the apparently abnormal phenomena which Roman religion attributed to the agency of incensed deities. That the world is completely governed by definite physical laws Lucretius sets forth with a profusion of vivid illustrations in the final book of the poem.

An interesting corollary to the Epicurean atomic philosophy is the theory of images, by which the poet explains sense perception—to him the source of all truth. According to this theory films of matter are constantly flying off from the surface of all bodies, and these films, composed of atoms, form a succession of images which cause sight, hearing, taste, or smell. The kind of feeling, pleasurable or distasteful, produced by a particular series of images is determined by the shape—smooth or rough—of the atoms composing it. Images, or combinations of images, finer than those perceptible to the eye and not necessarily emanating from actual physical objects may enter directly into the mind in the form of abstract thought, or, in sleep, as visions.

Along with his description of the physical world, Lucretius explains the nature of man and the development of his civilization. Man, like everything else in the world, is fashioned of lifeless atoms, differing from those which compose other types of matter only in being specially fine, specially shaped, and combined in special manner with one another. Man's life is dependent on the continued movement of his component atoms, and it ceases when that motion stops. The soul of man, like his body, is atomic in composition, being formed of the finest and smoothest of all atoms. Like the body it perishes with the cessation of appropriate atomic motion, as Lucretius goes to great lengths to attempt to prove in what are perhaps some of the least reasonable of his arguments. If, therefore, Lucretius reasons, the soul, as well as the body, is physical and mortal, there can be no conscious existence after death, and the fear of death, for the true disciple of Epicurus, is both groundless and foolish.

Although man's life is governed by atomic motion—for it is atomic motion in men which produces sensations of pleasure and pain, an orderly motion producing feelings of pleasure, while irregular or disorderly motion produces pain or displeasure—nevertheless, each man is endowed with an individual nature which allows him freedom of choice in his actions and makes him responsible for them. This notion of free will is an important part of Lucretius' philosophy, and according to the poet's reasoning follows logically upon the free will which he apparently attributes to the individual atoms, as they depart from their straight downward course eventually to unite with other atoms. It is the introduction of the concept of free will into his argument that makes Lucretius a moral teacher and leads him to advocate the deliberate conquest of fear, ambition, passion, love of luxury, and other human weaknesses as the only possible course toward achievement of the Epicurean ideal of happiness.

As a proponent of the atomic theory, Lucretius is far from being a true man of science as we think of the scientist today. In some respects he is little more than an eloquent mouthpiece for his predecessors Democritus and Epicurus. The atomic theory was to him, as has already been pointed out, primarily a tool rather than a final scientific truth, and his illustrations and arguments inevitably reveal inaccuracies and inconsistencies. But Lucretius is not without merit as a scientist. Surely it is to his credit that, in a day when the scientific aspects of the philosophy of Epicurus enjoyed small credence among the keenest of intellectual spirits, Lucretius had the perspicacity to seize upon an explanation of the composition and continued operation of the universe which has never been completely discarded, and which, upon its final acceptance centuries after the poet's death, became the hypothesis upon which modern theories of the physical world are based.

Lucretius was familiar with numerous other theories of cosmogony, for he devotes a considerable amount of space to refuting them in detail. Although Lucretius' method is not consistently the way of scientific inductive reasoning, nevertheless his logic is generally reasonable. His keen observation. his minute examination of natural phenomena, the aptness and validity of most of the examples of natural processes which he uses to prove the various steps in his argument, and finally, his insistence upon the universal operation of natural laws, all exhibit a temper of mind suggestive of scientific research, a quality which has been happily called his "scientific imagination." Certain it is that Lucretius' reasoning is far more to be esteemed for its anticipation of modern science than it is to be discredited for its fallacies.

Although Lucretius aims above all to erase the superstitious fear among his countrymen which he ascribed directly to the Roman concept of divine agency in the world, in the final analysis he does not deny the existence of the gods. He is attacking, essentially, not religion itself, or the spirit of reverence in its highest sense, but rather the superstitious aspects and abuses of the particular form of religion with which he was most familiar. The gods, according to the argument of *De Rerum Natura*, do exist. They are represented as immortal beings, of human form, living in a peaceful realm somewhere in the space between worlds, far removed from the distressing concerns of the world of mortal beings. Because the fixed laws of nature govern every sphere of existence, the gods have no need or opportunity to participate actively in the affairs of the universe. Instead they enjoy a life of calm and untroubled serenity which is perhaps an idealization of the Epicurean concept of philosophic happiness, deriving from freedom from care and danger. These immortal beings do exercise a certain indirect influence on men, however, for they give off images which enter men's souls, and may, in the case of minds which are intelligently free of superstitious fear, contribute to the realization of man's highest nature.

Despite his rejection of the idea of divine intervention in the affairs of the world, or perhaps, more accurately, in keeping with this iconoclasm, many readers have found in Lucretius an element of reverence in his poetic feeling for the operation of natural law, which might possibly be carried into a realm transcending human understanding and approaching a pantheistic concept. In explaining the manner whereby man may realize the Epicurean ideal of happiness, moreover, Lucretius keeps always before us a mode of existence which is in harmony with many of the tenets of religious faiths of all time. While he denies again and again the operation of a supernatural government of the universe and makes no appeal to a divine guiding power, Lucretius prescribes a code of behavior which shuns the vices prevalent in the Roman society—even the Epicurean society—of his day, and which in its moral principles bears the stamp of a religious faith.

Thus Lucretius is a moralist and a reformer as well as a scientist. And yet always he is a poet. His most outstanding gift from the modern reader's point of view is the almost incredible genius with which he gives expression that is genuinely poetic to a difficult and essentially prosaic subject. Even in some of the most abstruse of his scientific arguments and speculations, as well as in his feeling for the colossal grandeur of his subject, he shows a sense of beauty which he incorporates into verse that is at once lucidly factual and vividly imaginative.

That there should occur in a metrical exposition of complex and controversial material occasional instances of monotonous language and roughness and infelicity of phrasing, is hardly to be wondered at. The difficulties of accurately rendering science and ethics into poetry proved sometimes all but insurmountable for Lucretius, and when he found himself confronted with the necessity of choice between exactness of statement and effective poetic expression he generally chose to sacrifice the latter. The hexameter of Lucretius, while perhaps not keeping to the sustained heights upon which is carried the verse of Vergil—who frequently, in material and in phrasing, imitated Lucretius—nevertheless is consistently characterized by intensity and strength. It is in his numerous illustrative passages that Lucretius reveals most strikingly his true poetic genius. Here he skillfully interweaves science with poetry, showing himself a keen observer of nature, and an artist inspired with a pervading sensitivity to all forms of natural beauty.

It is probable that Lucretius would have smoothed out many of the crudities of expression in his verses had he been able to complete the revision of his work. Evidence that the poem was never really finished is to be found in a comparison of the final books with the first three, as well as in the abruptness with which the poem breaks off in the description of the plague at Athens. In the last books there are numerous instances of repetition, and passages in which the arrangement of material seems careless and illogical. The assumption is, therefore, that the poet's life was suddenly terminated before he had an opportunity to put the finishing touches on his work, and that it was published, after his death, in substantially the same condition in which he left it.

Lucretius' threefold claim to greatness, as a scientist, as a reformer, and as a poet, has been vindicated by the years. By applying the best in Epicureanism—a philosophy that came from another land and another time—to the spiritual and moral problems of his own people, Lucretius offered a practical program which, had its worth been recognized and accepted, might have contributed largely toward the furtherance of a loftier intellectual and ethical level at Rome. But this fact alone does not account for the timeless significance of *De Rerum Natura*. The three facets of his genius are, like the parts of one of his Epicurean atoms, inseparable one from the other. Only in their combination, in the incorporation of his message of freedom into verse of magnificent power and transcendent beauty, do the elements of the poet's genius together reach their greatest heights.

CHARLES E. BENNETT

Amherst, Massachusetts,
July, 1945.

TRANSLATOR'S PREFACE

THIS new translation of the *De Rerum Natura* of Lucretius is a by-product of more than a quarter of a century
of close association with the master-mind of Rome. The
present translator has long been aware of the need of an
English version of Lucretius which should not only re-
create in some measure the spirit and tone of the original,
but might have a certain independent value of its own as
literature. These combined aims, he feels, have not yet
been adequately achieved by any English version.

In the choice of verse as a medium for rendering verse,
the translator indorses whole-heartedly the sound position taken by William Ellery Leonard in the preface to his
metrical translation. Only by a subtle interweaving of
words and music can any version in an alien tongue hope
to approach the majesty and dignity of the Lucretian
hexameters. The translator has endeavored to keep constantly in mind the onward march of the poem as a whole.
Hence in many instances he has been less interested in
the rendering of the precise word or phrase than in at-
tempting to capture the spirit of the original. This has
involved, at times, a certain amount of expansion, which
seems justifiable in view of the larger aim. In the interest
of continuity and readability, the translator has not hesi-
tated to incorporate certain interpolated verses and
emendations proposed by competent commentators. In-

deed, in one or two instances, he has had the temerity to suggest emendations and interpolations of his own. In all such cases reference to the alterations has been made in the notes at the end of the volume. In the attempt to reproduce in so far as possible the slightly archaic diction of Lucretius, the translator has consistently employed language of a mildly archaic flavor. It would have been vastly easier to combine the use of "thee" and "thou" with "you," or third person singulars in –s with the Biblical third person forms in –th. This, the translator believes, would not be honest workmanship, and he has steadfastly resisted the temptation.

The text used is that of Bailey's Oxford edition. To the comparatively few instances in which departures have been made from this text attention has been called in the notes. The summaries of the individual books are from the Italian edition of Giussani, with slight changes and additions. The numbering of the verses follows Bailey's text.

The translator wishes to express his deep gratitude to David Morton, of Amherst College, whose encouragement and advice have been of inestimable value, and to Dr. Gerald F. Else, formerly of Harvard University, and Miss Marjorie Bennett, who have read the manuscript and contributed many thoughtful suggestions for its improvement.   C. E. B.

BOOK ONE

Proemium—Invocation to Venus, 1-145.

The nature of things in general, 146-634.
General principles concerning the existence of things,
146-482.
a) Substance is eternal: i.e. there exist eternal first
bodies or elements of things, 146-328; since nothing
is produced from nothing, 146-214; and nothing is
resolved into nothing, 215-264. The invisibility of
first bodies does not disprove their existence, 265-
328.
b) Void also exists, not only as space occupied by
bodies, but also as unoccupied space, 329-417.
c) Nothing has existence by itself except body and
void; all else is only accidents of that which has
independent existence, 418-482.
The first bodies are absolutely solid, indestructible, invisible, 483-634.

Refutation of Heraclitus, 635-704; of Empedocles, 705-829;
of Anaxagoras, 830-920.
Conclusion: The Universe is infinite in extent, 921-1117.

BOOK ONE

Thou Mother of our Roman race,[1] delight
Of men and gods, Venus, giver of life,
Who neath the wandering stars of heaven dost make
To teem the sail-filled sea, the bounteous earth;
To thee doth owe its birth each several tribe
Of living things that look upon the sun.
Thou, goddess, at thy coming, turn'st to flight
The winds, the clouds of heaven; for thee doth Earth,
The ancient fashioner, put forth her blooms
In sweet perfume; before thee Ocean's plains
Break forth in smiles; the sky, its anger past,
Gleameth with far-spread light. For soon as e'er
Doth stand revealed thy springtime's radiant face,
And loosed from out his bonds the freshening breeze
Of fruitful west wind bloweth free and strong,
Then first the birds of heaven herald thee
And thine approach, O Power divine, their hearts
Thrilled at thy touch; the while the stolid kine,
Wild with thy call, bound o'er the fertile plains
And swim the swollen streams; for each doth own
Thy mastery, and followeth with desire
Where'er thou goest before to lead him on.

1 Venus, Roman goddess of love and beauty, was the reputed ancestress
of the Roman race, through Anchises, father of Aeneas, the hero of
Vergil's *Aeneid*.

Thus thou dost pass, o'er seas and mountain heights,
Through ravening streams, amid the leafy haunts
Of birds, and o'er the newly greening plains,
And smiting every heart with fond desire
All breeds of living things constrain'st to yearn,
Each in his kind, their races to renew.
Since thou alone the universe dost guide,
Nor without thee doth aught to light arise
Or glad or lovely, thee I seek to be
The patron of these verses, which I strive
To build on nature's wide and wondrous works
As homage to our son of Memmius,[2]
Whom thou, O goddess, hast desired to shine
Through all his life, adorned with every grace.
Wherefore the more, divine one, lend thou charm
Eternal to my words, and grant the while
That war's wild works o'er every land and sea
May rest a little space; for thou alone
With tranquil peace canst soothe our mortal hearts.
For Mars,[3] high Lord of Hosts, whose might doth guide
The grim array of war, doth ofttimes fling
His wearied limbs upon thy lap, his mind
O'ermastered by the age-old wound of love;
And lying thus, with shapely neck thrown back

---

[2] Memmius: a Roman statesman of much disputed character, bitter political enemy of Julius Caesar. He was governor of Bithynia, in Asia Minor, in 59 B.C.

[3] Venus, as the goddess of love, is appealed to by the poet to exercise her charms on Mars, Roman god of war. It is quite probable that Lucretius has in mind some sculptured group, extant in his time, of the two figures. One is reminded of the painting "Venus and Mars" by Botticelli in the National Gallery in London.

To gaze upon thy face, his hungry eyes
With love he feedeth, while his very breath
Doth hang on thine. So, bending o'er him now
Thy holy body as he lieth, let fall
From thy sweet lips soft honey'd words, to crave—
For thou art great—the gentle boon of peace
For all our Romans; since mid war's alarms
We cannot hold our task with mind serene,
Nor can the noble son of Memmius
At such a crisis fail the common weal.[4]
Then for the rest, lend thou to Truth's appeal
A listening ear, a mind removed from care,
Lest thou shouldst leave in scorn, while still unknown,
My gifts, with faithful zeal before thee spread.
For I shall sing of heaven's high laws, of ways
Of gods, and of those primal elements
Wherefrom doth nature all things generate,
And bring them growth and increase, and whereto
Once more she doth resolve them at their death.
These elements,[5] in rendering our account,
It is our wont to note as matter, or
As generative germs of things, or else
The seeds of things, or yet again to name

ᴀᴠᴠᴠᴠᴠᴠᴠᴠᴠᴠᴠᴠᴠᴠᴠᴠᴠᴠᴠᴠᴠᴠᴠᴠᴠᴠᴠᴠᴠᴠᴠᴠᴠ

[4] There is a break here in the Latin text. When the discourse is resumed,
Lucretius is no longer addressing Venus, but his friend Memmius.
[5] Lucretius does not include here all his synonyms for the "primordial
bodies". In this text they will be variously described as matter, first bodies,
seeds or germs of things, first beginnings, primordial or primal bodies,
first principles, elements, or primal particles, all of which may be taken
to be equivalent to our "atoms". It is to be noted, however, that Lucretius never uses the word "atoms".

Primordial bodies, since 'tis these wherefrom
All things at first their birth and being take.

  When human life lay prone before men's eyes
Crusht down to earth beneath the heavy weight
Of superstition, which from heaven's own realms
Displayed her head, towering with aspect dire
O'er mortal destinies, a man of Greece [6]
First dared to lift to her his mortal eyes,
And first to stand against her. Such was he,
Whom neither fame nor fire of gods could daunt,
Nor heaven itself with threatening thunder roll
Could e'er dismay, but only roused the more
The eager courage of his daring soul
To be the first to break the close-drawn bars
Of nature's portals. So the fiery force
That urged his soul prevailed, and far beyond
The flaming barriers of the firmament
He fared, and in the far reach of his mind
Explored the vast immeasurable unknown,
Whence back to us triumphant doth he bring
The tale of what can, what can not arise,
How each thing's power is limited, and how
For each is marked its deep-set boundary.
So now in turn religion groveleth, crusht
Beneath our feet, and we once more are raised
To heaven's own stature by his victory.

∿∿∿∿∿∿∿∿∿∿∿∿∿∿∿∿∿∿∿∿∿∿∿∿∿

[6] Epicurus, famous Greek philosopher and the acknowledged master of Lucretius, was the founder of the Epicurean system of philosophy, which Lucretius adopts, and sets forth in his poem. It will be noted that Lucretius frequently pauses in his discourse to pay eloquent tribute to Epicurus.

Hereat I have this fear, lest thou mayst deem
My reasoning may lead thee to embrace
An impious philosophy, and set
Thy feet upon the road to sin. But no!
Religion's self, I ween, hath oftener proved
The mother of foul crime and impious deeds.
E'en as at Aulis, once in days of old,
Those chiefs of Greece, the foremost among men,
Did stain with Iphianassa's virgin blood [7]
The altars of the Maid of Crossways.[8] There,
When first the bands that bound her maiden brow
Hung down in even length on either cheek,
And she beheld hard by the altar's front
Her sorrowing sire, and close on either hand
His shrinking acolytes who strove in vain
The steel to hide, the while her townsmen's tears
Streamed at the sight, with sickening terror dumb
Down to the ground upon her knees she sank;
Nor could it profit aught that hapless one
In such an hour, that she had been the first
To bless the king with name of sire; for raised

‧‧‧‧‧‧‧‧‧‧‧‧‧‧‧‧‧‧‧‧‧‧‧‧‧‧‧‧‧‧‧‧‧‧‧‧

[7] Iphianassa, better known as Iphigenia, was the daughter of Agamemnon, king of Mycenae, one of the leaders of the expedition of the Greeks against Troy. When the expeditionary fleet became becalmed at Aulis, the oracles were consulted, and their reply seemed to indicate that Agamemnon should sacrifice his daughter to Diana to avert further displeasure of the gods. Accordingly Iphigenia was brought to Aulis, on the pretext of being wedded to Achilles, only to find herself confronted by an altar of very different import.

[8] Diana, goddess of the moon and of the chase, was often identified with Hecate, goddess of magic. In this aspect she was worshiped at shrines set up where three roads met.

By hands of men, all trembling was she borne
Before the altar—not that when the rites
Were duly done the clear-toned marriage-hymn
Might follow her, but, pure, by hands impure,
Upon her very bridal day to fall
A piteous victim of her father's slaying,
That so a fleet might find a prosperous wind.
To such base deeds could e'en religion urge.

The time will come when thou thyself, dismayed
By fearsome words of seers, mayst seek to part
From us; for even now how many a dream
They can invent for thee, to overthrow
The fastnesses of life, and to confound
With fear thy every fortune. And with right;
For if men could but see that bounds are fixt
To all the bitter sorrows of their life,
They might by some means have the strength to stand
Against religion and the threats of seers.
But now no means, no power can aught avail,
Since everlasting is the punishment
They needs must fear in death. For men know not
What is the nature of the soul: if it
Be born, or at our birth doth find its way
Into our frame; whether asunder torn
By death it perisheth with us, or flieth
To see the shades of Orcus, and the waste
Of dreary pools; or haply liveth on
To find, by heaven's aid, its devious way
Into the breasts of lesser breeds, as once

Of old our Ennius [9] sang, who first brought down
From the sweet heights of Helicon a wreath
Of fadeless foliage, to win bright fame
Among the tribes of our Italian land.
Yet even he in deathless verse proclaimed
That realms of Acheron exist, where dwell
No souls nor bodies, naught save hovering hosts
Of ghostly shadows, pale in wondrous wise.
And thence, he sang, there rose to him the form
Of ageless Homer, ever fresh and green;
With salty tears he spoke, and in his words
Revealed the riddle of the universe.

So then we needs must render well our tale
Of things on high, the paths of sun and moon,
And how they came to be; and what the power
That ruleth all the earth. Above all else,
With reasoning keen, our task will be to scan
Whence is the soul, the nature of the mind,
And what may be those visions strange that come
To affright us in our waking hours, or when
We toss with fever, or in slumber-drown,
That so we seem to see and hear once more
The dead, whose bones are wrapt in earth's embrace.

Nor doth the thought escape my mind how hard
A task it is to expound in Latin verse

ᴧᴧᴧᴧᴧᴧᴧᴧᴧᴧᴧᴧᴧᴧᴧᴧᴧᴧᴧᴧᴧᴧᴧᴧᴧᴧᴧᴧ

[9] Ennius (239-170 B.C.), called the "Father of Latin Poetry", was best
known as the author of a long epic, the "Annales", a narrative of Roman
history in verse. He exercised a profound influence on both Lucretius and
Vergil.

The dark discoveries of the Greeks; for first
We needs must treat of many hidden things
In novel words, since our own native tongue
Is poor, the subject new. And yet thy worth,
Good Memmius, and the joy I hope to win
Of thy sweet friendship, urge me to endure
All toil however great, and lead me on
To watch the calm nights through, the while I seek
What words and fitting measure I may choose
To shed the light of reason on thy mind,
That thou mayst search the heart of hidden things.

This terror, then, this darkness of the mind,
Not rays of sun nor shining shafts of day
Can e'er dispel, but nature's outward mien
And inward law. Let this, then, be for us
Our cornerstone—that ne'er, by power divine,
Doth aught rise out of nothing.[10] For this fear
Doth cramp all mortals with a cringing dread,
Since they behold in earth and heaven appear
Full many a sign whose inward cause their minds
Can nowise grasp, and so would fain believe
The source thereof to be a power divine.
Therefore, when we have seen that naught from naught
Can be created, then shall we perceive
The source wherefrom we must proceed, and whence

ᴧᴧᴧᴧᴧᴧᴧᴧᴧᴧᴧᴧᴧᴧᴧᴧᴧᴧᴧᴧᴧᴧᴧᴧᴧᴧᴧᴧᴧᴧᴧᴧᴧᴧ

[10] The basis of the physical system of Epicurus, hence of Lucretius, comprised three hypotheses: that nothing can be created out of nothing; that nothing can be destroyed to nothing; that space, or void, as well as matter, has actual existence.

Each several thing can take its rise, and how
All things exist without a will divine.

    For if from nothing things could take their birth,
From all would all things spring, nor need would be
Of seed. So men would rise from out the deep,
And from the land the finny tribes would spring,
Or birds from out the air; and hornéd herds
And flocks, and all the beasts of savage breed
Alike would hold the desert and the sown,
Their birth uncertain. Nor would fruits remain
True to the selfsame trees, but shift and change,
And all from all be gathered. For where'er
No fixt engendering bodies did abide,
How could a certain mother be assigned
To each? But since, as we observe, fixt things
From fixt seeds spring, each several breed is born
And riseth to the realms of light from that
Wherein doth lie its own peculiar stuff
And its own primal bodies. Thus it is
That from all things all things can not be born,
Since in each substance lieth a power distinct.
Again, why do we see the rose in spring,
The corn in summer's heat, or vines put forth
Their increase neath the autumn's mellowing sun,
Save that it be, when certain seeds of things
Have come together at their proper season,
What is to be brought forth doth take its mold,
While favoring skies look down upon its birth
And the warm earth in safety nurtureth up
Each tender thing into the coasts of light?

But if they sprang from nothing, suddenly
Would they arise, at no fixt interval,
And at strange times of year, since they would have
No primal elements, the which at times
Unfavorable to birth could be withheld
From generative union. Nor, forsooth,
Would there be need of time, in growth of things,
From union of the seed, if they could grow
From nothing. Thus from tiny babes would spring
At once strong youths full grown; and trees would leap
With growth abrupt arising from the ground.
But naught of this befalleth, since all things
Make gradual increase, as is meet, because
Their seed is fixt, and growing keep their kind.
From this, then, thou mayst know that every breed
Of things from its own substance doth increase.
Then, too, it doth befall that without rains
In proper season, earth could ne'er bring forth
Her fruits to glad men's hearts; nor yet, apart
From food could all the breeds of living things
Renew their kind, nor gain their livelihood.
Hence thou shouldst more believe that many seeds
Are found in common in all things—as words
Are formed of common letters—than suppose
That aught without beginnings can arise.
Once more, why hath not nature had the power
To raise up men of such expanse of limb
That they could cross the seas on foot, or tear
Apart with giant hands the mountain tops,
Or far outlive the span of mortal life?
Is it not because to each and every kind

Hath been assigned at birth its proper seed,
From which is foreordained what shall arise?
Therefore thou must confess that naught from naught
Can e'er be made, since there is need of seed
From which each thing can be begot, and brought
Into the light of heaven. And finally,
Do we not see the fields we duly till
To yield a richer increase to our hands
Than those untilled? There must, then, clearly be
Within the soil some primal germs of things
Which we, by stirring with the plow the clods
And taming to our will the stubborn earth,
Rouse into active being. But if these
Did not exist, each thing would plainly grow
Itself, of better mold, without our toil.

Then followeth this, that nature doth dissolve
Each thing again to its own elements,
Nor aught to naught destroyeth; for whate'er
Were mortal throughout all its inward parts
Would on a sudden from before our eyes
Be snatched and perish, nor would be a need
Of force to work its ruin and break down
The bonds that hold it fast. Whereas we see
That since of everlasting seed each thing
Abideth fast, until some force doth rise
Which can with sudden blow asunder tear,
Or penetrating deep within its voids
Break down its texture, nature suffereth not
The ruin of aught to meet our eyes. Again,
In that which time's slow passage doth undo,

If all its matter deep within should fail,
Whence, pray, doth Venus bring to light of life
The breeds of beasts after their several kinds?
Or whence, when thus renewed, doth Mother Earth
Bring them increase and growth, supplying each
With food according to his kind? Whence, too,
Do native springs and rivers risen afar
Nourish the sea, or ether feed the stars?
For all things that of mortal substance be
Would needs have been consumed in the slow roll
Of days long gone throughout eternal time.
But if through all the lapse of ages past
There hath been that wherefrom this sum of things
Hath been replenished, and so standeth fast,
Then surely must this residue be dowered
With deathless substance. Hence it is that naught
Can ever be dissolved to nothingness.

   Again, the selfsame force and cause would wreck
All things alike, did stuff imperishable
Not hold them fast with bonds or close or loose;
For but a touch would then suffice to be
A cause of death, since none would have a frame
Of mold eternal, but a texture frail
Which any force must needs asunder tear.
But this the truth is: since the fastenings
Of primal elements in various ways
Are set, and everlasting is their mold,
All things perforce endure with strength unharmed
Until a blow doth meet them of such power
That it can break the texture of their frame.

Therefore, once more, no thing that is can shrink
To naught, but all things at their perishing
Into the bodies of their substance melt.
So pass away the rains, when sky, the sire,
Hath flung them to the lap of Mother Earth;
But yet the bright-hued crops appear, the leaves
Grow green upon the trees, the trees themselves
Increase, and bend beneath their fruitful load.
'Tis thence are nourished human kind and beast;
And thence we see fair cities ringing glad
With childish laughter; and the leafy woods
Resound on every side with young birds' cries;
Thence, too, the cattle, wearied with their fat,
Lay down their limbs to rest in pastures green,
While from their swollen udders flow the streams
Of milky moisture. Thence their sportive young
With limbs unsteady gambol o'er the grass,
Their new-born hearts athrill with pure fresh milk.

Not wholly, then, doth perish what may seem
To die, since from one thing doth nature build
Another, nor will suffer aught to come
To birth without the death of some thing else.

And now, since I have proved that naught can e'er
From naught be born, nor, born, to naught dissolved,
Lest thou perchance shouldst choose my words to scorn,
Since primal bodies ne'er can be perceived
By sight of eye, know thou that there exist
In nature bodies which e'en thou thyself
Must needs confess have being, though unseen.

First, then, see how the winds with furious blast
Fall on the sea, and smite the ponderous ships,
And drive before them heaven's clouds; or now
In rapid whirl sweeping across the plains,
Leave in their wake a wrack of mighty trees,
And make the towering mountain tops to rock
With forest-crashing blasts. So, with shrill shriek
And wrathful roar, wildly doth rage the wind.
There are, then, clearly, bodies, though unseen,
In wind, which sweep o'er sea and land, and drive
The scudding clouds of heaven, and harry them
With sudden whirling blast. So stream they on,
And leave stark ruin in their wake, as when
A flood of water, though by nature soft,
Down rushing from some raging mountain stream
Swollen by copious rains, doth sweep along
The shattered branches of the woodland, aye,
And trees themselves uprooted; nor avail
Strong bridges in its way to stem its might.
So too, a mighty river, big with rain,
Will dash against its dikes, and roaring on
Spread wide destruction, rolling neath its waves
Huge rocks, and whatsoe'er would bar its flood.
Thus then the blasts of wind must make their way;
And when, like some strong stream, they turn their course
This way or that, they sweep all things before
With force resistless, or with eddying whirl
Will catch them up, and sometimes bear them far
Aloft in swiftly swirling vortices.
And so I say once more that winds are made
Of unseen bodies, since in deeds and ways

They will be found to rival mighty streams,
Whose substance standeth clear for all to see.

   Again, we catch the various scents of things,
Yet never to our nostrils doth there come
Aught we can see, nor can we e'er gain sight
Of withering heat, nor with our eyes see cold
Or look on voices; yet all these, 'tis sure,
Are formed with body's substance, since 'tis theirs
To strike upon our senses. For the power
Of touching and of being touched is given
To nothing else save body's self alone.
Then too, our garments, by a wave-washed shore,
Suspended, gather moisture, and when spread
In the warm sun grow dry. And yet our eyes
Can nowise see how came the dampness there,
Or how beneath the sun's hot rays it fled.
It must be, then, that moisture is dispersed
In tiny drops too small for eyes to see.
So too, with years of wearing will a ring
Grow thinner on our finger underneath,
And drip of water hollow out a stone;
The bended iron plowshare stealthily
Decreaseth in our fields; and oft we see
The hard stone paving of our streets worn down
By constant tread of crowds. And at the gates
Bronze statues show their hands worn smooth from touch
Of those that greet them as they pass them by.[11]

[11] A present-day analogy would be the foot of the famous statue of St.
Peter in St. Peter's Church in Rome, which is constantly being worn
down by the salutations of devout worshipers.

All these we see to be diminished when
They have been worn away, but e'en a glimpse
Of particles which at one time withdraw
The niggard nature of our sight hath banned.
And last, whatever time and nature add
By bit and bit to things, that they may grow
In due proportion, never sight of eye,
However strained, can see. Nor in those things
Which waste and wane with age, as rocky cliffs
That overhang the sea will slowly yield
Unto the gnawing brine, canst thou discern
How much at any instant each doth lose.
Thus nature worketh with her bodies blind.

And yet all things are not held closely packed,
By body's nature hemmed on every side;
For there is void in things. This to have learned
Will bring thee rich reward, nor suffer thee
To stray in doubt and futile questioning
Anent the sum of things, and scorn my words.
So, then, there doth exist pure space or void.
For if there were no void, no thing would move
In any wise, since that which standeth forth
As body's office, to resist and bar,
Would be in all things present at all times;
Hence naught could forward move, since naught would be
The first to yield its place. But we perceive
Through all the seas, the lands, the heights of heaven,
That many things, by various means, in ways
Diverse do move, the which, if void were none,
Not only would be robbed of restless stir,

But could in nowise have been born at all,
Since matter, closely packed on every side,
Would lie inert. Again, though certain things
Appear as solid, yet know thou from this
That they have void within: ofttimes in caves
The dripping moisture through the rocks will seep,
Till all around doth weep with heavy drops.
So food will force its way throughout the frame
Of living things; trees grow, and in due time
Put forth their fruits, because from deepest root
Through trunk and branch their sap doth find its path.
Then too, through walls of houses and closed doors
Do voices pass, and numbing cold will creep
Into our bones. But, were no voids within
Through which these bodies found a road to pass,
This could in nowise happen. Or again,
Why is it that we see one thing outweigh
Another, though its bulk is no whit more?
For if an equal store of matter lay
In ball of wool and lead, 'twere reasonable
That they should weigh the same, since 'tis the task
Of body to press downward every thing,
Whereas to nature of the void no weight
Is given. That body, then, of equal bulk,
But which is seen to be of lesser weight,
Doth clearly show it holdeth in itself
The more of void; in manner opposite
The heavier doth attest it harboreth more
Of body, less of space.[12] That, then, hath being,

[12] This clear and convincing argument would not be out of place in a
modern textbook of Physics.

Mingled in things, for which with reasoning keen
We now do seek—that which we call the void.

And now, lest that which some would falsely claim
Should lead thee from the truth, I must straightway
Forewarn thee. They contend that waters yield
And open up a liquid path before
When scaly creatures, swimming, forward press,
Because the fishes leave a space behind
To which the waters as they yield may flow.
And even so, they urge, can other things
Avail to move among themselves, and change
Their place, e'en though the sum of things entire
Be solid. But all this, in very truth,
Is based on reckoning false; for whither, pray,
Unless the waters leave an empty space,
Can creatures of the sea proceed to move?
Or where, again, can these same waters yield,
When motionless the fishes must remain?
So, either to all things we must deny
The power of motion, or we must confess
That void is mixt with body, whence each thing
May its first impulse toward a motion take.
Lastly, when two broad bodies, meeting, leap
Quickly asunder, air must needs rush in
To fill the space that doth appear between
The bodies. But, however swift the rush
Wherewith it streameth in, still all the void
Is not upon the instant filled; for first
The air must fill each portion of the gap
Successively, and last the space entire.

But if we hold that when two bodies meet
This through the air's condensing doth befall,
We go astray; for that is empty then
Which was not so before, and this is filled
Which late was empty. Nor in such a wise
Can air condense; nor even were it so,
Could it, I ween, apart from void, contract
And gather into one its several parts.

  So, then, however long reluctantly
Thou wilt hold back, thou must at last confess
That there is void in things. And much besides
I could adduce to prove my words are true.
But these slight hints may now suffice a mind
Alert, since through them thou mayst learn the rest.
For even as hounds, roaming a mountain side,
When once they catch the traces of the trail,
Ofttimes with nostrils keen scent out the lair,
Deep hid in leafy dell, of savage game,
So thou thyself from facts new facts shalt know,
And in such arguments shalt learn to creep
Into the secret lairs of hidden things
And thence drag forth the truth.

                But if mayhap
Thou'rt loth to hear, and shrinkest from my theme,
This, Memmius, can I surely promise thee:
So large will be the draughts my tongue will pour
Of sweets from out my heart's pure wellsprings deep,
That I must fear lest sluggish age may steal
O'er all our limbs, and loose the bonds of life

Ere I can pour, upon one single theme,
Into thine ears my store of proofs entire.

But now, to take again the web my words
Have once begun to weave, all nature, then,
As it hath being itself, of elements
Dual is builded—bodies, and the void
In which they stand, and in their diverse ways
Do move. For body's being is declared
By all our general sense; wherein if we
Cannot repose our certain trust, no ground
Will there be left whereto we may appeal
On things unknown, nor prove by reason's ways
The truth of aught.[13] Then too, were there not room
And empty space which we have termed the void,
Nowhere could bodies stand, nor here and there
In various paths could they avail to move,
As even now I have revealed to thee.
And naught besides is there which thou canst claim
Hath being, apart from body, and from void
Distinct, to form, as 'twere, a third domain.
For whatsoe'er hath being must itself
Be somewhat, be it great, or be it small
If only it exist; and if so be
It suffer touch however small and light,
It will to body's sum an increase bring
And add unto its count. But if perchance
It is not to be touched, since from no side

ᴡᴡᴡᴡᴡᴡᴡᴡᴡᴡᴡᴡᴡᴡᴡᴡᴡᴡᴡᴡ

[13] Lucretius here speaks as an orthodox Epicurean in affirming the trust-
worthiness of the senses.

Can it bar aught from passing through itself
And going on its way, then this forsooth
Will be that which we call pure space or void.

Once more, whate'er hath being by itself
Will either act, or suffer other things
To act upon it, else it needs must be
Of such a sort that other things may rest
Or act within it. And yet naught can act,
Or can it suffer action, save it be
Of body's nature; or again make room
Except it be pure void or vacancy.
Aside from body, then, and empty void,
There can be left no nature, as it were,
To form a third in all the count of things;
Not such as neath our senses' ken can fall
At any time, nor even be conceived
By any man through reasoning of his mind.
For whate'er things have claim to being, these
Unto these twain, body and void, are linked,
Thou'lt find, as their essential properties,
Or else are found to be their accidents.
A property is that which in no case
Can be from body sundered or withdrawn
Save with extinction of the thing itself,
As weight from rocks, or burning heat from fire,
Moisture from water, or from body's kind
The power of touch, or touching-not from void;
While slavery, or poverty, or wealth,
War, liberty, and peace, and all things else
Which come and go, and leave behind unharmed

The essence of all things, these we are wont
With reason sound to call their accidents.
So too, time hath no being by itself,
But 'tis from things we grasp a sense of that
Which in the past was set, or what for us
Today doth hold, tomorrow hath in store.
Then too, thou must perforce confess that none
Can e'er perceive time by itself, apart
From things which move or stand in quiet rest.
And so, when men shall name as things the rape
Of Tyndarus' daughter,[14] or the vanquishment
Of Trojan tribes in war, we must take heed
Lest they perchance constrain us to avow
That these are things existing by themselves,
Since ages past have borne beyond recall
Those tribes of men whereof these were in truth
But accidents. It were as well to claim
Whate'er hath happened as an accident
Of those domains, or of those realms of space.
Again, had body's substance never been,
Nor space and room wherein all things might move,
Ne'er, fanned by Tyndaris' beauty, would the flame
Of love have burned deep in the Phrygian breast
Of Alexander, till it set ablaze
Grim war's destruction. Nor in dead of night
Spawning from out its secret womb a brood

---

14 Tyndarus' daughter: Helen, also called Tyndaris in the following passage, wife of Menelaus, king of Sparta, whose abduction by Paris (also
called Alexander), son of King Priam of Troy, was the cause of the
Trojan War.

Of Grecian warriors, would that oak-ribbed horse [15]
Have spread the flame through Ilion's lofty towers.
So thou mayst clearly see that all events,
Where'er they rise, have never by themselves
Existence, as hath matter, nor, again,
Can they lay claim to being as doth void;
But with more reason shouldst thou say that these
Are accidents of matter, and of space
In which things live and move and have their being.

　Again, all matter doth consist in part
Of primal bodies, and in part of those
Which by the union of these elements
Have been created. But these seeds of things
No power can e'er destroy, for to the end
Strong in their solid frame do they prevail;
Albeit 'twould seem to challenge our belief
That aught with solid body can be found
In the sum of things: for heaven's bolt doth pierce
Through walls of houses, as do shouts and cries;
Hard iron doth glow white hot within the flame,
And rocks neath fire's fierce onslaught oft will seethe
And crack asunder. Yea, e'en stubborn gold
Will yield and flow with heat; the ice of bronze
Surrendering to the flame will liquefy.
So too, through silver stealeth genial warmth

---

[15] The well-known stratagem by which a band of Greek warriors concealed in the belly of a huge wooden horse, advertised by a cleverly planned piece of Greek trickery as an offering to the goddess Athena. entered the city and made possible its capture and destruction.

Or piercing cold, since each our hands can feel
Whene'er we duly hold the cup to catch
The sparkling dew of liquid poured within.
So surely doth it seem that naught in all
The realm of things can be of solid frame.
But since true reason and e'en nature's self
Compel, attend while in brief words I show
That there are things which ever stand unmoved
With solid and eternal frame—that store
Of matter which I name the seeds of things
And their first principles, wherefrom the sum
Of things entire was born and standeth fast.

First, inasmuch as dual hath been found
And far diverse the nature of these twain,
Body, and void wherein all things take place,
Each must exist apart, pure and unmixt.
For where doth lie that space we call the void,
There can no body dwell; nor in the place
Where body is can empty space abide.
First bodies, then, are solid, without space.
Again, since there is space in bodies formed,
There must be solid stuff to ring it round,
Nor can true reasoning prove that aught can hide
Space prisoned in its frame, except thou grant
A something solid which doth shut it in.
Now clearly nothing save it be a mass
Of matter can avail to hold enclosed
The void in things. Matter, therefore, compact
Of solid texture, can eternal be

Though all things else dissolve to nothingness.
Moreover, if nowhere lay vacant space,
All would be solid; and, contrariwise,
Were there not certain bodies which could fill
All places which they hold, the sum of things
Would be but void and empty vacancy.
So, then, we may be sure, body from void
Is clearly marked, and void from body, since
Our world doth stand neither completely full
Nor yet quite empty. Hence there needs must be
Bodies determined which can serve to mark
The void of space from matter's ample store.
These bodies, though assailed by hammering blows
That smite them from without, can ne'er be crushed,
Nor will they yield to aught that deep within
Their frame would penetrate, nor when assailed
In any wise beside will they give way,
As I but now have shown thee. For 'tis clear
That naught, were there no void, could e'er be crushed
Or torn asunder, or be cleft in twain
By cutting, or again would entry give
To moisture, creeping cold, or stabbing flame,
Whereby all things are brought unto their doom.
And since the more a body hath of void
Within its frame, the more, when thus assailed,
'Twill yield and die, our primal bodies, then,
Being of solid nature, without void,
As I have shown, must be imperishable.

Or once again, if matter had not been
Of everlasting texture, long ere now

All things to naught had wholly passed away,
And all from naught in turn had been reborn.
But since I have revealed that naught from naught
Can be begot, nor, born, to naught recalled,
The primal elements must needs be made
Of stuff immortal, whereinto all things
At their last hour can be dissolved, that so
Their matter for the birth of other things
May be supplied. These primal bodies, then,
Are solid, single, indivisible;
Nor could they else throughout the eternal roll
Of endless time now gone have been preserved,
And of their substance build all things anew.

Once more, if nature had ordained no end
To breaking up of things, all bodies formed
Of matter would ere now so far have ebbed
That naught therefrom could be conceived, to rise
In proper season to its life's full span.
For, take whate'er we will, and we can see
Its life at swifter pace doth ebb away
Than it can be rebuilt. So, what the lapse
Of time's long endless days by now had quenched,
Disordering and dissolving, ne'er in all
The time that doth remain could be renewed;
But in the world we know, a certain end
Hath been assigned to breaking, since we see
All things reborn, and for all things likewise
According to their kind a season fixt
Wherein their life's full flower they may attain.

This, too, we add, that though the seeds of things
Stand fast with solid body, yet all things
Of yielding nature, earth, air, water, fire,
How they are formed, and by what power they move
Can be explained, when once we hold that void
Is mixt in things. But if, contrariwise,
The seeds of things were soft, no way would be
To show whence spring hard flint and strength of iron;
For thus their nature from the first would lack
Beginning of foundation. There are, then,
These unseen bodies, strong in singleness,
Whose union, when close-packed, can cause all things
To stand firm knit and show their stalwart strength.

Once more, if unto bodies hath been set
No limit for their breaking, it must be
That in each body from eternal time
Even till now there doth survive some stuff
That hath not yet by danger been assailed;
But since these bodies stand with nature frail,
It scarce can be that they have lingered on
Through time eternal, vext by countless blows.

Again, since for each thing in its own kind
There hath been fixt an end of growth and life,
And since what each by nature's laws can do,
And what it cannot do, doth stand ordained,
Nor doth aught suffer change, each several thing
So standing fast that even the various birds,
Each in his order, on their bodies show
The markings of their kind, so must their seed

With frame of changeless nature be endowed.
For if in any wise the primal seeds
Could be o'ercome and suffer change, then, too,
It would be doubtful what could come to being
Or what could not, or in what way for each
Its proper power is limited, or how
For each is marked its deep-set boundary;
Nor could the various breeds after their kind
So oft recall the nature, habits, life,
Yea, e'en the gait of those that gave them birth.

Then, too, since each least thing our eyes can see
Doth show a boundary point, so in like wise
That body which beneath our senses' ken
Doth lie must in its turn possess a point
To set its bound. This point, we may be sure,
Existeth without parts, and must consist
Of frame the most minute; nor hath it e'er
Had being by itself, nor can exist
Alone hereafter, since the point itself
Is but a part of something else, both first
And single. After it in order due
And close array come other and other parts
Of pattern like, to build the tiny frame
Of that first body. And since by themselves
They have no being, so it needs must be
They cling to that wherefrom by no assault
Of violence can they be torn away.

'Twill follow, then, that these first elements
Are solid in their singleness, close-packed

And dense with their least parts, yet never framed
By union of those parts, but holding fast
In their eternal oneness; nor one jot
Doth nature suffer to be torn away
Therefrom, or be removed, keeping them safe
As seeds of things. Besides, if there were not
Some smallest thing, each tiniest body must
Of infinite parts consist, since halves of halves
Will still have halves, nor aught will set a bound.
How then will differ the full sum of things
From least of things? No difference thou wilt find;
For, hold the sum unbounded as thou wilt,
Each tiniest thing will equally be formed
Of infinite parts. But since true reason crieth
That this is false, forbidding mind belief,
So must thou yield forthwith and own the truth:
That there exist those things which must be formed
With nature truly least. Since these are such,
Thou must confess the primal particles
Are solid and eternal. Nor again,
Had nature, the creatress, e'er been wont
To cause all things into their smallest parts
To be resolved, could she by now avail
To build up aught therefrom, since whatsoe'er
Itself is without parts can ne'er possess
The properties creative matter needs
Must have—bonds, weights and blows diverse,
Meetings and motions, whereby all things act.

Wherefore, those who have seen the stuff of things
As fire, and out of fire alone have deemed

The sum of things created, these, 'twould seem,
From truth and reason mightily have fallen.
First among these, in forefront of the fight,
Is Heraclitus,[16] winning more renown
For his dark sayings amongst empty heads
Than with those sober Greeks who seek for truth.
For fools are prone to admire and love the more
Whate'er they can perceive lurking beneath
Wry-twisted words, and to set up as true
What is contrived to tickle handsomely
Their silly ears, tricked out with clever sound.

For how, I ask, could things so varied be,
If out of fire, alone and pure, they stand
Created? For 'twould be of no avail
That ardent fire became condensed or made
More rare, if still its parts maintained the while
The selfsame nature of the fire when whole;
For, with its parts drawn close, there would but be
A fiercer ardor, and contrariwise
A milder when dispersed and spread abroad;
But naught beyond this shouldst thou e'er conceive
Could happen in such cases, and much less
Could such a varied range of things take rise
From fires condensed and rare. And only thus,

16 Heraclitus, an early Greek philosopher, who lived from about 535 to
475 B.C., based his philosophic work "On Nature" on three cardinal
principles: that all knowledge is based on perception by the senses; that
everything is in a continual state of change from one condition to another;
that fire is the principle from which all things arise, and into which they
again resolve themselves. It is the third of these doctrines with which
Lucretius takes most violent issue.

If they admit that space is mixt in things,
Can fires become condensed, or be left rare.
But since they see that many a doubt doth rise
To baffle them, they hold their peace, and shrink
From leaving unmixt void in things. And so,
Fearing the steeps, they lose the rightful path;
Nor, on the other hand, do they perceive
That, void being stript from things, all bodies then
Would be condensed, and from all pass to one,
Such as could ne'er in eager haste send forth
Aught from itself, as genial fire doth shed
Abroad both heat and light; so thou mayst see
It was not formed of parts close-packed. But if
They think that fires in any other wise
Are quenched in union, and their substance change—
Yea, if forsooth they stoutly do insist
On this belief, their fire must clearly fall
To utter nothing, and from naught once more
Whatever things are born must take their rise.
For whatsoe'er doth suffer change, and pass
Beyond its boundaries, straightway will prove
The death of that which did exist before.

Besides, somewhat in these must needs live on
Unharmed, lest into utter nothingness
All things around thee sink, and up from naught
Reborn arise the sum of things entire.
Now then, since there are bodies definite
And certain, which forever stand unchanged,
Keeping eternally their selfsame mold,
Which come and go in order new, and so

Change things in form and texture, thou shouldst know
Their substance is not fiery. For, be sure,
'Twould naught avail that some withdraw and go,
And others come, or some their order change,
If yet they all retained the soul of fire;
For whatsoe'er they might contrive to form
In any wise would still be fire. But this
I hold to be the truth: bodies exist
Whose unions, motions, order, place, and shape
Build fire; but with their order changed, they change
The nature of the thing, nor yet are like
To fire, or aught besides which hath the power
To send off bodies to our sense, and strike
Our touch with contact.

              And to say besides
That fire is all, and no true thing is found
In all the count of things save it be fire,
As this same Heraclitus saith, stark mad
Doth seem; for from the senses' ranks himself
Would fight against the senses, and o'erthrow
Those very things whereon his creed entire
Doth hang, and whence to him hath been made known
The very thing to which he giveth name
Of fire. For he would hold the senses grasp
Aright the body of fire, but other things
No whit less clear to see they cannot know;
And this to me both vain and mad doth seem.
For where, then, shall we turn? What can we find
More sure than sense itself, whereby we judge
Between the false and true? And why should one

Remove all else, and choose to leave untouched
Heat's nature, rather than deny that fire
Hath being, and grant existence to aught else?
For either claim doth equal madness seem.

Wherefore, they who have thought to find in fire
The stuff of things, and out of fire the sum
To rise, those too who as the primal cause
For birth of things have set the airs of heaven,[17]
And they who fancy moisture by itself
Can fashion aught, or earth can all create
And pass into all nature's various forms,
These seem from truth's plain path to have strayed afar.
Add, too, those who combine the seeds of things,
Link air to fire, and moisture join to earth,
And those who hold that all things can arise
From natures four—earth, water, air, and fire;
Foremost of whom doth stand Empedocles [18]

[17] Anaximenes (about 560-502 B.C.) supposed air to be the fundamental material out of which everything arose by rarefaction and condensation. Thales (640-550 B.C.) seized upon water as the basic element. It is worth noting that these, and the other Greek philosophers whom Lucretius here attempts to refute, are significant not because of the particular substance or substances which they chose as the basis of matter, but because they chose *something*. In other words, they were breaking away from the old notion of a divinely created and operated universe, and groping for a truly scientific explanation. They may thus justly be viewed as pioneers of modern science.

[18] Empedocles, of Acragas, or Agrigentum, in Sicily (the "tri-cornered" island), who flourished about 450 B.C., assumed as the basis of matter four elements, earth, water, air, and fire, operated on by two opposing forces: Love, which attracts and binds, and Hate, which repels and separates. Lucretius' admiration for the genius of Empedocles is evidenced by the glowing terms of his praise in this passage.

Of Acragas, he whom an island bore
On her tri-cornered coasts, where sweeping round
With many a winding, the Ionian sea
Splasheth the spray from its cerulean waves,
And roaring through its narrow strait, doth part
From her own shores the lands of Italy.
Here grim Charybdis [19] sitteth, here the might
Of Aetna gathereth in a thunderous threat
That he will rouse once more the bellowing ire
Of his fierce fires, and from his gaping jaws
Belching again his bursting blazes, hurl
At heaven's heights his fiery flames anew.
While great and manifold to human kind
Those wonders seem, that draw men to her shores,
Though rich in goodly fruits, and girt with might
Of valiant men, yet naught hath she possessed
Within her realm, I ween, than this one man
More famed, more holy, wondrous, or more dear,
From out whose breast divine still thunder forth
Those sacred utterances that sound abroad
The clear truths he hath found, till he doth seem
Scarce sprung from human stock. Yet even he,
And those I named before, far, far below
His worth, yea, less in every wise than he,

ᴨᴧᴧᴧᴧᴧᴧᴧᴧᴧᴧᴧᴧᴧᴧᴧᴧᴧᴧᴧᴧᴧᴧᴧ

[19] Scylla and Charybdis, according to an ancient tradition, were two
fabled monsters which had their abodes on either side of the Strait of
Messina, between the "toe" of Italy and the island of Sicily. The tradition
was doubtless based on the presence, on the mainland side, of a dangerous
sunken reef, and, on the island side, of an equally dangerous whirlpool.
Hence the proverbial statement that he who seeks to avoid Scylla is likely
to fall a prey to Charybdis.

Though fair and godlike were the truths they found
And forth from out their hearts' pure shrine did pour
In holier wise, with wisdom far more sure
Than ever Pythian priestess [20] spake her rede
From Phoebus' laureled tripod—yea, e'en these
In dealing with the seeds of things have tript,
And, howe'er great, with great and heavy crash
Have fallen there; for motion they assume
With void removed from nature, and would leave
Things soft and rare, as air and moisture, fire,
Earth, and the beasts and fruits of earth, but yet
Admit no void within the frame of things.
Then, too, they err in this, that they would have
No limit set to breaking up of things,
No pause in their destruction. So, they claim,
There is no least in all the sum of things;
Albeit we see that each thing's boundary point
Is that which to our senses' measure least
Doth seem. Thus, then, from this thou mayst infer
That boundary points of things thou canst not see
Must be endowed with nature truly least.
Again, they wrongly name as elements
Things which are soft, and which we can perceive
To be of body born and frail; for thus
The sum of things to naught must needs return,
And out of naught reborn the store entire

<hr />

[20] The priestess of the oracle of Apollo at Delphi. Her seat was placed on
a high gilded tripod set over a chasm from which issued vapors which
had the power of inducing ecstasy and supposedly prophetic vision.

Must rise and flourish; but by now, I ween,
How far from truth stand both thou wilt perceive.
Besides, these very things in many ways
Are hostile, yea, are poison each to each;
Wherefore, once joined, they needs must perish, or
Fly wide apart, e'en as, when storms arise,
Lightnings and wind and rain asunder fly.

And last, if out of fourfold elements
All things are made, and into these once more
Are all resolved, why, pray, should these be called
The elements of things, rather than things
Be thought to be the elements of these?
For each from each they rise, and change their hue,
Yea, and their very nature, through all time.
But if perchance thou deemst that fire and seeds
Of earth, or e'en the windy air and dew
Of rain can so unite that none of these
In union doth its nature change, then naught,
Thou mayst be sure, can e'er from them be born,
Nor living thing, nor lifeless, as a tree;
For each, forsooth, in all the mingled mass
Of varied matter; will at once reveal
Its own peculiar nature; so will air
With earth be seen commingled, heat conjoined
With moisture. But the primal particles
Should bring to bear a nature all unseen
And secret power in birth of things, that naught
May be at hand to hamper and to bar
Whate'er is born from being its own true self.

But they, forsooth, would e'en go back to heaven
And heaven's fires, and first would hold that fire
Doth change into the airy breezes, whence
Rain is begot, and out of moisture, earth;
And once again, with order changed, all things
From earth retrace their course, first dew, then air,
Then heat, nor ever cease to change about,
But pass from heaven to earth, from earth once more
Unto the stars of heaven. But primal seeds
In nowise thus should act; for there is need
For somewhat still unchanging to abide,
Lest all things sink to utter nothingness.
For whatsoe'er doth suffer change, and pass
Beyond its boundaries, straightway will prove
The death of that which did exist before.
Wherefore, since those we e'en but now have named
As elements are wont to suffer change,
They must themselves consist of other things
Which can in nowise altered be, lest so
Thou see all things to utter ruin sink.
Why not, then, rather hold that seeds exist
Endowed with such a frame that if perchance
They have created fire, these same avail,
With some removed and others joined thereto,
Their rank and movement altered, to upbuild
The breezes of the heavens, and that thus
From each to each all things have power to change?
'But,' thou wilt say, 'doth not fact clearly prove
That all things take their nurture and do grow
Upward from earth into the airs of heaven?
And were it not that in its favoring time

The season fostered them with teeming showers,
Till e'en the cloud-drenched treetops bend and rock
Beneath the flood, and in his turn the sun
Warmed them with kindly heat, no living thing
Could grow, crops, trees, or creatures of the earth?'
Aye, and our bodies, were they nurtured not
By food and tender moisture, needs must lose
Their flesh, yea, e'en the life from every bone
And sinew would be loosed. For, past all doubt,
As we do draw our body's nourishment
From things determined, so do all things else
In turn from things determined take their growth.
'Tis certain, then, if diverse things on food
Diverse are nurtured, that the cause must lie
In many elements in many ways
Common to many things, among them mixt.
And oft it mattereth greatly with what sort
Of other seeds these selfsame elements
Are linked, and in what order, and again,
What mutual motions they do give and take.
For selfsame seeds build sky and sea and earth,
Rivers, the sun, likewise the crops and trees
And living creatures; but they needs must move
With varied minglings and in various ways.
Nay, even in my verses everywhere
Thou must confess that words and verses both
In sense and ring of sound stand far apart.
So much can letters do, if we but change
Naught save their order; but the seeds of things
Have powers more manifold to bring to bear
Whereby they can create each several thing.

Now let us scan the homoeomeria
Of Anaxagoras; [21] for so the Greeks
Do term it, though our scanty native speech
Will not permit our tongue to give it name,
Albeit the substance of his creed with ease
Will lend itself to words. For when he thus
Doth speak of homoeomeria of things,
He would declare, no doubt, that first of all
Our bones of small and tiny bones are formed,
And flesh of small and tiny bits of flesh;
Blood, too, is formed of many drops of blood
That meet in mutual union; and again,
He fancieth gold of tiny grains of gold
Can be upbuilt; that e'en the earth can grow
From little earths; that fire is made of fires,
Water of water drops, and all the rest
With kindred reasoning doth he feign to hold,
Yet nowhere in the sum of things will grant
That there is void, nor is a limit set
Unto the breaking up of things. Wherefore,
On either path, 'twould seem, he goeth astray,
E'en as did they of whom I spake before.

wwwwwwwwwwwwwwwwwwwwwwwww

[21] Lucretius quite possibly does not treat with complete fairness the
theory of Anaxagoras (about 500-430 B.C.) with regard to the constitu-
tion of matter. Anaxagoras seems to have held that all *substances,* not all
objects, are made up of indivisible, imperishable particles which have the
same nature as the substances which they form. It is extremely dubious
that Anaxagoras would seriously have held to the odd notion that eyes
are made up of little eyes, hands of little hands, etc. Even Lucretius seems
a little puzzled over this wide application of Anaxagoras' doctrine. It may
be that we have here a suggestion of a molecular theory.

Add this: that he would make his primal seeds
Too frail, if those be primal seeds, forsooth,
Which, being endowed with nature wholly like
To things themselves, like them must suffer harm,
Yea, e'en must perish, since there will be naught
To rein them back from ruin. For which of these
Beneath resistless strain can still stand fast
To 'scape from death in ruin's very jaws?
Will fire? or dew? or breezes? Which of these?
Will blood, or bones? Not one, I ween, since all
Alike will wholly mortal be, as e'en
Those things we clearly see give way beneath
Some strain, and yield to death before our eyes.
But that no thing to naught can e'er return
Nor rise again from naught, I summon here
As witness truths I heretofore have proved.
Moreover, since 'tis food that bringeth growth
And nurture to our body, so 'tis clear
That veins and blood and bones, yea, sinews, too,
Are formed of alien stuff; or if 'tis claimed
That all our foods consist of parts diverse
Together mixt, holding within themselves
Small bits of sinews, bones, yea, even veins
And drops of blood, then must we take all food,
Both moist and dry, to be itself composed
Of substance alien to itself, to wit
Of mingled bones and sinews, gore and blood.
Again, if whatsoe'er doth grow from earth
Be in the earth, then earth must be compact
Of alien things which from the earth arise.
Or, change the field, the selfsame argument

Will still apply: if flame and smoke and ash
Lie hid in logs, then logs must needs be formed
Of things of alien kind. So every breed
Of body nourished by the earth must grow
From alien things which rise from out the ground;
And likewise whatsoe'er doth issue forth
From logs, by matter alien to itself
Is fed, which from the logs doth take its rise.

   Yet here is left one little nook wherein
To hide, whereof our Anaxagoras
Himself availeth, holding that all things
Are mingled, though in hiding, in all things;
But that alone is manifest whereof
Most parts are mixt therein, and hold their place
Ready to hand and in the foremost rank.
But this from reason's realm is banished far;
For then 'twere meet that corn, when crushed beneath
The millstone's ponderous strength, should often show
Some trace of blood or other humors nursed
Within our body; and from blades of grass
Likewise, when rubbed by stone on stone, should ooze
Small clots of gore, e'en as their juices ought
To yield sweet drops, of savor similar
To milky richness of the fleece-clad flocks.
So, too, 'twould seem, when clods of fruitful earth
Are crumbled, various grasses, grains, and leaves
Should oft appear, hiding within the sod
Their dwarfed and scattered shapes. And last, 'twere meet
That ash and smoke should be at once revealed
In faggots, sudden snapt, and little fires

Should secret lurk; but since plain fact doth show
That none of these befalleth, so be sure
That things themselves are not so mixt in things,
But common seeds of many things lie hid
Mingled in things in many and various ways.

'But yet,' thou sayest, 'on mighty mountain heights
It oft will chance that, swayed by strong south winds,
The neighboring tops of lofty trees will rub
Each upon each, till with a sudden blaze
They burst into a mass of flowery flame.'
So be. But yet 'tis not that fires abide
Implanted in their wood, but many seeds
Of heat are there, which, gathered into one
With rubbing, set the forests all aflame.
But if within the forests flame had lurked
All ready-made, its fires could not be hid
One single moment, but would burn them all
In general conflagration, and consume
The trees to ashes. So then, seest thou not
What I have said but little while ago,
That it doth matter greatly what the sort
Of seeds with which these selfsame elements
Are linked, and in what order, and again
What mutual motions they do give and take?
And that the same, a little changed, produce
Both fire and wood? E'en as the words themselves
Are formed with letters little altered, though
We name with sound divergent *fir* and *fire*.
And, lastly, shouldst thou think whate'er thou seest

In things clear to our sense can come to birth
Only if thou dost fancy bodies framed
With nature like the whole, then wilt thou find
That first beginnings fade away to naught;
Nay, it will come to pass that they will shake
With quivering mirth, yea, e'en will laugh aloud
Till face and cheeks are wet with briny tears.

Mark now what doth remain, and lend thereto
An ear more keen. Nor doth it 'scape my mind
How dark the way; but in my heart great hope
Of praise hath set its quickening spur, and struck
Into my breast a sweet desire to woo
The Muses' favor; whereby now inspired
With eager feet I thread dim pathless haunts
Of the Pierides,[22] ne'er trod before
By foot of man. My joy it is to seek
Springs yet untasted, and to drink my fill.
I long to pluck fresh flowers, and crave to win
A glorious coronal to crown my head
Whence heretofore the holy sisterhood
Hath never wreathed the brows of mortal man;
First, since I teach of great and wondrous things,
And haste to free the mind from close-knit bonds
Of superstition; then because I shed
On darksome ways verses so full of light,
Touching all things with music's magic charm,
Since, this, I ween, with reason doth accord.

wwwwwwwwwwwwwwwwwwwww

[22] A name sometimes given to the nine Muses, from the name of their
father, Pieros.

For even as healers, when they would essay
To give to ailing children bitter draughts
Of noisome wormwood, first will overlay
The cup's rim round with the sweet golden dew
Of honey, that thereby the trustful age
Of childish innocence may be beguiled
To ope the portal of the lips, and all
Unwitting swallow down the nauseous draught
Of wormwood, thus deceived, though not betrayed,
But rather by such means may be restored
And once again made strong; so now do I,
Since these my teachings oft too bitter seem
To those who have not known their taste, and since
The common herd doth shrink from them in dread.
For I have chosen in sweet-tongued melody
The Muses know to frame my reasoning
For thy delight, and as it were to touch
My theme with honey'd sweets of poesy,
If so perchance I might avail to hold
Thy mind upon my verses till thou come
To grasp the nature of the world entire
And mark the mold whereto it hath been framed.

But now, since I have shown how firm abide
Those particles of matter which through time
Eternal wing their ceaseless flight, nor e'er
Are vanquished, come, and let us now unfold
Whether there be an end unto their sum
Or no; and likewise that we know as void,
Or place or space, wherein all things do move,
Our task shall be to see if it doth lie

With boundaries hedged about on every side,
Or stretcheth vast, unmeasured, fathomless.

　First, then, we do maintain the universe
In no direction of its various ways
Is hemmed with bounds; for so it needs must have
An outmost rim. But clearly there can be
No outermost of aught, unless there be
Somewhat beyond to set the bound, that so
We may discern some point beyond whose range
The nature of our sense can ne'er pursue
The object of its search. Whereas in truth,
Since we must needs concede that there is naught
Beyond the Whole, it hath no outermost,
And hence must lack all limit and all bound.
Nor mattereth aught where thou wilt take thy stand
In all its realms, so true it still will be
That wheresoe'er one hath his place, 'twill leave
The Whole no less unfenced on every side.
Nay, e'en suppose all space to have been set
About with bounds, were one to run afar,
E'en to its edge, and hurl a flying dart,
Which wouldst thou have—the weapon hurled amain
Would fly afar, and reach its destined goal?
Or thinkst thou aught would check and bar its way?
For this or that thou needs must choose to hold.
Yet both cut off escape for thee, and force
Thy mind to grant the universe doth stretch
Abroad with every prisoning bound removed.
For whether there be somewhat there to halt

Thy speeding dart, and bar its onward course,
So that it flieth not forth to reach its goal,
Or if it forward fare, in either case
It hath not started from the outmost bound.
Thus I shall follow thee, and wheresoe'er
Thou setst thy farthest coasts, I still shall ask
How fareth now thy dart. Nay, it will prove
That nowhere can a bound be set, but room
To fly will still extend the chance of flight.

Again, were all the space within the sum
Of things shut in on every side, and set
With bounds determinate and limited,
Ere now the store of matter everywhere
By virtue of its solid weight must all
Have flowed together to the bottom, nor
Could aught beneath the heavenly canopy
Have power to act; nay, heaven would be no more,
Nor light of sun, since there inert would lie
All matter in a heap, where it had sunk
Eternal eons ago. But as it is,
No rest, we may be sure, hath been allowed
To bodies of the primal elements,
Since there can be no bottom absolute
Whereto they may as 'twere flow down, and there
Remain in quiet rest. Nay, evermore
In ceaseless movement, and from boundless space
Bodies of matter, churning endlessly,
Rise up from depths below. And, last of all,
Before our eyes one thing is seen to bound

Another: air doth wall apart the hills,
And mountains fence the tracts of air. Again,
Lands bound the sea, sea lands; but for the Whole
Nothing is there without to hem it in.

Void, then, and depths of space have nature such
That e'en the lightning bolt in its bright course
Could ne'er traverse their boundless realms, nor yet
Make one whit less the sum of space to go;
So far on every side doth spread vast room
For things, freed from all limits everywhere.
Nay, more, 'tis nature's self that doth forbid
The universe to set unto itself
A bound, since she doth e'er constrain the void
To limit body, body in its turn
To bound the void, and thus by interchange
Doth leave the Whole unbounded; else would one,
Did not the other bound it, spread afar
Immeasurable, with nature all unmixt.
But space, as I have taught above, doth stretch
Illimitable. If, then, the sum of things
Were bounded, then would neither sea nor earth,
Nor heaven's bright dome, nor race of mortal men,
Nay, nor the holy bodies of the gods
Avail to last for e'en one little hour;
For from its unions all asunder driven
The store of matter headlong would be borne
All uncompounded through the vast abyss;
Nay, rather it could ne'er have been conjoined,
Nor given birth to aught, since scattered far
It ne'er could be assembled. For in truth

Not with design or reasoning shrewd did all
The first beginnings take their divers posts
Each in his proper place; nor yet, forsooth,
Did they by mutual compact fix upon
Their several movements; but in numbers vast
Shifting now here, now there, throughout the Whole,
Harried by blows relentless down the course
Of endless time, trying now this, now that
Of motion and of union, they at last
Came into patterns such as those whereby
This world of ours is built, and standeth fast.
And so, preserved through many a lingering age,
When once to movements fit it hath been set,
It sendeth rivers with their bounteous streams
To feed the sea, and maketh all the earth,
Warmed by the genial sun, to teem anew
With increase, while the race of living things
Doth rise and flourish, and the gliding fires
Of heaven glow and live. Nor could this be
In any wise, did not a bounteous store
Of matter rise from out the infinite
Whence they are wont their losses to repair
In season due. For as, when reft of food,
All living things will lose their flesh, and pine,
So too, must fail the Whole, when, turned aside
From its due course, matter hath ceased to come
For its supply.

              Nor yet can raining blows
From every side without preserve the sum

Entire of things, once into union brought;
For they can only smite upon it, blow
On blow, and stay a part till others come
To aid, and so the sum may be maintained.
Yet these perforce must now and then rebound
And on the instant yield both time and space
For flight to the first bodies, that forthwith,
Freed from their unions, they may fly abroad.
Wherefore I say once more, it needs must be
That bodies rise in numbers passing great;
Nay, for the blows to fail not doth require
A store of matter boundless everywhere.

Herein withhold, good Memmius, thy belief
From those who would assert that all things strive
To reach the center of a mass,[23] and thus
The nature of the world doth stand, unhelped
By blows external; that no top can e'er
Be set apart from bottom, since all things
Are pressing toward the center (if, indeed,
Thou canst believe that aught can ever stand
Upon itself); and that all heavy things
Beneath the earth press upwards, and are held
Set upside down upon the earth, as when
We see in water images of things.
Likewise these folk maintain that living beings

wwwwwwwwwwwwwwwwwwwwwwwwwwww

[23] Lucretius' utter scorn of a centripetal theory, i.e. attraction toward the center of mass, is based on two misconceptions: that gravity always pulls downward, and that the earth is flat.

Head downward walk, nor can they fall from off
The earth into the regions of the sky
That stretch below, e'en as our bodies ne'er
Of their own will into our heaven's realms
Can fly. So, too, they claim, when these behold
The sun, we see the stars of night,
And that in turn with us they share the hours
That sweep the sky, their days, our nights being one.
But error vain this reasoning hath fixt
In minds of stupid folk, since they hold fast
Their false beliefs with logic all awry.
For there can be no center, since the Whole
Hath been created boundless; nay, forsooth,
If there were center, why should aught be deemed
To linger there rather than hold its place
In any other part, howe'er remote?
For all that room and space we call the void
Through center and non-center must give place
Alike to weights, where'er their movements tend.
Nor is there any spot or place whereto
Bodies may come, and yielding up their weight
Stand still in empty space; nor doth it suit
The quality of void to give support
To aught, but rather must it needs give way
Continually, as doth its nature crave.
So then, we may be sure things cannot thus
Be held in union, smitten with desire
For center.

        And again, they falsely hold
That not all bodies toward a center strive,

But only those of earth and water, such
As moisture of the sea and mountain streams,
And those as 'twere with earthy substance bound;
But airy winds, they claim, contrariwise,
And burning fires as well are cast abroad
From out the center; and 'tis from this cause
The vasty ether sparkleth bright with stars,
And through the azure deeps of heaven is fed
The sun's clear flaming orb, since all their heat
Doth flee the center and hath gathered there;
Nor could the topmost branches of the trees
Bud forth in leaves, unless by bit and bit
Up from the earth were food for each supplied.
But reasoning thus they wander far astray,
For naught save matter infinite in store
Can keep from utter ruin the sum of things;
Lest on a sudden, like wingéd flames, the walls
Of our great firmament asunder fly
And scatter blindly through the vast inane,
And lest the dome of heaven above our heads
Come thundering down, and e'en the solid earth
Give way beneath our feet, and mid the wrack
Of earth and sky, with bonds asunder torn,
Go ruining through the deeps of space, till naught
In one brief moment will be left behind
Save barren void and sightless elements.
For on whatever side thou'lt hold that first
The bodies fail, this side will be the gate
Of death for things, and by this path will all
The rout of matter pour itself abroad.

Thus shalt thou come, by labor slight and fond,
These truths to know; for each shall catch a gleam
From that which went before. Dark night no more
Shall steal away thy path, but thou shalt see
Deep into nature's inmost mysteries.
So things will light the lamp for other things.

BOOK TWO

Proemium, 1-61.

Atomic motions, 62-332.
    a) Incessant motion of the atoms, 80-141; 308-332.
    b) Velocity of the atoms, 142-166.
    c) Their movement by gravity, 184-215.
    d) The *clinamen,* or swerve of the atoms, 216-293.
    e) Conservation of matter and motion, 294-307.

Shapes of the atoms; their combinations, 333-729.
    a) Indefinite number of atomic shapes, 333-477.
    b) But not infinite, 478-521.
    c) Yet an infinite number of atoms of each shape, 522-580.
    d) Widely diverse, but not unlimited combinations of atomic shapes in *concilia,* or unions, 581-729.

Absence of secondary qualities of the atoms (color, odor, sound, heat, sense), 730-990.

Worlds are infinite in number, and are continually being created and destroyed, 991-1174.

BOOK TWO

How sweet it is when stormy winds assail [1]
The mighty main, safe on the shore to view
Another's sore distress; not that 'tis joy
To feel another's woe, but that 'tis sweet
To know thyself from like afflictions free.
Sweet, too, to scan war's panoply far-flung
Across the plain, thyself from danger free.
Yet naught more gladsome than to hold secure
Those heights serene, by wise men's doctrine reared,
From which thou mayst look down, and all about
Behold thy fellows, wandering here and there,
Search for the way of life and find it not,
Striving with native wit and noble birth,
Straining both night and day with toil supreme
To master wealth and stand forth Lords of Things!
O wretched minds of men! O blinded hearts!
In what dark way of life and perilous,
Is passed this span of years, brief though it be!
Can ye not see nature doth crave but this—
That from distress the body may be free,

~~~~~~~~~~~~~~~~~~~~~~~~~~~~~~~~~~~~~~

[1] In this beautiful passage, Lucretius sets forth the real significance of
Epicureanism as a code of conduct. It will be noted that he expressly dis-
claims the "eat, drink and be merry, for tomorrow we die" interpretation
of the philosophy of Epicurus, which was becoming prevalent even in his
own day.

The mind at peace, apart from care and fear?
So for our body's nature do we find
But little needful, that may banish pain,
And sometimes take the place, to our content,
Of many a rich delight. Nor aught of loss
Doth nature feel, if through our splendid halls
No gilded effigies of youths appear
With hands upraised to hold bright-burning lamps
That shed their light on midnight revelries;
Nor if the house gleam not with glint of gold
Or silver's sheen, nor fretted golden vault
Resound to music of the lyre, whenas
On some soft bank of verdure men may lie
Flung at their length in friendly wise beside
A running stream, or neath the sheltering arms
Of some tall tree, and with delight procure
From nature's bounty all their bodies crave;
And most of all when springtime's smiling face
Hath strewn the greening grass with flowers. Nor e'er
Do fiery fevers sooner quit thy frame
If thou dost toss in broidered bravery
Of blushing purple, than if thou must lie
In poor man's coat. Since, then, of no avail
For body's needs are riches, nay, nor birth,
Nor pomp of kings, so, too, they must be deemed
To profit not the mind; unless, perchance,
When thou dost view thy legions swarming o'er
The Campus [2] sward, waging their mimic wars

~~~~~~~~~~~~~~~~~~~~~~~~~~~~~~~

2 The Campus Martius, the military exercise ground of Rome, lay on the
level plain between the Capitoline and Quirinal hills and the Tiber river.

In all their strength of horse and foot, each man
Alike full armed, alike with spirit high;
Or when thou dost behold thy fleet to crowd
The main and wander far and wide—that then
Thou deemst religion's anxious scruples fly
Far from thy mind, dismayed by things like these,
Or then the fears of death will leave thy heart
Swept clean and free from care. I tell thee no!
For if we see these thoughts to be but mirth
And idle mockery, and that in truth
The fears of men and cares that dog their heels
Dread not the sound of arms or war's array,
But boldly stalk mid potentates and kings,
Unawed by gleam of gold and dazzling sheen
Of purple raiment; why, then, dost thou doubt
That all this power doth lie in reason? Yea,
Since life is but a struggle in the dark.
For e'en as children tremble with affright
At darkness' unseen terrors, so at times
Do we ourselves in broad daylight have fear
Of things which we in truth should dread no more
Than those vain fancies children in the dark
Do tremble at, and fear will come alive.
This terror, then, this gloom that doth enshroud
The troubled mind, not piercing rays of sun
Nor day's bright shining beams must needs dispel,
But nature's outward mien and inward law.

　　And now, give ear, the while I shall disclose
What are the movements manifold, whereby
Creative particles of matter bring

To birth each several thing; and how, once born,
They can again dissolve it; what the force
That thus constraineth them; and with what speed
They trace through deeps of space their course assigned;
And thou, fail not to hearken to my words.

For of a surety matter doth not cling
Close-packed together, since we see this thing
And that to wane, and, as it were, perceive
All things to ebb with time's slow lapse, as age
Doth steal them from our sight; and yet the sum
Is seen to bide unlessened, since those bits
That leave one body cause decrease in that
From which they pass away, but increase bring
To that whereto they come; so will they make
One wane with age, the other flourish; yet
They stay not there. 'Tis thus the sum of things
Is e'er renewed, and mortal beings live
Each at another's cost; some races wax
And others wane, and in brief space the tribes
Of living things change, and like runners toss
To others' outstretched hands the torch of life.

Now if thou dost believe the sum of things
Can lag inert, and by its lagging breed
In things new movements, so thou strayest far
From reason's path. For since 'tis through the void
They range, all first beginnings needs must move
By their own weights, or else mayhap at times
By impact of another. For whene'er
'They meet in sudden clash, 'twill come to pass

That with a swift recoil they leap apart
This way and that; nor is it strange, forsooth,
Since hard their bodies and of solid weight,
Nor aught is there to bar them from behind.
And that with clearer vision thou mayst see
All bodies tossing, tossing, call to mind
That in the sum of things no lowest bound
Is set, nor have the first beginnings place
Where they may come to rest, since I have shown
With many words, and reason sound hath proved
That void doth stretch unlimited and vast,
Immeasurable on every side. So then,
No rest, we may be sure, hath been assigned
To first beginnings through the deeps of space,
But rather with relentless movement driven
In paths diverse, some, when together dashed,
Leap back great space apart, while some are thrust
But short way from the blow. And whichsoe'er,
In union more compact together brought,
Bound back but little space, each unto each
Entangled by their close-locked shapes, these form
Strong roots of rock, or iron's savage strength,
And all else of their ilk. Others, again,
There are which wandering through the boundless void
Leap far apart, and far again retrace
The distant paths between. These build for us
Thin air and gleaming light of sun. And last,
Many besides go drifting through the void
Flung off from matter's unions, nor could e'er
Their motions link harmoniously with these.
And of this truth whereof I speak, doth move

Ever before our eyes an image clear.
For look, whene'er the sun's bright streaming rays,
Pouring his light within, pierce through the gloom
Of our dark houses; there thou mayst discern
Mingling in various wise throughout the rays
A throng of tiny bodies in the void,
That as in strife unceasing wage their wars
And tiny battles, struggling troop with troop
Nor ever pausing; such the ceaseless urge
That driveth them to frequent skirmishings
And hot retreats; so thou from this mayst gain
Some shadow dim of how the primal seeds
Forever toss throughout the great inane.
Thus in some wise a little thing can give
A hint of great, and shadow of the truth.
Again, for this 'twill profit thee the more
To note these bodies which are seen to swarm
In the sun's bright beams—since tossings such as these
Give hint of movements secret and unseen
In matter underneath. For thronging there
Thou wilt behold thy motes, beneath the lash
Of blows unseen, face suddenly about
And change their path, shifting now here, now there
To every side their restless wandering course.
This aimless shifting, be assured, doth rise
In all from first beginnings underneath.
For first the primal bodies of themselves
Do move, and next those bodies which are formed
Of tiny groupings, closest, as it were,
To powers of primal seeds, are roused and stirred
By blows unseen from these, and in their turn

They set in motion bodies of a bulk
A little greater. So the movements rise
From first beginnings upward, and by bit
And bit come forth unto our senses' ken,
Till e'en those bodies move that we perceive
In motion in the sunbeam, yet can ne'er
With sure discernment note the blows whereby
They are constrained to act in such a wise.

Now what the speed of movement that is given
To matter's first beginnings thou mayst learn,
Good Memmius, in compass brief, from this:
When first the dawn doth spread her new-born light
O'er all the lands, and birds of every hue
Flitting about the pathless wood do fill
All the soft airs with their sweet minstrelsy,
How swift at such a time doth spring the sun,
And in the warming mantle of his light
Doth clothe all things is clear for all to see.
But yet that warmth the sun doth shed abroad
And his calm light pass not through empty void;
Wherefore more slowly do they move, the while
They part, as 'twere, the waves of air; again,
The particles of heat do ne'er advance
By one and one, but massed and tangled; thus
They are at once retarded each by each
And from without impeded, in such wise
That they must move at slower pace. But since
The seeds of things in solid singleness
Pass through the empty void, with naught without
To check their course, and each as single whole

With all its parts go hurtling toward the mark
They first had set, be sure they needs must be
Surpassing swift in movement, aye, must fly
With speed far fleeter than the light of sun,
E'en so that many times the tract of space
They could traverse in that brief moment while
The sun's bright flashing beams run o'er the sky.
For not with forethought, surely, were it meet
That first beginnings linger and hold back,
Or pass in single file that each might scan
The why and wherefore of each several thing.

   Yet some there be who, blind to all the ways
Of matter, cling perversely to the creed
That not without a power divine in ways
So nicely tempered to the needs of men
Could nature bring her changing seasons round
And rouse to birth the crops, and all beside
Which goodly Pleasure, guide of life, doth tempt
Mankind to approach, and with her kindly hand
Still leading on, doth lure them with the arts
Of love their generations to renew,
Lest human kind should perish from the earth.
But when they dream that gods all this have framed
In man's behoof, in every way they seem
From truth and reason to have fallen far.
For howe'er scant may be my little lore
Of what the first beginnings are, yet this
From heaven's own workings would I dare affirm,
Yea, prove with many an argument besides:
That in no wise the nature of our world

Was made for us by will divine; for oh
How great the faults wherewith it is beset!
But this to thee, good Memmius, anon
I shall explain. Now what is left to tell
Of matter's movements I would fain unfold.

Here is the place, I ween, in our discourse,
To prove thee this as well: that naught endowed
With body's nature can by its own power
Be upward borne, or travel upward; lest
The stuff of flames lead thee astray herein.
For upward do they spring, and upward grow,
E'en as the smiling crops and trees, that take
Their increase upwards, though their weight entire,
Small though it be, tend downward. Nor, when fires
Leap high unto the house-tops, and anon
Lick beams and rafters with swift fiery tongues,
Should they be thought of their own will to act
In such a wise, without some force beneath
To drive them upward; even as from a wound
Upon our body the unprisoned blood,
Doth start, and with a sudden spurt leap high,
Scattering its gory humors far and wide.
And seest not too with what a mighty thrust
Soft water's nature doth disgorge great planks
And timbers? For the deeper, end on end,
Striving with might and main we thrust them down
Beneath the flood, the more with eager spring
'Twill spew them forth and fling them back again,
Till oft they leap up half their length and more.
Yet these things each and all, we make no doubt,

As far as in them lieth, are downward borne
Through empty void. So then, must flames avail,
When outward prest, to rise into the air,
Albeit their weights, so far as they have power,
Struggle to drag them downward. And again,
The nightly firebrands of the sky that fly
Above our heads, seest not how they do trail
Long tracks of flame behind them, wheresoe'er
Nature hath given a path? Dost thou not see
E'en stars and meteors falling to the ground?
Yea, and the sun from heaven's high dome doth shed
On every side his warmth, and sow the fields
With fruitful light; thus e'en to earth his heat
Doth downward tend as well. The lightnings too
Thou wilt perceive to fly athwart the rain,
When here and there their fires burst from the clouds
And rush together. Thus the force of flame
Doth commonly tend downwards toward the earth.

This truth besides I fain would have thee learn
Ere thou proceed: when downwards through the void,
Straight on by force of their own weight, are borne
The primal bodies, quite at random times
And random places, some will push aside [3]

wwwwwwwwwwwwwwwwwwwwwwwww

[3] This curious theory of the "swerve" of the atoms in space was a necessary, if somewhat violent, expedient which Epicurean physicists were
forced to adopt in order to account for the first combinations of atoms,
which, according to their theory, are to be generally viewed as falling
"downwards" in parallel lines. Once this deadly parallelism has been up-
set even to the slightest degree, all sorts of combinations become possible.
Even Lucretius seems to shrink from possible implications of thi

A little space, yet only just so much
As thou mightst call the slightest change of trend.
Were they not wont to swerve, then must they all
Like drops of rain straight down through space profound
Forever fall, nor could there e'er arise
A single meeting, or a single blow
Among the first beginnings; so in all
The realm of nature naught would come to birth.
But if perchance one hold, since bodies framed
With heavier weight more swiftly through the void
Are borne, that thus they can at times o'ertake
And fall upon the lighter from above,
And in such wise can bring to birth the blows
That mold creative motions, he, 'tis sure,
From reason's path doth wander far astray.
For whatsoe'er doth fall through water, aye,
Or through the air, 'tis true, will speed its fall
At quickened pace proportioned to its weight,
Since water's body and the texture thin
Of air can ne'er with equal force resist
Each several thing, but will more quickly yield
Unto the conquering might of heavier things.
But empty void, contrariwise, can ne'er
At any time, at any point, afford
Support to aught, but rather as its bent
And nature tend, must needs forthwith give place.
All bodies, then, that once have set their course
Through the calm reaches of resistless void,

"swerve" as implying a First Cause, yet he is glad to seize upon it as an
explanation of Free Will.

Though in their weights unequal, must be borne
With equal speed. Hence ne'er can heavier fall
On lighter from above, nor of themselves
Engender blows that shall in turn create
Those movements manifold whereby the works
Of nature are sustained. Wherefore, I say
Once more, these bodies needs must move aside
A little, so that little be the least,
Lest we be seeming to assume therein
A sidewise movement, and the solemn truth
Rise up to say us nay. For this we see
Clear and distinct—that naught of weight can e'er
Of its own will be sidewise borne, since all,
So far as thou canst see, fall from above.
But that naught whatsoe'er can swerve aside
From its straight path, who, pray, can e'er discern?

Once more, if motions rise linked each on each,
New springing from the old in order fixt,
Nor e'er by swerving do first bodies make
Some start of movement which may break the bonds
Of fate's decrees, that so from endless time
Cause follow not on cause—whence cometh, pray,
O'er all the earth this freedom of the will
To living creatures? Whence, I say, that power
Wrested from fate, whereby we forward move
Each where his fancy leadeth? For like them
We turn our paths aside, at random times
And random places, where our will hath sped.
For his own will, I doubt not, to each one

Doth give the impulse to these acts; and thence
Through all the limbs the movements flow apace.
Seest not, moreover, how, when open fly
Their barriered stalls, the horses' eager might
For one brief breathless space doth seem to pause,
Nor can their lagging bodies forward leap
To match their surging minds? For all the store
Of matter through the frame entire must needs
Be stirred, that, roused through all the limbs, it strive
Amain to follow at the mind's behest.
Thus thou mayst see that from the heart doth spring
The start of movement: yea, from out the will
Of mind it cometh first, and thence through all
The frame and all the limbs doth spread abroad;
Yet not as when, driv'n by the whelming force
Of powerful blows dealt by another's hand
We forward move; for then 'tis clear as day
That all our body's substance is astir,
Urged on in our despite, until at length
Our will hath curbed it back throughout the limbs.
Dost not, then, see by now that though ofttimes
A force without doth drive men on, and e'en
Against their will doth thrust them headlong, still
There doth remain a something in our breast
Which hath the power to hamper and to thwart—
Something at whose behest our matter's store
May be at times constrained to turn its course
Now here, now there, throughout the limbs, or now,
Spurred headlong forward, feel the curb and rein
And once again be brought to stand at rest?

Hence in the primal seeds, thou must confess,
Doth other cause of motion lie than blows
And weights, whence come these powers inborn,
For that we see that naught from naught doth spring.
For weight itself it is that doth forbid
All things to come to pass by blows, as though
From force without. But that the mind itself
Hath no constraint within in all its acts,
Nor like a conquered thing is bound for aye
To suffer and endure—this power the swerve,
Though slight, of first beginnings doth ensure.

Nor e'er at any time was matter's store
More closely packed, nor yet more wide apart
In space; for naught doth come to bring thereto
Increase, nor ever passeth aught away.
Therefore the movements which first bodies take
Differ no whit today from those they knew
Ten thousand yesterdays ago, nor e'er
Will everlasting morrows find them changed;
Nay, neath the selfsame law that gave it birth
Each thing will still be born, and live and grow
And stoutly thrive, as unto each is given
By nature's laws. Nor any force can change
The sum of things; for naught is there without
To which, escaping from the boundless Whole,
Matter of any kind may flee, nor whence
May rise unwonted force to burst within
The Whole, and change the scheme of things entire,
Confounding all its motions each with each.

Herein we need not marvel that, though all
The first beginnings are in motion, still
The Whole in deepest rest doth seem to stand,
Save when a body with its bulk entire
Doth forward move; for all first bodies keep
Their natures hid far, far beneath the ken
Of mortal senses. Therefore, since themselves
Thou canst not see, they must conceal as well
Their movements from thee; most of all, since e'en
Things we can look upon, yet when withdrawn
Some little space, their movements oft will hide.
For oft on some far hill the fleecy flocks
Cropping the pleasant pastures, onward creep,
Each where the fresh-dewed grass with jeweled gleam
Doth lure it on, the while the full-fed lambs
Gambol with playful buttings—yet to us
From far all this doth seem a blur, and stand
A still white blot upon the green hill side.
Then, too, when mighty legions swarm across
The level plains, charging now here, now there
In mimic warfare, up to heaven doth rise
A glint of arms, and all the earth around
Doth gleam with brass, and echo to the tread
Of marching men, while the far mountain-tops
Roll back to heaven's high stars the thunderous shouts,
As, wheeling round with sudden sweep, the knights
Charge full across mid-field, and shake the ground
With thunder of their onslaught—yet a place
There is upon some distant mountain side
Whence all doth seem to be at rest and lie
As but a glimmer on the plain below.

Come now, as thy next task proceed to learn
What nature the beginnings of all things
Display; how widely varied are their forms,
Of shapes how manifold they are possessed;
Not that but few with like form are endowed,
But that they all stand not of selfsame mold,
Each like to each. Nor need we find it strange;
For since their number is so manifold
That neither end nor sum hath e'er been set,
As I have shown, then surely scarce will all
With selfsame texture and with form alike
Have been endowed. For e'en the race of men,
The silent shoals of scaly things that swim
The seas, the gladsome herds, the savage breeds
Of woodland beasts, the birds of varied hue
That round the joyous watering-places throng
By river bank and spring and pool, or haunt
The pathless forest, flitting here and yon—
Of these, go take whichever one thou wilt
From out his kind, so shalt thou surely find
That each from each doth differ. Else could ne'er
Offspring its mother know, or mother own
Her offspring; yet we see they thus can do,
Nor less than human kind each other know.
For oft before some holy sculptured shrine
Hard by the smoking altars slain, doth fall
A calf, forth breathing from his panting breast
The warm tide of his blood. But wandering through
The verdant glades, the orphaned dam doth seek
O'er all the ground the trace of hoofprints left

By little cloven feet, and anxious-eyed
Each place doth scan, if here, perchance, or there,
She may behold her vanished babe; or now
She halteth, and her mournful lowings fill
The leafy grove, and ever and anon
Back to the stable doth she turn once more,
Sore stabbed with heartsick yearning for her young.
For her no tender willows, or lush grass
Fresh bathed with dew, nor streams that once she knew
Gliding with brimming banks, can soothe her heart
Or turn aside the care that lingereth there.
Nor can the sight of other calves among
The gladsome pastures aught avail to turn
Her mind to other things, or bring surcease
Unto her woe. So keen her sense of loss
Of that which was familiar and her own.
So too, the little tender kids that cry
With tremulous voices know their hornéd dams,
And butting lambs the flocks of bleating ewes,
Thus as their natures tend they run to find
Each one a milk-filled udder of its own.
Again, take any corn thou wilt, and see
How e'en within its kind each several grain
Is not like to its fellow, but through all
Doth run some difference in their outward form,
E'en as we see in shapes of shells that paint
The lap of earth, where with its gentle waves
The sea doth beat upon the thirsty sand.
By reasoning similar, it needs must be,
Since the first bodies are by nature formed
And ne'er were shaped by hand to the fixt mold

Of one alone, that they too fly about
With shapes of unlike pattern each to each.

'Tis easy, then, for us by reason's aid
To see wherefore the lightning's fire doth strike
Far deeper than our grosser fires that rise
From brands terrestrial. For the heavenly fire
Of lightning hath, as thou mayst say, a mold
More subtile, and is formed of finer web,
And thus doth make its way through holes wherethrough
This fire of ours, of logs and pine-brands born,
Can nowise pass. Again, through lantern horn
Light findeth passage, but with sudden hiss
Raindrops are spat away. And wherefore so,
Save that it be the particles of light
Are finer far than those whereof is formed
The kindly dew of water? And, again,
We see that wine will through a strainer flow
With utmost ease, while in quite other wise
Thick olive-oil doth lag, its particles
Being or larger or more hooked, and meshed
With one another; hence it doth befall
Its first beginnings cannot each from each
So quickly be disjoined and one by one
Flow through each single and appropriate pore.
This too thou well mayst note: that liquid draughts
Of honey and of milk stray o'er the tongue
With pleasing taste, whereas, contrariwise,
The bitter gall of wormwood and the juice
Of wild centaury twist the mouth awry
With noisome savor; so that thou mayst know

That formed of bodies round and smooth are things
Which touch the senses sweetly, while all those
Which harsh and bitter do appear, are held
Together bound with particles more hooked,
And for this cause are wont to tear their way
Into our senses, and on entering in
To rend the body. Lastly, good or bad
In touch unto our senses, all things fight
Each against each because of different shapes
They stand composed. Lest thou perchance believe
The strident discord of a shrieking saw
Is formed of elements of smoothness like
To muted melodies that harpists wake
With practised fingers o'er the slumbering strings.
Nor shouldst thou deem that first beginnings built
In pattern similar do make their way
Into men's nostrils, when the flames are fed
With reeking carcasses, and when, fresh strewn
With sweet Cilician saffron, all the stage
Doth smile, and from the nearby altar breathe
The scents of Araby. And judge not, too,
That goodly colors, which can feast the eye,
Are formed of seeds of texture like to those
Which pierce the pupils and compel our tears.
Or dire or loathsome seem, of aspect dread.
For whate'er shape doth soothe the senses, this
Without some smoothness in its elements
Hath ne'er been brought to being; nor again
Hath that which harsh and hurtful doth appear
Without some roughness in its grain been found.
And some there are which can be rightly judged

Not wholly smooth, nor altogether hooked
With points bent round, but rather, as it were,
With little angles slightly jutting forth,
That so they can but titillate the sense,
Whiche'er it be, and hurt it not. Whereof
Are lees of wine, and endive's pungent taste.
And last, that burning fires and chilling frost
Do stab our senses toothed in different wise,
'Tis touch in either case doth give us proof.
For touch, yea, touch, by holy powers divine,
Is body's sense, when somewhat from without
Doth find its way within, or some thing born
Within our body, passing out, will pain
Or pleasure bring, as neath the blandishments
Of Venus; or mayhap when, by some shock
Disturbed within our bodies, seeds will clash
Against each other and our sense confound;
As if but now perchance thou shouldst thyself
Strike with thy hand whatever part thou wilt,
And trial make. Wherefore, it needs must be
That shapes of first beginnings differ far,
So manifold the feelings they create.

And finally, those things which seem to us
Compact and hard must be composed of shapes
More hooked, and as it were with branching arms
Held deeply anchored each to each. Whereof
In foremost rank doth stand the diamond stone,
And stubborn flint, and iron's hardy strength,
And brass that on our doors doth shriek aloud
Its protest. But of grains more smooth and round

May well be formed whate'er doth chance to be
Of liquid nature, that will stream and flow;
For being round, its several globules ne'er
Are held back each by each; so in like wise
Will draught of poppy seed [4] as lightly move
As one of water, since the slightest jar
Will send it likewise rolling down apace.
And last, of things thou seest to fly abroad
Upon the instant, smoke and cloud and flame,
It needs must be that e'en if not compact
Entire of bodies smooth and round, they still
Are not entangled by their close-locked shapes,
And so can prick the body, or invade
The heart of rocks, and yet not each to each
Cling fast. So, then, whate'er we see doth drift
Apart with ease, and likewise doth present
A pricking to our senses, this, be sure,
Is formed of elements not closely linked
But sharply pointed. Or when thou dost see
The selfsame things both fluid and bitter, e'en
As ocean's brine, count it no miracle;
For being fluid, these are formed of shapes
Both smooth and round, but intermixt therewith
Are bodies that are rough, and seeds of pain;
Yet these, forsooth, can ne'er be closely knit

wwwwwwwwwwwwwwwwwwwwwwww

[4] Lucretius doubtless has in mind a simple game, still played by children
in some districts of Italy. The game consists in piling up a pinch of poppy
seed on the palm of the hand, and carefully bringing the hand to the lips,
where the heap of seed is drawn into the mouth by a quick intake of
breath. The winner is the one who can first accomplish this delicate feat
without allowing any of the fine round seeds to become spilled.

By hooks, but clearly are both round and rough,
And thus avail at once to roll and hurt
Our senses. And that thou mayst be more sure
That bodies rough are mingled with the smooth,
Whence cometh the bitter body of the brine
Of Neptune, there hath e'en been found a way
To part them each from each, and so discern
How even brackish waters, trickling through
The spreading sands, flow sweet into a well,
Their harshness lost. For left behind are all
The elements of bitter saltness, since,
Being rough, they cling more closely to the earth.

Since I have taught thee this, I shall proceed
To link thereto a truth, which with it joined
Will win therefrom belief: that seeds of things
Are limited in number of their shapes.
Were this not so, then, once again, some seeds
Must needs be boundless in their body's bulk;
For in the selfsame single tiny frame
Of any seed thou wilt, the shapes can ne'er
Be greatly varied, each with each. For grant
First bodies formed of three least parts, or e'en
Add a few more; 'tis clear when thou hast tried
In order every grouping of the parts
Of that which is itself a single whole,
Exchanging top for bottom, right with left,
To find what form or figure of a whole
Each plan doth give, if thou wouldst further go,
And wish perchance to change the shapes still more,

New parts must be assigned. 'Twill follow, then,
That in like manner such arrangements call
For other parts, if thou perchance wilt still
Make other shapes. And so each change of form
Is followed by increase of body. Hence
It cannot be thou shouldst believe that seeds
Have endless variation in their forms,
Lest some thereof thou shouldst constrain to be
Of magnitude unbounded—which can ne'er
Acceptance win, as I have taught before.
For thou wouldst straightway see barbaric robes
And ruddy Meliboean purple, tinged
With costly dyes from shells of Thessaly,
And golden broods of gay-hued peacocks, steeped
In smiling beauty, all neglected lie,
Their place usurped by some new hues of things.
Likewise the scent of myrrh and honey'd sweets
Would be despised; the swan's melodious song,
And e'en the artful strains that once did sound
From Phoebus' strings would mute and smothered lie.
For ever something better than before
Would be arising; and in selfsame wise
All things would wane unto the worser side,
E'en as we showed that toward the better all
Would rise. For equally to nose and ear,
Eyes and the taste of mouth would one thing prove
More loathsome than all else. But since we see
This is not true, but e'er on either side
A limit fixt assigned to things doth mark
Their boundaries, so must thou needs confess
That primal matter too is limited

In difference of its shapes. And, finally,
From fires e'en down to numbing frosts the way
Is limited, and likewise back again
An equal space is measured. For all heat
And cold, and gentle warmth between, do lie
'Twixt this and that, filling the scale entire
In order due. Therefore their natures stand
With measured difference, since at either end
They are marked off by these twin points—on this
By flames beset, on that by stiffening frost.

Since I have taught thee this, I shall proceed
To link thereto this truth, which with it joined
Will win therefrom belief: that seeds of things,
Though formed in patterns similar, must be
In number infinite. For since the tale
Of difference in their shapes is limited,
It needs must be that those which are alike
Are infinite in number, else the sum
Of matter would abide with limits set,
Which I have proven false, and have revealed
In these my verses how the particles
Of matter from the infinite do keep
The sum of things intact, unceasingly
Raining their yokéd blows from every side.
For while thou dost observe that certain breeds
Of beasts are found more rare and as it were
Of nature less productive, yet in climes
Remote and regions sundered far in space
There may be many of the selfsame breed,
And thus the count made up; e'en as among

The foremost of four-footed beasts we see
The breed of elephants with snakelike hands,
Whose thousands upon thousands palisade
All India with a wall of ivory
That none may penetrate within; so great
The multitude of these strange beasts, whereas
We see but few ensamples of their kind.
Still let me grant this point, that there may be
Some single thing, unique, alone from birth,
With ne'er a twin in all the world beside;
Yet even so, except there be a store
Of matter infinite, whence it can be
Conceived and born, it ne'er can come to being,
Nor what is more, find nourishment and grow.
Nay, e'en suppose the bodies that create
One single thing to toss about the Whole
In number limited: whence, where, I ask,
Or by what force, or how, will they contrive
To meet and join as one in that vast sea,
That rout of alien matter? For, 'tis sure,
No plan have they of union, but as when
From many a mighty wreck, the vasty sea
Doth toss now here, now there, thwarts, ribs and spars,
Prow, masts, and drifting oars, till all along
The shores of many a land men may behold
The floating wreckage, and being warned thereby
Resolve to shun the treacheries of the sea,
Her might and guile, nor e'er to heed her wiles
When, falsely calm and calmly false, her face
Doth wear its temptress smile; e'en so, shouldst hold

The first beginnings of a certain kind
Once limited, then scattered far apart
Through all the range of time, they needs must toss
This way and that, on all the diverse tides
Of matter, so that ne'er together driven
Can they unite, nor cling in union—nay,
Nor find increase and grow. Yet all these things
Do clearly come to pass, as facts will prove,
Since things can be created, and once born
Can grow. So then, in whatsoever kind
Of things thou wilt, 'tis clear that there abide
First bodies infinite, wherefrom their needs
Are all supplied.

    And so the powers of death [5]
Cannot prevail forever, and entomb
Life evermore; nor yet can powers of birth
And increase endlessly bring things to life
And keep them safe. So from eternal time
With equal issue goeth the ceaseless strife
Of first beginnings, as now here, now there,
The vital forces conquer, or in turn
Are conquered. Mingled with the funeral dirge
Riseth the cry of babes that wail to see
The shores of light. Nor night hath followed day
Nor day on night that hath not heard, conjoined
With infants' sickly wailings, the laments
That wait on death and the black funeral.

[5] In this magnificent passage are summarized, as perhaps nowhere else in
the poem, the hope and the despair of Lucretius.

This truth besides 'twere well to keep deep sealed
Within the guarded chambers of thine heart:
That naught is there in things whose natures stand
Clear marked for all to see, which hath been made
Of first beginnings of a single mold,
Nor aught which holdeth not well-mingled seed;
And whatsoe'er hath in itself the more
Of powers and forces greater, doth reveal
That in its frame it hath more numerous kinds
Of first beginnings, and more varied shapes.
So, first of all, earth hath within herself
Those primal bodies whence the bubbling springs
Pour out their cold and never-failing streams
To feed the boundless sea; and she doth hold
As well the seeds whence fires are born; for oft
In many places, kindled into flame
The soil of earth doth blaze, while deep, deep down
The might of Aetna rageth with its fires.
Then too, she holdeth seeds whence she can rear
For human kind bright crops and smiling trees,
And give to every breed of beasts that range
The lonely mountain heights their streams and leaves
And pleasant pastures.

                    Wherefore Earth alone
Is named Great Mother of the Gods [6]—alone

[6] Cybele, also called Magna Mater, the Great Mother, was a Phrygian
deity, whose worship was imported to Rome during the period of the
Second Punic War. The impressive but barbaric ceremonies which at-
tended her triumphal "progresses" through cities and towns on the occa-
sion of her festivals have nowhere been better described than here.

Mother of beasts, yea, and the parent, too,
Of our own frames. Of her in days of old
The poet sages of the Greeks did sing
How from her sacred shrine borne high aloft
Upon her car, twin-yokéd lions she drave,
To teach the world that in a boundless space
Of air the world doth hang, nor e'er can earth
On earth repose. And beasts of savage breed
They yoked unto her car, since they would show
That offspring howe'er wild by loving care
Of parents may be tamed to softer ways.
And round her head they set a castled crown,
Since fortressed on their glorious heights men's towns
She keepeth safe. So with this emblem dowered
E'en now in awful state through many a land
Is borne the Holy Mother's symbol stone.
This, then, it is the diverse tribes acclaim
Mother of Ida in the ancient rite
Of worship, and assign it Phrygian bands
To bear it company, since in those lands
First rose, men say, to spread through all the world
The boon of corn; and eunuch priests besides
They give to tend it, since they fain would teach
That whoso hath the Mother's godhead scorned
And thankless to his parents hath been found
Must needs be judged unworthy to beget
A living brood to see the shores of light.
So neath their palms the taut-stretched timbrels sound
Their thunder, hollow cymbals clash, the horns
Breathe their hoarse menace, and the Phrygian strains
Of the caverned flute stir deep their maddened minds.

Sharp weapons, too, they bear before, as sign
Of fateful frenzy, that the thankless minds
And impious hearts of the unhallowed throng
May shrink dismayed before the awful power
Of her majestic presence. So when first
Through the great towns she rideth, high in state,
In stony silence blessing all mankind
With wordless greeting, all her journey's path
They strew with bronze and silver, dowering her
With bounteous store of alms, and everywhere
Rose blossoms fall like snow, till shadowed o'er
Alike are Mother and her thronging train.
Next goeth an armed band, named by the Greeks
The Phrygian Curetes,[7] since, 'twould seem,
They join in mimic strife and leap on high
In rhythmic movements, hailing with delight
The sight of blood, while on their wagging heads
The fearsome crests are set agog. And thus
Those Curetes of Dicte they recall
Who once in Crete, 'tis said, the wailing drowned
Of infant Jove,[8] as, armed, around the boy
In boyish glee their dizzying dance they whirled,
Beating with brass on brass in measured rhythm,

---

[7] The triumphal car of the Great Mother was accompanied by a band of armed attendants, the Curetes or Corybantes, who performed a wild barbaric dance in her honor.

[8] According to an early legend, Jove (Jupiter), the infant son of Saturn and Rhea, the Mother Goddess of Crete, was concealed by his mother from the jealous eyes of his father on the slopes of Mt. Dicte in Crete. To protect him, his mother assigned a band of earth-born demons, the Curetes or Corybantes, armed with weapons of bronze, who drowned the crying of the child by clashing their spears against their shields.

Lest Saturn seize and grind him in his jaws,
And strike an everlasting wound deep down
Into the Mother's heart. 'Tis for this cause
They leap in arms in the Great Mother's train;
Or else they would proclaim the goddess' will,
That men with arms and valor should resolve
To guard their native land, and ever prove
A bulwark and an honor to their kin.
All this, though well devised and bravely told,
Yet from true reason's realms is banished far.
For in its very nature all the host
Of heavenly presences must needs enjoy
Life without end and peace ineffable,
Far sundered from this little world of ours.
For free from every pain, from danger free,
Strong in its own great might, nor needing aught
Of us, it is not won by virtuous deed
Nor touched by wrath. Nay, earth itself doth lack
All feeling from all time; and 'tis because
It holdeth elements of many things
That it can bring its creatures manifold
In many ways into the sun's clear light.
Herein should any man prefer to give
The name of Neptune to the sea, or choose
To think of corn as Ceres, or abuse
The name of Bacchus rather than to speak
The true name of the vine-juice, let us yield,
And grant him leave to babble o'er and o'er
That earth is Mother of the Gods, if so
In very truth he doth himself forbear
To soil his mind with superstition's stain.

So, oft the fleecy flocks and warrior breed
Of horses, and the hornéd herds will crop
Grass from the selfsame field, beneath one arch
Of heaven's high dome, and from one single stream
Of water slake their common thirst, yet live
Their lives with different aspects, and retain
The nature of their parents, and their ways
Will counterfeit, each in his several kind;
So great the difference that matter hath
In any kind of grass thou wilt; so great
In every stream. Hence, too, in all the tale
Of living creatures any single one
Is made of bones, blood, veins, moisture and heat,
Sinews and flesh; and these in turn are found
Far different each from each, since they are formed
Of first beginnings varying in their shapes.
Then once again, whate'er is set ablaze
And burned by fire hath in its body stored,
If naught besides, at least those elements
That give it power to send out fire, shed light,
Shoot sparks, and scatter embers far and wide.
So too, if all things else thou wilt but scan
With reasoning similar, thou'rt bound to find
That in their bodies seeds of many things
And diverse shapes are held concealed. Again,
Full many a thing thou dost observe whereto
Alike have been assigned color and taste
Along with smell; whereof in foremost rank
Are offerings that on the altars burn
And touch each separate sense in different wise.
These, then, of shapes diverse must needs be made;

For scent thereof doth find a way within
Our body where their colors cannot pass,
And e'en as by this path doth color steal
Into our senses, so the taste by that.
Hence thou mayst know they differ in the shapes
Of their first principles. Thus, then, do forms
Unlike collect into a single mass,
And out of mingled seeds are all things made.
Nay, even in my verses everywhere
Thou wilt discover letters manifold
Common to many words, and yet perforce
Thou must admit that words and verses both
Are formed of different letters each from each.
Not that but letters few run through them all
In common, or no two of letters like
Are fashioned, nay, but that they stand not all
Like each to each. So, too, in other things
Though there are found first bodies manifold
Common to many things, yet in their sum
They may exist far different each from each;
Hence 'tis with reason due we say that sprung
From elements diverse are human kind
And corn and trees that glad the hearts of men.

And yet thou must not hold that elements
Of every sort can be in every wise
Together linked, else rising everywhere
Strange monsters wouldst thou see, misshapen forms
Seeming half man, half beast, and e'en at times
Tall branches from a living body grown,
Or limbs of earth-born beasts linked on with those

Of creatures of the sea, while through the realms
Of earth, the common Mother, would be nursed
Chimaeras,[9] breathing flame from their dread jaws.
But naught of this befalleth, since we see
All things of fixt seeds and of parent fixt
Are born, and in their growth preserve their kind,
And this, be sure, must come to pass by law
Unalterable. For every breed doth draw
From all its food its proper elements
That pass into its limbs, and there conjoined
Induce appropriate movements; but no less
We see their nature cast out on the ground
Things alien to their living; much besides
Of unseen substance, driven by blows, doth flee
From out their body, which could ne'er be linked
To any part, nor following within
The vital motions, tune thereto its ways.
But lest perchance thou fancy living beings
Alone by these laws bound; know that all things
By this same principle are limited.
For e'en as all begotten creatures live
Unlike in all their natures each to each,
So it must be that each thereof is made
Of first beginnings of a different shape;
Not that but few with like form are endowed,
But that they all stand not of selfsame mold,
Each like to each. Moreover, since the seeds

wwwwwwwwwwwwwwwwwwwwww

9 The Chimaera was a fabled fire-breathing monster having the fore-part
of a lion, the rear part being a serpent or dragon, and the middle part a
goat.

Are thus diverse, so, too, must differ far
Their spaces, paths, linkings and weights and blows,
Meetings and movements, sundering not alone
Bodies of living things, but earth and sea,
Yea, holding heaven itself apart from earth.

  Come now and list unto a theme pursued
With pleasant toil, lest thou perchance shouldst hold
That those white objects which before thine eyes
Thou seest to shine are of white bodies made,
Or black of black seeds born, nor e'er believe
Aught else tinged with whatever hue thou wilt,
To bear this hue because the primal seeds
Of things are dyed with colors similar.
For primal seeds no color have at all,
Or like to things, or unlike. But perchance
If it seem not to thee that searching minds
Can enter in and come to comprehend
These bodies, thou dost wander far from truth.
For as those blind from birth, who ne'er have viewed
The sun's clear light, can still by touch gain sense
Of things which ne'er for them since life began
Have been with color linked, so mayst thou know
That for our minds as well can bodies touched
With ne'er a trace of color yet become
A concept clear. Again, whate'er ourselves
May touch in sightless darkness we feel not
To be with color clothed. Since, then, I win
The day, and prove this true, I now will show
That first beginnings with no hue are dyed.
For every hue, no matter what, doth change

To every other. But the primal seeds
In nowise thus should act, for there is need
For somewhat still unchanging to abide,
Lest all things sink to utter nothingness.
For whatsoe'er doth suffer change, and pass
Beyond its boundaries, straightway doth prove
The death of that which did exist before.
So then, forbear to dye the seeds of things
With color, lest before thee all things fail
And pass away to utter nothingness.
Besides, if naught of color hath been given
To primal elements, and yet they stand
Endowed with various forms whence they beget
All things of various colors, since we see
That it doth matter greatly with what sort
Of other seeds these selfsame elements
Are linked, and what their order, and again
What mutual motions they do give and take,
Thou canst at once with utmost ease explain
Why objects which but little while ago
Were black in hue, may on a sudden change
To marble whiteness; as, when mighty winds
Have stirred its smooth tranquillity, the sea
Doth change to foaming breakers, flashing forth
A hue of marble. So, thou mayst declare,
A thing we oft see black, its substance mixt,
With order of its first beginnings changed,
Will gleaming white appear. But if so be
That waters of the sea of azure seeds
Were made, in no wise could they change to white;
For in what way soe'er thou wert to stir

Seeds blue in color, never would they pass
To marble's hue. But if the seeds that make
The single unmixt brightness of the sea
Were tinged with various colors, e'en as oft
Of different shapes and forms diverse is framed
Some object square in pattern, it were meet
That as within the square we can perceive
The forms unlike, so in the ocean's plains
Or aught thou wilt of pure bright hue besides,
Colors diverse and differing each from each
We should discern. But though the unlike shapes
In no wise thwart and hinder our whole square
From being square in outline, yet the hues
Diverse in things do block, yea, e'en forbid
A single brightness from the whole to shine.

Again, the reason which doth lead us on
And tempt us sometimes colors to assign
To first beginnings, all doth fail, since white
Is not made out of white, nor that called black
Of black, but out of various colors. Yea,
Far sooner will things white be born and rise
From none at all than from a color black
Or any else which doth that whiteness thwart.

Then, further, since no color can exist
Apart from light, whereas the seeds of things
Come not into the light, so mayst thou know
These are not clothed in color. For what sort
Of color can there be in darkness blind?
Nay, e'en in light a hue will change, as struck

By straight or slanting beam it doth reflect
The light it borroweth, e'en as we behold
The irised plumage on the necks of doves
That like a jeweled ring set round their throats
Doth gleam in the sun; for now with garnet bright
'Twill glow, or now will shift and shimmer, till
'Tis very emerald set in coral'd rose.
So too, a peacock's tail, when it hath caught
The bounteous light, doth shift and change its hue
With every movement; so, thou mayst be sure,
Since all these hues from some appropriate stroke
Of light are born, they scarce can be conceived
As having being without it. And again,
Because the pupil of the eye doth take
Into itself a stroke of certain kind
When it is said to sense a hue of white,
And still another when it doth perceive
Black or aught else, nor mattereth a whit
What hue in all the varied range doth paint
The things we touch, but rather what the form
Wherewith they have been furnished; so, be sure,
The first beginnings have no need of hues,
But by their varied forms they are empowered
To bring to being touch of various kinds.

    Besides, since to fixt shapes hath been assigned
No special hue, and any shape thou wilt
Of first beginnings may exist in hues
Of any sort, why, then, I ask, doth not
Whate'er is made of them, in every breed,
Appear likewise infused with every kind

Of hue? For 'twould be meet that flying crows
From their white wings should oft reflect a gleam
Of white, or swans of jet-black hue be born
Of seeds of black, or any hue thou wilt
Or single or diverse.

And once again,
The more each thing is finely cleft apart
To tiny particles, the more thou'lt see
Its color bit by bit to fade away
And e'en be quenched, as when a purple robe
Is plucked apart to tiny shreds; for so,
When it hath been unraveled thread by thread,
The Punic purple, king of colors all,
Is scattered all abroad. So thou mayst know
That with their dying breath the slender shreds
Breathe out their little store of color ere
They pass away into the seeds of things.
And, last, since thou thyself dost not assert
All bodies send forth either sound or smell,
'Twill follow, then, that not to every thing
Dost thou ascribe odor and sound. E'en so,
Since with our eyes we cannot all things see,
Be sure that some exist bereft of hue,
E'en as do others scentless, aye, and some
Devoid of sound; and yet a mind alert
Can come to know them, e'en as it can mark
Things that are stript of other qualities.

But lest perchance thou deem that reft of hue
Alone are primal bodies, know as well,

That these lie wholly sundered from all warmth,
And cold, and fiery heat, and ever move
Barren of sound, and starved of taste, nor cast
From out their body odor of their own.
Yea, e'en as when thou dost prepare to blend
The essence sweet of marjoram or myrrh,
Or flowery scent of nard, breathing sweet balm
Unto the nostrils, first 'twill be thy task
To seek, if so be thou canst find it, oil
Of scentless nature, which may send no breath
Of odor to the nostrils, lest it give
The least slight trace of its strong scent, and so
Corrupt those rarer odors mingled in
And boiled with its own substance. So, I ween,
From this same cause the primal particles
Must ne'er contribute to the birth of things
Scent of their own, nor sound, since they can cast
Naught from themselves abroad; nor can they bring
The smallest trace of taste, or cold, or warmth
Of fiery heat, or aught besides; for these,
Since they are mortal in their frames—the soft
Of yielding body, brittle of body frail,
Hollow of rare,—so must they one and all
Be far remote from primal elements
If we would lay beneath created things
Foundations everlasting, whereupon
The whole of life may rest, lest thou behold
All things sink back to utter nothingness.

   And now must thou confess that whatsoe'er
We see hath sense, is yet of elements

Insensate formed; nor e'er do open facts,
Clear marked for all to see, this truth refute
Or fight it back; but rather of themselves
Do lead us by the hand, and force belief
In what I say—that living things are born
Of things insensate. For do we not see
How worms come forth alive from filthy dung,
When, soaked by endless rains, the flooded earth
Doth reek with moisture? So we may perceive
The round of things each to another change;
Streams, leaves, and pleasant pastures are transformed
To cattle; cattle change their form and pass
Into our bodies; while our bodies oft
Give nurture to the strength of savage beasts
Or strong-winged birds. Thus, then, doth nature change
All foods and living bodies, and from food
Create the senses of each living thing,
In no far different wise than she doth turn
Dry logs to flame, and into fire all things.
Dost see not, then, how greatly mattereth
The order wherein first beginnings lie,
And with what others mingled they do give
And take their mutual movements?

                              Then, again,
What is it that doth strike upon the mind,
And, stirring it, constraineth it to frame
Its various thoughts, that thou mayst disbelieve
This very truth, that sentient things may spring
From things insensate? Clearly, stones and wood
And earth, all mixt in one, can ne'er produce

A vital sense. At just this point, therefore,
It will behoove thee to remember this:
I make no claim that all at once from each
And every substance which can bring to birth
Things that are sentient doth sensation spring;
But that 'tis of great moment, first of all,
How small the bodies are that constitute
The sentient thing; then with what shape endowed,
And what their movements, order, and their place.
But naught of all these substances we see
In logs or sods; yet these, when, as it were,
They soften with the rain, bring forth young worms,
Because the bodies of their matter, stirred
By new conditions from the order old,
Are brought to fruitful union, in such wise
As living beings must be brought to birth.

Again, they who would hold a sentient thing
Can spring from sentient things, which in their turn
Are wont to draw their sense from others—these
Would render mortal e'en the very seeds
Of their own senses, when they make them soft.
For all our sense with sinews, flesh and veins
Is linked; and these we see are soft, upbuilt
Of mortal body. But e'en suppose that these
Forever can endure: still must they have,
I make no doubt, the feeling of some part,
Or else be deemed of feeling similar
To that of living things entire. But meet
It were that parts alone can have no sense;
For all our general feeling doth deny

A separate alien sense in every limb;
Nor hands, apart from us, nor any part
At all can keep sensation by itself,
So like are they to living things entire.
Thus it must be they feel what we do feel,
That so in every part they may enjoy
Their share appropriate of our vital sense.
How, then, can these be called the seeds of things,
And shun the paths of death, since one and all
Are living beings, and living creatures stand
One and the same with mortal things? Still, grant
They may: yet naught e'en so will they create
Meeting in union, save a thronging rout
Of living things, e'en as we know that men,
Cattle and savage beasts naught e'er could breed
In mutual union. Nay, e'en if perchance
Seeds lose their proper sense from their own frame
And gain another, what avail to grant
That which they straightway lose? And then besides,
As we have said before, since we observe
The eggs of birds to living fledglings turned,
And worms to swarm when flooding rains have fouled
The earth with slime, so may we know that sense
From that which hath not sense may be begot.

But should one claim perchance that sense may rise
In any case from that which hath not sense
By change, or as it were by birth, whereby
'Tis framed and brought to active being, so
It will suffice to bring to such an one
Clear proof that never can a birth have place

Save when a union hath been formed before,
Nor without union can aught e'er be changed.
For, first of all, no sense will ever be
In any body ere the living thing
Hath been itself begot, because, 'tis clear,
Its substance, scattered far abroad, is held
In air, in streams, in earth, and e'en in things
From earth created; nor in living mold
Hath it yet come together, and combined
Its proper mutual motions, by whose aid
The all-discerning senses, lamps alight,
Keep watch and ward o'er every living thing.

   Again, take any living thing thou wilt:
A blow too heavy for its frame to bear
Will on a sudden fell it, and confound
Its every sense of body and of mind;
For torn is all the fabric of its frame,
And, deep within, its vital motions stayed
Until its matter, shaken from its throne
In every limb, doth slip the vital bonds
That anchor soul to body, and abroad
Doth scatter all its substance, streaming forth
Through every pore. For what more should we judge
A blow on meeting with each thing can do
Than break it down and shatter it to bits?
Yet oft it chanceth, when a blow less harsh
Is dealt, the vital forces that remain
Are wont to win—aye, win, and lull to rest
The wild disorders rising from the blow,

And to its wonted post each vagrant part
Recall, that all the urgency of death
Which even now had all but set its seal
Upon our frame, is loosed, and sense that now
Was almost spent is made to flame anew.
For howe'er else, I ask, could living things
Back from the very gates of death return
With wits recovered, to the light of life,
Rather than reach that goal whereto their race
E'en now was almost run, and pass away?

Again, since there is pain when by some force
Disturbed throughout the living flesh and limbs
The bodies of our matter, all confused
In their abode within, lie ill at ease;
And when once more they settle to their place
We feel a bland relief, so mayst thou know
The first beginnings ne'er by any pain
Can be assailed, nor yet within themselves
Can any pleasure find; for they, be sure,
Are not themselves of first beginnings made,
Through whose new movements they may be distressed
Or in some soothing pleasure take delight.
Thus with no sense they needs must be endowed.

Once more, if to insure all living things
The power of feeling, sense must be assigned
Unto the first beginnings, what of those
Wherefrom the race of men in its own kind
Doth take its birth? Yea, surely, they will shake

With quivering mirth, and e'en will laugh aloud
Till face and cheeks are wet with briny tears;
And much besides they shrewdly will discourse
Of matter's varied minglings, and will ask
What in their turn are *their* first bodies, pray,
Since, being fashioned like whole mortal men,
They too must in their turn be likewise built
Of other particles, and these again
Of others, till nowhere thou darest to stop.
Nay, I shall follow; and whate'er thou say'st
Doth speak and laugh and think will be composed
Of other particles which likewise do.
But if we see this argument to be
But madmen's raving, and a man can laugh,
Without a store of laughing elements,
And think, and discourse all in learned lore,
Unblest with seeds discreet and eloquent,
Why, then, should things which as we see have sense
The less be able to exist, compact
Of seeds which lack all feeling from all time?

  Again, we all of heavenly seed are sprung;
Heaven is the sire of all, by whom the earth
Our kindly mother, when she hath conceived
The drops of watery moisture, big with life,
Doth bring to birth the smiling crops, and trees
That glad men's hearts, and race of mortal men;
And every kind of beast she bringeth forth
And giveth to each his meat, whereon they feed,
Drawing therefrom a pleasant sustenance,

And breed their offspring. Justly, therefore, earth
Hath won the name of mother. So what once
From earth arose doth sink to earth again,
And what from heaven's high coasts hath fallen doth go
To find once more its home in realms of heaven.
Nor e'er can death destroy things in such wise
That all the bodies of their matter fall
To ruin, but their union sundereth; then
One with another doth it join anew,
And thus it is that all things change their forms
And shift their colors, and sensations gain
And in a fleeting moment yield them up.
So thou mayst know it is of import great
What are the seeds wherewith these elements
Are linked, and in what order, and again
What mutual motions they do give and take.
Nor shouldst thou think that what we see to float
Upon the surface of created things,
Or now to birth arising, and at once
Passing away to naught, can e'er abide
Possessed of bodies of eternal mold.
Nay, in the letters of my verses here
It is of moment with what others each
Is joined, and how their mutual order lieth;
For with the same few letters we denote
Sky, earth, sea, streams, and sun, and yet again
Grains, trees, and living creatures. Of all these
The letters, if not all, yet in great part
Are similar, but order 'tis doth mark
Their different sound. Likewise it is with things:

When meetings, motions, order, place, and form
Are altered, things themselves must needs be changed.

Now lend thy mind, I pray, to truth's appeal;
For mightily do strive to win thine ear
A tale till now untold, and truths that wear
An aspect strange. Yet naught there is, I ween,
So quick to win our trust but that at first
It scarce can be believed; and likewise naught
So great and fraught with wonder that by bit
And bit all men cease not at length thereat
To marvel. Chief of these, the pure bright blue
Of heaven, and all it holdeth—stars that trace
Their wandering paths now here, now there, the moon,
The sun's bright burnished radiance—each of these,
If now to mortal eyes it should appear
First of its kind, and on a sudden burst
Upon our startled view, what tale would e'er
Be told more wonderful than this? Or what,
While yet unseen, would less command belief
In tribes of men? Naught, as I think; so strange
A marvel would these sights appear. But now,
Outwearied with the boredom of our seeing,
Not one will lift his eyes to heaven's bright realms!
Cease, then, dismayed by novelty alone,
To cast out reason from thy stubborn mind;
But rather with keen judgment weigh each thing,
And if it true appear, throw up thy hands
And yield thereto; but if thou find'st it false,
Gird up thy loins and fight it! For the mind

Doth seek to reason, since the store of space
Outside the ramparts of this world of ours
Doth stretch immeasurable, what is beyond
Whither the mind would follow, and the wings
Of our untrammeled spirit fain would soar.

Now, first, we find that through the general Whole,
In all its regions and toward every side,
On this hand and on that, above, below,
No limit hath been set, as I have shown,
And e'en the truth itself doth cry aloud,
And from its very deeps the boundless void
Doth shine forth clear. And, next, it should be thought
In no wise likely, since on every side
Doth stretch wide empty space, and seeds of things
Vast in their sum, in number numberless,
Flit here and yon in ceaseless movement driven,
That this our earth and sky have been alone
Created in their kind, while all the host
Of matter out beyond doth lie inert;
And most of all, since this our earth was made
By nature, and the seeds of things themselves
Blundering where'er they might their way along,
Huddled in many an aimless random mass,
Until at length some met, to be for aye,
Through their swift union, seeds of mighty things—
Earth, sea and sky, and tribes of living beings.
So, then, I say once more, we must confess
That elsewhere matter hath its other worlds
E'en such as this of ours, which e'er doth stand

Close clasped within the ether's warm embrace.
Besides, when ample stretcheth matter's store
Ready at hand, and space there is as well,
Nor any force or cause doth stay, 'tis clear
That things must come to action and be brought
To their full growth. If, then, the store of seeds
So vast doth stand that e'en the life entire
Of living beings could ne'er their number tell,
And if the selfsame laws of nature hold
Which have the power to cast the seeds of things
Together in their several places, e'en
As here they are together thrown, perforce
Thou must confess that other worlds exist
In other realms of space, and divers tribes
Of human kind and breeds of savage beasts.

This, too, we note, that in the Whole is found
Naught that doth stand alone, singly begot
And growing solitary and apart
From others of its kind, but each doth live
One of a class, with others of its ilk.
So, first of all, recall unto thy mind
The various living creatures; thou wilt find
In such sort are begot the breeds of beasts
That roam the mountains, thus the seed of men,
And thus again are born the silent shoals
Of scaly creatures, and the bodies too
Of flying fowl. Wherefore thou must confess
That likewise sky and earth, sun, moon and sea,
Yea, and all else besides, are not unique,

But rather of a number numberless,
Since e'en for them life's deep-set boundary-stone
Likewise doth surely wait, and they are born
With forms as mortal as the earthly breeds,
That teem with countless numbers of their kind.

So if thou holdest deep within thy heart
This well-learned truth, straightway is nature seen
Rid of her haughty lords and free at last,
Working her will in all things, asking naught
Of aid from gods. For by the holy hearts
Divine, that pass their lives in tranquil peace,
Secure and calm through the untroubled years,
Who can avail to rule the vast domains
Of the Immeasurable? Or who can hold
Within his hand the strong reins of the deep
To guide its course? Who hath the power to turn
All firmaments at once in every place,
That he may bring the darkness by his clouds,
Or make the bright clear ways of heaven to shake
Beneath his thunders, and anon hurl forth
His lightning bolts and bring red ruin down
On his own temples, then in baffled rage
Receding to the desert, practise there
The shaft which oft the guilty passeth by
And striketh down the pure and innocent?

But since the hour that saw the world begot
And the first birthday of the sea and earth
And rising of the sun, an ample store

Of bodies hath been added from without
And seeds from every side, which the great Whole
Hath brought together, tossing here and there,
Wherefrom might be increased the sea and lands,
And whence the dome of heaven might lift afar
Its lofty canopy high o'er the earth,
And air rise up between. For everywhere,
Each to its own, all bodies neath the rain
Of blows are parceled, and unto their kind
They all must pass, moisture to moisture; earth
From earthy substance groweth, fires forge fires,
Ether from ether waxeth, till at length
Nature, the author and the finisher,
Hath brought all things unto the end of growth,
As doth befall when no whit more can pass
Within the veins of life than what doth ebb
And so is lost. Here at this point the growth
Of every thing must cease, for at this point
Doth nature by her powers its increase curb.
For whate'er things thou seest wax and thrive
With glad increase, and climb at steady pace
The steps that lead to life's fruition, these
Take in more matter than they spend, while still
Their food with ease doth pass into their veins,
And their own bulk is not so broadly spread
That much they lose and more of matter waste
Than that whereon their life is nourished. Yea,
For we must grant that many bodies ebb
From things and pass away; yet more must come
Till they have reached their topmost peak of growth;
Then slowly time doth break their full-grown powers

And sap their strength, and life doth thenceforth take
The downward path. For verily the more
Of bulk a thing possesseth, and the more
Its surface spreadeth wide, the more, when once
Its increase hath been stopt, it needs must shed
Its outworn matter, sloughed from every side;
Nor easily, I ween, to all its veins
Is food supplied, nor doth the store suffice,
So vast the tide of matter that doth stream
From out its body, to repair its loss.
For food for their renewing must all things
Supply, yea, food support, and food sustain.
Yet all for naught, when veins cannot receive
Or nature bring whate'er is needful. Thus
'Twere meet things perish, when by constant ebb
Of their own substance they grow thin and rare,
Or neath the rain of blows without give way,
Since food at last doth fail their tottering age,
And from the outer world relentlessly
Squadrons of hostile matter, hammering home
Upon each thing with ceaseless beat their blows,
Break down its strength and conquer it at last.

Thus, then, the mighty walls that ring our world
Will be assaulted, and come tumbling down
In crumbling ruin. Yea, e'en now, forsooth,
Its life is broken, and our earth, outworn,
Will scarce bring forth her tiny creatures—she
Who once bore every breed, yea, brought to birth
Huge beasts with towering bodies. For, I ween,

No golden rope from heaven did first let down
The living races to the fields of earth,
Nor sea did cast them forth, nor waves that beat
Against the rocks; but 'twas the selfsame earth
Conceived them, who doth now from out her store
Yield them their nourishment. And all unasked
Of old she bore for mortals smiling fields
Of corn, and vines to glad their hearts, and gave
From her own hand sweet fruits and pleasant meads,
Which now, e'en aided by our labor, scarce
Will reach their growth. Meanwhile our oxen's toil
And planters' strength we waste, and though we wear
To naught our iron plowshares, scarce can win
From out our fields a scanty livelihood,
So grudging is their yield, so great our toil.

So ever more and more, with shaking head,
The aged plowman sigheth that in vain
Is spent his weary round of toil, and oft,
Matching the present times with times gone by,
Is wont to praise the fortunes of his sire.
Thus too the vineyarder, viewing with gloom
The aged, shriveled vines his hands have drest,
Doth curse the age, and all its evil ways,
And, wearying heaven with incessant prayers,
Mumbleth his plaint of how in olden days
Folk lived good pious lives, and easily
Could win a living from their little plots,
E'en though the measure of each man's demesne
Was less by far. Alas! he doth not grasp

That all things, wasting day by day, approach
Their grave, outwearied with the lingering years.[10]

wwwwwwwwwwwwwwwwwwwwwwwwww

[10] This gloomy picture of the decline of agriculture in Italy in the last
century before Christ, while accurate in its details, is entirely wrong in its
attribution of the real cause. Lucretius, with most of his contemporaries,
failed to see the true reasons for the sorry plight of the small farmer of
his day. The appalling loss of man-power during the long series of bloody
civil wars, the enormous increase in taxation, the competition of cheap
slave labor, the utter lack of a consistent governmental economic policy,
the protection of large land-holders whose estates were often acquired
and maintained by questionable practices—all these contributed in no
small degree to the impoverishment of the small independent farmer.

BOOK THREE

BOOK THREE

O thou who first from out the depths of night
Didst raise aloft so clear a lamp to shed
Its light upon the blessings of our life,
Thee now I follow, brightest star of all
The Grecian race, and in the well-worn paths
Thy feet have trod I set my eager steps;
Not that I fain would match my worth with thine,
But rather from the love I bear thee yearn
To follow thee afar. For how, I pray,
Should swallow hope to vie with swan, or how
In test of speed should kids aspire to match
The slender strength of their uncertain limbs
Against the might of some fleet-footed steed?
'Tis thou, O Father, hast the keys of truth;
Thou unto us thy children dost vouchsafe
A father's precepts; and from out thy scrolls,
O glorious one, as bees in flowery glades
From every bloom their nectar sip, so we
Likewise do feed upon thy golden words—
Golden, and blest with life forevermore.
For soon as e'er thy doctrines, sprung from out
Thy godlike heart, begin to cry aloud
The nature of all things, the fears that haunt
The mind disperse, and wide asunder fly
The ramparts of the firmament, till far

Across the reaches of the heavens I see
All things in restless motion through the void.
There, clothed in majesty, stand forth revealed
The heavenly presences, and those calm realms
Where never wind doth blow, nor stormy clouds
Send down in drenching floods their showers of rain,
Nor chilled to icy whiteness falleth e'er
The stain of snow; but ever-cloudless skies
Arch high above, and bathed in far-flung light
They smile serene. Never a need have they
But nature doth supply, nor aught doth e'er
Assail their calm untroubled peace of mind.
Yet nowhere to my vision do appear
The realms of Acheron, e'en though our earth
No bar doth set to hide the view of all
That through the void beneath our feet doth move.
So on my soul is laid a holy awe
And ecstasy divine, that nature thus
Unveiled by thee, O mighty one, doth stand
Revealed on every side to light of day.

And now, since I have taught thee heretofore
What nature the beginnings of all things
Display, and how with widely varying shapes,
Each as it will, they take their random flight
With ceaseless movement driven, and how therefrom
Each several thing can be created—next
I hold my task must be in clear-tongued verse
To show the nature of the mind and soul,
And forth in headlong haste to drive that fear
Of Acheron, which from its deepest roots

The life of man doth utterly confound,
Casting death's somber shadow on before
O'er all his path, nor doth it leave him e'en
One little joy untinged and unalloyed.
For though men oft declare that body's ills
And life of infamy must needs be feared
More bitterly than Tartarus and death,
And though they claim to know the mind is built
Of blood, or e'en of wind, if so perchance
Their whim doth tend, and hence they have no need
Of our philosophy—from this know well
These are but idle boasts to win applause
Rather than utterance of well-tested truths.
For oft these selfsame boasters, banned from out
Their native land, far from the sight of men,
Deep stained with some foul crime, and plunged in woe,
Live on, and still where'er their hapless way
They take, vows to the dead they pay, or now
Black cattle slaughter, and their offerings send
To gods below. Thus in their bitter plight
With keener diligence their hearts they turn
Unto religion. Wherefore 'twere more meet
To judge a man in doubt and danger, aye,
At fortune's ebb to weigh his worth; for then
At last true words are wrung from out his heart,
The mask is shed, the face of truth revealed.

So too, base greed and blind ambition's goad
Which drive unhappy mortals oft to leap
Beyond the bounds of right, and e'en at times
As willing tools sharing another's guilt

To strive both night and day with toil supreme
The heights of power to reach—these sickening sores
That wound our life in no small part are nursed
By fear of death. For oft the bitter scorn
Of other men, and pinching want appear
Far sundered from the pleasant, ordered ways
Of settled life, and lingering, as it were,
Before the gates of death. Thus neath the spur
Of terrors false, seeking to flee afar
From these same woes and drive them far abroad,
Men pile their substance high in civil strife,
And count with greedy hands the mounting heaps
Of riches earned with blood, and mid the tears
That drench a brother's bier, their cruel hearts
Beat high with joy, while cowed with conscious guilt
They hate and shun the tables of their kin.
And oft likewise by this same fear beset
They waste with envy and bewail their lot,
That they must see another rise to hold
The honored place of power, another draw
The gaze of men and in the brilliant glare
Of recognition move, while they themselves
Are wrapt in mire and darkness. So ofttimes
They give their lives for statues and a name!
And oft from fear of death, hatred of life
And looking on the light doth fix on men
So firm a grasp that in their deep despair
They seek their doom, forgetful that the source
Of all their ills in this same fear doth lie;
That this it is that doth their honor stain,
This that doth burst the bonds of friendship, aye

All sweet affection's uses overthrow.
For oft ere now, in their desire to shun
The realms of Acheron, men have betrayed
Their native land and those that gave them birth.
For e'en as children tremble with affright
At darkness' unseen terrors, so at times
Do we ourselves in broad daylight have fear
Of things which we in truth should dread no more
Than those vain fancies children in the dark
Do tremble at and fear will come alive.
This terror, then, this gloom that doth enshroud
Our troubled minds, not piercing rays of sun
Nor day's bright shining beams must needs dispel,
But nature's outward mien and inward law.

First, then, I say the *animus,* which oft
We term the mind, or intellect, wherein
Is set the reasoning and control of life,
Is part of man, no less than hand or foot
Or eyes are part of living beings entire.
Yet some there be, forsooth, who would maintain
That mind's sensation nowhere hath been set
In place determined, but can only be
A certain vital habit, as it were,
Of the living body, which the Greeks have termed
A 'harmony', since it doth make us live
As sentient beings, though no single part
Itself hath mind; e'en as one oft will say
Good health is of the body, yet nowise
Is it a part of him whose body's health is sound.
So they place not the mind's intelligence

In any part determined; but herein
They seem to me to wander far astray.
For oft the body, which is plain to see,
May suffer pain, the while some hidden part
May give us pleasure; and contrariwise
The opposite will oft be true, as when
One wretched in his mind will pleasure feel
In all his body, in no other wise
Than when a sick man's foot will twinge with pain
And yet his head may suffer not at all.
Again, when all the limbs to slumber soft
Are yielded up, and the tired body lieth
Relaxed and reft of sense, something besides
There is within us which e'en then is moved
In various ways, and in itself doth feel
Stirrings of joy and idle cares of heart.

And now, that thou mayst learn that what we term
The *anima*,[1] or soul, doth likewise dwell
Among the limbs, nor is the body wont
To feel by 'harmony', consider first
How oft 'twill happen that despite the loss
Of many a member, life will linger on
Within the frame; or how again, when but
A few small particles of heat have fled
Abroad, and from the lips only a breath

~~~~~~~~~~~~~~~~~~~~~~~~~~~~~~~

[1] It is not always easy to draw a sharp line between Lucretius' conception of *animus* and *anima*. In general it may be said that *animus* is synonymous with intelligence or mentality. *Anima*, although usually to be taken in the sense of soul, appears at times to signify the life principle, or even consciousness.

Of air hath issued forth, this selfsame life
Forthwith doth flee our veins and leave our bones.
So mayst thou learn from this that every kind
Of body hath not equal function, nay,
Nor equally do all support our life;
Rather 'tis those that are the seeds of wind
And gentle warmth that keep life lingering on
Throughout the limbs. 'Tis therefore warmth and breath
Of life within our body which forsake
The dying frame. So, then, since mind and soul
Are in their nature found a part of man,
Give back that name of 'harmony', brought down
Among those fiddlers, from high Helicon
Or wheresoever else they dragged it forth
And clapped it on to that which lacked a name.
Whate'er it be, let it be theirs to keep;
And thou, give ear unto my theme anew.

Now I contend that mind and soul are held
In union each to each, and of themselves
Make up a single nature; but the head,
As I would term it, and the ruling power
In all our body is the reason, yea,
That which we call the mind or intellect.
And this doth have its fixt abode midway
Within the region of the breast: [2] for here
It is that fear and terror throb, and here
Sweet soothing joys maintain their dwelling-place.

[2] It seems strange to us that the function of the brain was all but completely ignored by ancient philosophers.

Here, therefore, is the mind, the *animus;*
But all the part which doth remain, of soul
Or *anima,* lieth dispersed abroad
Throughout the frame, and doth obedience yield
Unto the mind, moved at its touch and will.
And unto mind alone is given the power
To know itself, and in itself rejoice
When naught doth soul and body stir as well.
And as when head or eye, assailed with pain,
Doth hurt us, yet in all the body else
We suffer no distress, so doth the mind
At times feel pain or thrill with joy, the while
Its twin, the soul, by no new sense is stirred
Throughout the limbs and members. But ofttimes
When by a fear more violent the mind
Is shaken, we perceive the soul as well
To suffer with it through the frame entire,
And sweat and pallor on a sudden start
On all the limbs, the tongue is thick, the voice
Doth falter, eyes are dimmed, ears ring, and limbs
Grow faint, and at the last we often see
Men fall to earth from terror of the mind.
Thus any man from this may well believe
That soul is linked with mind, since by the force
Of mind impelled it thus straightway can thrust
The body forward, yea, e'en strike it down.

So too, this selfsame reasoning will show
The nature of the mind and soul to be
Corporeal; for since 'tis seen to move
The limbs, to snatch from sleep our frame, to change

The countenance, yea even guide and turn
The man entire, not one whereof we see
Can come to pass apart from touch, nor touch
In turn apart from body, must we not
Perforce confess that mind and soul are formed
Of body's nature? And thou seest besides
That mind doth oft with body suffer, yea,
Its feeling share. And if the grisly shock
Of some deep-driven weapon hath laid bare
Sinews and bones, yet, howe'er narrowly,
Hath failed to reach the life, there doth ensue
A faintness, and a strange half-sweet desire
To seek the ground, and on the ground a surge
Of swift confusion, and from time to time
A wavering will to rise as if from sleep.
Therefore the nature of the mind must be
Corporeal, since it doth suffer harm
From weapons and from blows corporeal.

　　Now of what kind of body doth the mind
Consist, and out of what it hath been formed
I shall proceed to render thee account
In my discourse. First, then, I do assert
It is exceeding fine in texture, shaped
Of bodies most minute. That this is so
Give ear and learn from what I next proclaim.
No thing is there we see to come to pass
So swiftly as a thought within the mind
Is pictured and at once in motion set.
More swiftly, then, doth mind itself bestir

Than aught besides in all the tale of things
Whose natures stand forth clear for all to see.
But being so nimble it must needs be formed
Of seeds exceeding round and passing small,
That by the tiniest impulse struck they move.
For so with but the slightest impact stirred
Will water start and tremble, since 'tis formed
Of tiny bodies, round and quick to roll;
But honey's nature, quite in other wise,
Is firmer, and more sluggish is its fluid,
Its movement more reluctant; for the mass
Of all its matter doth together cling
Because, no doubt, of particles less smooth
It doth consist, and seeds less fine and round.
So e'en a breath, however light and held
In balance delicate, can yet constrain
A high-piled heap of poppy seed [3] to fall
Apart from top to base before thine eyes;
But quite in other wise a pile of stones
Or heaped-up corn ears it can ne'er dislodge.
Thus, then, will bodies of a finer mold
And smoother, with proportionate nimbleness
Be dowered; but on the other hand, all things
Found heavier and more rough so much the more
Are firmly set. Now, therefore, since the mind
Is in its nature found of nimbleness
Beyond all else, so must it needs be formed
Of bodies passing small, and smooth, and round.

wwwwwwwwwwwwwwwwwwwwwww

[3] See note 4, p. 77.

This truth to hold well grasped, good friend, will serve
Thee well in many ways, and useful prove.
Again, this fact as well will clearly show
The nature of the mind, how thin must be
Its texture, and how small the space wherein
It might be held, could it be gathered there:
When once the untroubled peace of death hath crept
Upon a man, and stolen away is all
The mingled nature of his mind and soul,
Naught canst thou there discern of loss of all
The body's sum, in aspect or in weight;
But death doth keep all save the sense of life
And living warmth. And so it needs must be
Of seeds exceeding small and fine is formed
The soul, linked on through veins and flesh and thews,
Since when from out the frame entire it now
Hath wholly fled, yet doth the outward mold
Of every limb remain unchanged, nor lost
Is one least jot of weight. E'en so it is
When fled from wine is all its rare bouquet,
Or vanished into air the fragrant breath
Of perfume, or the savor spent and lost
From aught besides; still no whit less doth seem
Unto our eyes the thing itself, nor aught
Is seen to be diminished from its weight,
Because, be sure, many and tiny seeds
Make up the flavor and the scent in all
The body of things. Wherefore I say once more
We can be sure the nature of the mind
And soul is formed of seeds surpassing small,
Since, fleeing, no jot of weight doth it withdraw.

Yet not unmixt this nature must we deem,
For 'tis a certain slender breath doth leave
The dying, mixt with heat, and heat in turn
Doth with itself draw air; nor is there heat
Which hath not air commingled in its frame.
For since rare is its nature, it must be
That many seeds of air will move about
Within it. Thus already we have found
The nature of the soul to be threefold.
Yet e'en all these will scarce suffice, I ween,
To bring to birth sensation, since the mind
Will not admit that aught of these can breed
Sense-bringing motions or the thoughts that surge
Within the mind itself; nay, there must be
Some nature else thereto assigned, to make
A fourth as well. Yet this is all unnamed,
Though naught existeth nimbler or more fine,
Or formed of smaller or of smoother seeds.
For first itself is roused, being framed of shapes
Minute, then heat the motion doth receive,
And hidden power of wind, then air in turn,
And next in order due are all things else
To movement stirred: the blood is roused, and all
The flesh is waked to feeling, till at last
To bones and marrow doth it pass, as sense
Of pleasure, or a pang of other kind.
But yet not idly pain or biting ill
May thus far make its way; but that all things
Are so disordered that no place is left
For life, and out through all the body's pores
Scatter abroad the particles of soul.

And yet most often it will chance that there
At body's very surface, as it were,
The fatal motions halt, and by such means
We can avail to keep the life within.

Now as I long to give account of how
Commingled each with each, and in what forms
Together bound they live and flourish, all
Against my will the far too slender store
Of this my country's tongue doth hold me back.
Yet even so, as my poor powers permit,
I shall take up the theme in compass brief.
For to and fro with movements that accord
With first beginnings do their primal seeds
Concurrent paths pursue, nor e'er can one
Be set apart alone, nor can its powers
Be put in play sundered by empty space
Far from the rest; but, as it were, they form
The many forces of one substance. E'en
As in the flesh of any kind ye will
Of living creatures, there is smell and tinge
Of certain color, aye, and savor—yet
From all of these is built a single bulk
Of body, so do heat, and air, and power
Unseen of wind, together mingled, form
One nature, blended with that nimble force
Which doth disperse among them from itself
The first impulse to motion, whence arise
Sense-bringing movements throughout all the flesh.
For deep, deep down beneath and deeply hid
This nature lieth, nor doth aught abide

Below in all our body, nay itself
As soul of all our very soul doth dwell.
E'en as infused through limbs and all our frame
The force of mind and power of soul doth lurk
Unseen, being built of bodies small and rare,
So, I would have thee learn, this force unnamed
Of tiny bodies fashioned, all unseen
Doth lie, and likewise in its turn doth dwell
As very soul of all our soul, and hold
Dominion in our body's frame entire.
In such wise, too, it needs must be that wind
And air and heat together act, infused
Throughout the limbs; yet one will lag behind
The rest, or crowd in front, that so each thing
Though formed of all will yet appear as one;
Lest heat and wind, and power of air, apart
One from another, all sensation end
And by their severance scatter it to naught.

Thus hath the mind that heat which it doth show
When roused to anger, and from flashing eyes
Bright fires do leap; but spirit chill it hath
As well, that doth attend on fear, and spread
A shivering o'er the limbs, yea, e'en doth move
The frame entire. And last there is an air
Of calm, that doth prevail whene'er the breast
Is tranquil, and the countenance serene.
But greater store of heat those creatures hold
Whose fiery hearts and minds impassioned blaze
To sudden rage. Whereof in foremost rank
Doth stand the furious force of lions, that oft

With groan and roar would burst their very hearts,
Nor can they shut within their prisoning breasts
The full tide of their wrath. But more of wind
The deer's cold heart doth hold, and through its flesh
More swiftly doth it speed the chilling airs
That set its limbs a-tremble with affright.
But oxen's nature more from placid air
Its life doth draw; nor e'er o'ermuch is roused
By touch of anger's smoldering fires that spread
Their murk of dusky darkness, nor benumbed
With dread, transfixt by frozen shafts of fear;
But midway doth it stand, between the breeds
Of deer and raging lions. So it is
With human kind. E'en though their training bring
To certain men an equal culture, still
'Twill leave some early traces of the bent
Of each one's mind. Nor must we think those ills
Can be uprooted and cast out entire,
But that one man will run at headlong pace
To bitter anger, and another yield
More readily to fear, while yet a third
Will take some things more gently than is meet.
In many ways besides it needs must be
Men's natures differ, and the habits too
That spring therefrom; whose causes all unseen
I can not now set forth, nor seek out names
To match the number of the elements
Wherefrom doth rise this varied store of things.
Yet this herein I clearly can affirm:
So small the traces of these natures left

Within, which reason's power can not dispel
That naught may bar the living of our lives
In manner worthy of the gods themselves.

This nature, then, of soul is kept within
The body's wholeness, and itself doth stand
As guardian of the body and the cause
Of life within us. For by common roots
They cling together, nor can e'er, 'tis clear,
Without the ruin of both be torn apart;
And e'en as 'tis not easy from a lump
Of frankincense to tear away the scent
But that its nature too will pass away,
Likewise the nature of the mind and soul
Can not with ease from out the body's frame
Entire be banished save with ruin of all.
So from their first begetting do they move
With primal bodies intertwined, and dowered
With life they share in common; nor, 'tis clear,
Can power of body or of mind apart
Have aught of feeling, either for itself
Without the other's aid, but linked in one
By common motions of these twain is sense
Kindled and fanned to life throughout our flesh.
Again, at no time by itself apart
The body is begotten, nor alone
Doth grow and thrive, nor is it seen to last
Beyond the final day of death; for ne'er—
As water's moisture oft will render up
Its borrowed heat and yet itself thereby
No dissolution suffer, but remain

Unscathed—never, I say, in this same wise
Can the abandoned frame avail to bear
The sundering of the soul, but all unknit
Will sink to dissolution and decay.
So from their earliest hour body and soul
In mutual bonds the vital motions learn,
Yea, e'en while hid within the mother's womb,
That so no sundering may they know, apart
From hurt and ruin to themselves. Wherefore,
Since closely linked the cause which doth ensure
Their very life, so mayst thou surely know
Their natures too must needs be joined in one.

    And furthermore, should one incline to hold
That body can not feel, and to believe
'Tis soul blent with the body that doth catch
This motion which we call sensation, so
He taketh arms against plain truth. For who,
I pray, will e'er bring proof of body's sense
If it be not what fact itself hath taught
And shown us? 'But,' thou sayst, 'when soul is fled,
Body doth everywhere sensation lack.'
Aye, for it loseth what in life was ne'er
Its own; and gone are many things beside
When it is driven from the bounds of life.

    To say, moreover, that the eyes can naught
Behold, but that as through an open door
The mind through them doth see, is hard to win
Belief, since e'en the feeling of our eyes
Must tend against it; for their sense doth draw,

Yea, e'en compel toward the pupils, when
Objects too bright we oft cannot perceive
As vision keen to keener light doth yield.
But 'tis not thus with doorways; for the doors
Through which we see ne'er suffer aught of ill
When they are opened. Further, if our eyes
But serve as doors, so should the mind discern
All things more clearly with the eyes removed,
Yea, with the very doorposts torn away.

Herein thou couldst in no wise hold as true
That doctrine, sprung from out the holy heart
Of our Democritus,[4] that each by each
The first beginnings of body and of soul
In order alternate are set, and thus
They weave the patterned fabric of our limbs.
For as the particles of soul are found
Smaller by far than those whereof are framed
Body and flesh, so, too, they needs must yield
In number, and but thinly through the limbs
Be scattered, yet so thou wilt warrant this:
That small as are the tiniest bodies which

---

4 Democritus, born about 460 B.C., and said to have lived more than a hundred years, was called "the most learned of the Greeks before Aristotle". He was the real founder of the atomic theory, that is, the doctrine that the universe was formed out of atoms, operating in space or void. These atoms are infinite in number, indivisible, indestructible, and their difference in size, form, and arrangement accounts for the difference in created things. The soul consists of smooth round atoms, which in their motion, penetrating the whole body, produce the phenomena of life. It is evident that the system of Epicurus is, of all ancient systems, the most closely connected with that of Democritus.

When cast upon our limbs can first arouse
Sense-bringing motions in our frame, so great
The intervals first bodies of the soul
Preserve between. For oftentimes when dust
Hath gathered thick upon our body, yet
We feel it not, nor know when on our limbs
Doth drift fine-sifted chalk; nor do we sense
A mist at night, nor feel the slender threads
By spider spun, that drift athwart our face
And snare us as we move, all unaware
That on our head hath fallen her tattered web.
So, too, a feather wafted from the wing
Of flying bird we feel not, or the seeds
That float from thistles in such airy wise
That scarce they seem to fall. Nor yet the trace
Of every crawling creature do we sense,
Or mark each tiny footfall one by one,
As gnats or other breeds minute do move
Across our body. Such indeed must be
The store of things within us stirred, or e'er
The seeds of soul commingled in our limbs
Throughout the frame may feel the surging shock
Of stirring elements, and speeding down
Their wonted ways may rush together, meet
For one brief instant, and in turn leap back.

But mind at life's far barriers doth keep
A closer ward, and mightier mastery
O'er life doth wield than all the power of soul;
For reft of mind and understanding ne'er
Can e'en the smallest part of soul maintain

For one brief breath of time within our frame
Its dwelling-place, but following in its train
With ne'er a backward look, will fly abroad
Into the air, leaving the chilling frame
In the cold clasp of death. Yet he whose mind
And understanding have stood fast, himself
In life doth firmly stand; for howe'er much
The trunk is mangled, yea, though all the limbs
On every side are lopped, and soul be torn
And reft from every member all about,
Yet will he live and draw the breath of heaven
To give him life. Aye, stript, if not of all,
Yet of a great part of his soul, he still
Doth linger on and cling to life. E'en as
When all around the eye is torn, if yet
The pupil hath remained unharmed, then still
Abideth firm the living power of sight;
(But only shouldst thou not outright destroy
The whole ball of the eye, and cutting round
The pupil, leave it by itself; for that
Will not be done without the ruin as well
Of all the eye.) But if that tiny part,
The very center of the eye, is gnawed away,
Straightway the light is gone, and in its place
Darkness doth fall, howe'er in all the rest
Of its bright orb the eye may whole remain.
By such a compact, then, body and soul
In mutual union bound forever dwell.

Come now, that thou mayst learn how mind and soul,
Light though they be, of living creatures, yet

Are born and die, I shall proceed to strike
For thee chords that I long have sought, and found
With joyous toil, to match thy life's dear worth.
Be thine to link these twain as one beneath
A single name, and when, to choose a case,
I henceforth speak of soul, and prove its state
Is mortal, make no doubt I speak as well
Of mind, since each with each they are at one,
And form a single nature. First of all,
Since I have shown it hath a texture fine
Built up of tiny bodies, yea of seeds
Far more minute than those whereof are formed
Soft water's moisture, cloud or smoke; so these
In speed of motion doth it far surpass,
And sooner will it move by some slight cause
Impelled; since e'en by images of smoke and cloud
It oft is stirred, as when in slumber wrapt
We seem to see high altars breathe aloft
Their clouds of steam and smoke (for past all doubt
It is as idols [5] these are to us borne);
Now, therefore, since, when shattered all in bits,
Doth lie a vessel, forth from every side
Thou'lt see the water pour, its limpid streams
Spreading this way and that; and seeing that clouds
And smoke scatter in air, so, be assured,

[5] The "simulacra", idols, or images of things, which in the Epicurean
system form the basis of the physical sensation of sight, were conceived
as thin films of atomic matter which were constantly thrown off in every
direction from the surface of all things. These material emanations were
thought to be borne through the air more or less intact, and to strike the
eyes. This curious "corpuscular" theory is discussed at length in Book IV.

Doth soul as well disperse, and sooner far
Will perish and in briefer space dissolve
Into its primal bodies, once withdrawn
From limbs of mortal man and fled away.
For since the body, the vessel, as it were,
That held the soul, no longer can avail
To keep it in, shattered by some mischance
Or thinned and weakened with the loss of blood
From out its veins; how then canst thou believe
It can be held together by an air
More thin and less entrammeling than our frame?

Again, feeling doth prove that mind is born
Along with body, and with it step by step
Doth grow, and equally must waste with age.
For e'en as children totter with a weak
And tender frame, so doth a slender wit
Attend thereon; but as with riper years
Their strength doth wax, wisdom will grow apace
And force of mind gain increase. And at last,
When time's stern strength hath sapped the frame, and
    loosed
Are all the limbs, their powers benumbed, anon
The wits are lamed, tongue raveth, mind is shaken,
All things give way and in one breath are fled.
'Tis meet, then, that the nature of the mind
Should all be scattered likewise, e'en as smoke
Into the high-flung breezes of the air;
Since side by side with body do we see
It brought to birth, and side by side they grow,
And worn with age together droop and fade.

Next there is this: as body's self we see
To suffer fell disease and piercing pain,
Mind hath its carking cares, and grief and fear;
Wherefore 'twere meet it share as well in death.
Nay, oft in ills of body doth the mind
Go wandering astray: the sufferer's wits
Are all unstrung—he raveth, and at times
O'ercome by heavy lethargy will sink
Into a deep unending sleep, wherefrom
No voices doth he hear, nor can he know
The faces of his kin who stand about
Calling him back to life, while face and cheeks
Stream with their tears. Wherefore thou must confess
That mind itself may dissolution know,
Since deep within doth penetrate the taint
Of sickness; for alike disease and pain
Are fashioners of death, as long ere now
We have been taught by many a man's decease.

Again, when once the fiery potency
Of wine hath stolen into a man and spread
Abroad through all his veins its liquid fire,
Why is it there doth follow in the frame
A heaviness, as the uncertain limbs
Stagger and stumble, tongue becometh thick,
The mind is sodden, eyes are bleared; meanwhile
Shouting, sobbing, and quarreling grow apace
And all the signs that go along therewith?
Why come all these to pass, except it be
The mastering might of wine is wont to throw
The mind in turmoil, e'en within the frame?

But things which in such wise can fall a prey
Unto confusion and disorder, these
Bear witness that were yet some other cause
A little greater to strike root within,
They needs must perish, reft henceforth of life.
Nay, oft before our eyes some man, struck down
By fell distemper,[6] all at once will fall
As by a lightning stroke, the while his lips
Are stained with froth, groaning and shuddering rack
His frame, his wits are lost, muscles grow taut,
Writhing and gasping scourge him, while his limbs
He wearieth with their tossing to and fro.
And thus because, no doubt, the cruel force
Of the distemper, loosed throughout the limbs
Doth all the soul confound and lash to foam,
E'en as upon the briny plains the waves,
By fierce winds whipt, flash white with seething froth.
As for his groanings, these are from him wrung
Because his limbs are racked with pain, and most
Since all the particles of voice, when thrust
From out the mouth, go crowding forth apace
Where lieth, as 'twere, the paven path they knew.
And loss of wits doth follow, since the power
Of mind and soul is all confounded, yea,
Torn wide apart, and tossed this way and that,
As I have shown, by that same taint unhinged.
But when at length the fever that provoked
The baneful seizure hath its rancor spent,

––––––––––––––––––––––––––

[6] This vivid description of a sufferer from epilepsy bespeaks the true scientific observer.

And back into its dark retreats hath crept
The bitter humor of the cankered frame,
Then first with drunken staggerings doth rise
The luckless sufferer, and bit by bit
His senses rally and his soul once more
Will take its wonted place. When, therefore, these
Within the very body by such ills
Are racked and torn, and in such dreadful wise
Do suffer, why wilt thou believe that reft
From out the body they can keep their life
In unfenced air, among the warring winds?

Again, since we do see that ailing minds
No less than sickly bodies can be cured
And changed by healing potions, so in this
We read a warning that the mind doth live
A mortal life. For whosoe'er would seek
To change the mind, or strive to alter aught
Of other nature, first must add thereto
Yet other parts, or shift their place, or take
From the whole sum one tiny jot at least;
But that which is immortal suffereth not
Its sum to be diminished or increased.
For whatsoe'er doth suffer change and pass
Beyond its boundaries, straightway will prove
The death of that which did exist before.
If, then, the mind doth sicken, it doth show
Signs of a mortal nature, as but now
I have disclosed, or if by physick healed.
So promptly doth true fact catch up its arms
Against false doctrine, and cut off retreat

From him who fleeth, and with the twin-edged sword
Of truth pursue and prove him false of heart.

  And often, too, we see a man let go
By bit and bit his life, and limb by limb
The vital feeling lose; for first the toes
And nails upon his feet grow livid, then
The feet and legs will die, and last through all
The frame besides, on creeping step by step,
Steal the slow footprints of benumbing death.
Yet since the nature of the soul is rent,
Nor e'er at once doth issue forth entire,
It must be reckoned mortal. But perchance
Shouldst thou believe that soul from all the frame
Can shrink away, and to a single place
Gather its several parts, and so withdraw
Its sense from all the members; still that place
Whereto is mustered such a store of soul
Should be discerned to boast a keener sense.
But since such place is nowhere found, 'tis clear,
As I have claimed but now, that it is torn
And scattered all abroad, and so is lost.
Nay, e'en should we be minded to concede
A premise false, and grant 'twere possible
For all the soul to gather in a mass
Within the body of a dying man,
As bit by bit from his dim eyes doth fade
The light of day, yet even so the soul
Must be accounted mortal, nor one jot
Will matter if it perish, blown abroad
Into the airs, or, gathered into one

From all its parts, to brutish stupor sink,
When more and more in every part the sense
Doth fail the man entire, and less and less
Of life in every part doth linger on.

　　And since the mind is found a proper part
Of man, and hath its habitation fixt
In place determined, e'en as ears and eyes
And other instruments of sense which hold
The helm of life, and as the hand or eye
Or nose, sundered from us, can nowise feel,
Nay, e'en exist, but in brief space dissolve
In base corruption, so the mind alone
Cannot live on without the body, nay,
Without the living man himself, who is
Its vessel, as it were, or whate'er else
Thou'lt choose to figure e'en more closely linked,
So firm thereto are body's fastenings set.

　　Again, by mutual union do prevail
The living powers of body and of soul,
And thus avail to live. For ne'er, apart
From body, can the nature of the mind
Alone give birth to vital motions; nor
Bereft of soul, can body's self avail
To hold to life and know the joys of sense.
Nay, in such wise as by itself the eye
Torn by its roots away can naught discern
Apart from all the body, so, 'tis clear,
No virtue by themselves have soul and mind;
And this because, no doubt, through veins and flesh,

Sinews and bones infused, their primal seeds
Are by the body's wholeness kept secure
In union close, nor can they leap apart
Unhindered, with long intervals between;
And in such wise confined they can give rise
To those sense-bringing motions, which no more,
When, once outside the body after death,
They fly into the breezes of the air,
Can they produce, since then they are not held
Close bound in equal wise. For air, forsooth,
Will be a body, yea, a living thing
If soul can shut itself therein, and curb
Its powers to those brief motions it doth make
Within the sinews and in all the frame.
Wherefore I say once more, with all the ward
Of body loosed, the vital breath gone forth,
We must confess that sense of mind doth sink
To dissolution, yea, and soul as well,
The cause of death being closely linked in both.

   And further, since the body cannot bear
The severing of the soul, but to decay
And noisome stench doth melt, why dost thou doubt
That all the force of soul from deep within
Hath gathered, and forth trickling bit by bit
Scattered like smoke abroad; and body, too,
A changed and shapeless thing, doth lie in vast
And crumbling ruin, since its very walls
Are shaken from their place, as more and more
The soul doth stream from out the limbs through all
The body's devious ways, and issueth forth

From every pore? So, then, in many a wise
Thou mayest learn that through the frame hath **passed**
The nature of the soul, sundered in parts;
Aye, e'en within the body was it all
In fragments torn, ere it could issue forth
To drift upon the breezes of the air.

For none, 'tis clear, doth feel at death his soul
Go forth entire from out his body, nay,
Nor rising first to throat and mouth above,
But rather failing in its wonted place,
E'en as he doth perceive each several sense
As well in its appointed place to fade.
But were the mind immortal, in the hour
Of death its grief were less that it must melt
To dissolution than that it must pass
And like a snake leave but its slough behind.

Nay, e'en while held within the bounds of life
The soul ofttimes, by some mischance assailed,
Is seen to struggle to escape, and loose
The fastenings of the body, while the face
Sunken and pale doth grow, as in the hour
Of death, and all the failing limbs fall limp
Upon the bloodless frame. For so it is
When men will say 'the heart hath had a shock',
Or else 'the heart hath failed', when all about
Is swift confusion, and the frightened house
Strive each and all to clutch the last slight link
Of lingering life. For then sore shaken lie
The mind and all the potency of soul,

And with the body's self totter and fall;
So would a cause a little graver bring
Destruction unto both. Why, then, still doubt
So frail a thing, outside the body driven
Into the fenceless air, all shelter lost,
Could not abide, not through all time alone,
But ne'er for one brief moment could endure?

Again, why is it mind's intelligence
And power of reason ne'er is born in head,
Or feet, or hands, but to a single spot
In all alike doth cling, and keepeth e'er
A fixt abode, except that to each thing
Hath been assigned its place appropriate
Where it may come to birth, and where, once born,
It may live on and keep its place as one
Of many members, so dispersed that ne'er
Confusion in their order will prevail?
So surely from each cause doth spring effect
Appropriate, nor e'er are wont to rise
Flames out of floods, nor frost to spring from fire.

And further, if the nature of the soul
Immortal doth abide, and soul itself
Sundered from body hath the power to feel,
Then must it be conceived as being endowed
With five-fold senses; nor in other wise
Can fancy shape for us the souls that flit
Through realms of Acheron below. For thus
Painters and bards of old their tales have told
Of souls endowed with senses. But in truth

Nor eyes, nor nose, nor hand itself can e'er
Apart exist for souls, nor tongue nor ears
Sundered from body. So must we deny
Feeling, yea, even being, to the soul.

And since we see that in the frame entire
Doth dwell the vital feeling, and the whole
A living thing abideth, should some force
Cleave through its midst with swift and sudden stroke
That left each sorry half to lie apart,
So, too, no doubt, the soul that dwelt therein
Must needs be cleft in twain, riven and torn
E'en as the body. But whate'er is cleft
And sundered into parts doth, past all doubt,
Disclaim eternal nature. So, 'tis said
That oft in shock of battle, where doth rage
The fiercest carnage, with so swift a stroke
Will scythe-shod chariots lop the unwitting limb
From some stout warrior, that the sundered flesh
Shorn from its trunk, abandoned on the ground,
Is seen to twitch and quiver. Yet the mind
Of eager youth, unheeding, feeleth naught
Of pain, so sudden is the stroke, so rapt
His very soul with fervor of the fight.
So with his lessened limbs straight doth he make
For where the fight is thickest, recking naught
Of lost left arm, that, shield and all, the wheels
Have borne afar amid the weltering ruck
Of horses and devouring scythes. And one
There is who knoweth not his good right arm
Hath dropt, but once again doth mount, and leap

Into the fray. And one, bereft of leg,
Will strive to rise, while by him on the ground
His severed foot doth twitch its dying toes.
So, too, lopt from the warm and living trunk
And rolling on the ground, a head will keep
The look of life, with wide and staring eyes,
Until at length it hath surrendered all
Its residue of soul. Nay more, shouldst choose
To hew in pieces with an axe the length
Of some sleek snake with forked and flickering tongue
And tail a-lash, so wilt thou straight perceive
The several parts each writhing neath the stroke
And spattering all the ground with gore, as head
With mouth agape doth make for tail, that so,
Sore smitten by the burning pains that sear
Its grievous wounds, it may assuage their hurt
With biting. Are we then to say that souls
Exist, whole and entire, in these small bits
Of body? But from reasoning like to this
'Twill follow that a single living thing
Doth in one body many souls conceal;
Therefore divided is that soul which once
Was one together with the body. Thus
Both must be reckoned mortal, for that each
Alike in many fragments hath been cleft.

Moreover, if the nature of the soul
Immortal doth abide, and at our birth
Doth pass into our body, why will ne'er
A memory stir us of that time which passed
Ere we were born, or why do we retain

No trace of deeds then done? For if the power
Of mind hath been so changed that gone is all
Our memory of the past, that state, I trow,
Is but a little step removed from death.
Wherefore thou must confess the soul which was
Of old hath passed away, and this which now
Doth hold its place hath been but now new-born.
Once more, if, when our body hath received
Its form complete, the living power of mind
Is wont to enter, as we come to birth
And ope the door to life, so 'twere not meet
It should be seen to grow with body, yea,
With all the limbs and in the very blood;
But meet it were that it should dwell apart
As in a cage alone, yet in such wise
That body's self no less be rich in sense.
Wherefore I say once more, we must not think
Souls know not birth and shun the laws of death;
For souls, be sure, were scarce so closely linked
Unto our bodies, if from source without
They were engrafted. (But clear fact doth show
That thus they cling, since through the web entire
Of veins and flesh, sinews and bones, doth run
The thread of soul, that so e'en teeth withal
Sensation share, as oft an ache will show
When water's chill doth bring a sudden twinge,
Or when, unwitting, in a piece of bread
We bite upon the fragment of a stone.)
Nor yet, I ween, with web so closely woven
Can souls come forth entire, and all unmarred
Unweave themselves from sinews, bones and joints.

But if perchance thou deemst the soul is wont
To be engrafted in us from without
And then to make its way through all the limbs,
So all the more it needs must perish, fused
With body's frame. For what doth permeate
Must needs dissolve, and so must pass away,
Spread all abroad throughout the body's veins.
For e'en as food, when once it hath been poured
Through all the limbs and members, doth dissolve
And from itself provide a nature new,
So mind and soul, with frame howe'er unmarred
They pass into a new-formed body, still
In passing through must needs dissolve, the while
Through all the limbs are filtered, as it were,
Those particles whereof are fashioned all
This nature of the mind that now doth hold
Its sway in all our body, born from that
Which in its turn hath perished, spread abroad
Among the limbs. So, then, 'tis plain to see
The nature of the soul is neither reft
Of day of birth, nor yet exempt from death.

Again, are seeds of soul left lingering on,
Or no, within the lifeless frame? For so,
If they be left, and still abide therein,
'Twill follow that the soul can scarce with right
Be held immortal, since reduced and reft
Of certain parts it hath resigned the frame.
But if we hold that it hath fled the limbs
And flown away, nor in the body left
Aught of itself, how cometh it to pass

That rotting flesh of corpses oft doth teem
With worms? Whence come, I say, these multitudes
Of living creatures manifold that surge
Boneless and bloodless through the heaving frame?
But if perchance thou deemst that from without
Souls in the worms are grafted, and can find
Each several one his body, nor dost e'er
Consider whence it is that myriad souls
Of living things have gathered where but one
Hath flown, yet this there is which doth appear
Worth while to ask thyself and put to test:
If ever souls go hunting for the seeds
Of little worms, and build themselves a home
Wherein to dwell, or find a lodging place
In bodies as it were all ready-made?
Yet why they thus should do, or wherefore choose
A harder lot, it is not mine to say.
For from a body free, they wing their way
Untouched by sickness, cold, or hunger; aye,
Since body's self from these same ills is prone
To suffer more, and mind hath many pains
Which spring from taint of body. Yet e'en so,
Grant it may serve them well to build a frame
When they would enter in, yet will no way
Be seen whereby e'en this they might achieve.
Souls, then, toil not to fashion for themselves
Bodies and limbs, nor yet in any wise
Can they an entry into bodies find
When fully formed; for thus they cannot lie
Inwoven with so fine a web, nor e'er
Will common feeling from their union arise.

Again, why doth an untamed fierceness run
Through all the lion's grim breed, or on the fox
Doth craft attend? Or why to stags is given
Their fathers' heritage of flight, that so
Their limbs are spurred by fear their sires have known?
And other humors, too, of kindred sort,
Why do we find them planted in the limbs
And tempers from the very hour of birth,
Except it be a power of mind deep fixt
By its own seed and breed doth take its growth
Together with the body of each one?
But if the soul were deathless, and were wont
To change its bodies, then would living breeds
Be found of doubtful tempers; so would dogs
Of seed Hyrcanian oft turn tail and flee
The onset of the hornéd hart, the hawk
Would fly in terror through the airs of heaven
Before the dove; so men would witless be,
And wise the untamed beasts of savage breed.
For false the reasoning whereby men will say
That altered is a deathless soul, whene'er
It doth its body change; for what is changed
Will be dissolved, and so will pass away;
For shifted are its parts, and changed doth stand
Their order; wherefore through the limbs as well
They needs must be dissolved, that so at last
They perish with the body, each and all.
But should they claim that souls of men to none
Save human bodies pass, still I shall ask
Why, once it hath been wise, can one same soul

Become dull-witted? Why a child hath not
A ripened wit, or new-foaled colt doth prove
Less knowing than a horse with strength full-grown?
They will, be sure, take refuge in the plea
That weakened minds to bodies weak belong;
But this, if true, will force thee to confess
The soul is mortal, since so great a change
It suffereth throughout the frame, and all
It once possessed of life and sense doth lose.

Or in what wise will power of mind avail
With each and every body to wax strong
And reach life's longed-for bloom, except it be
A partner with the body at its birth?
Or wherefore doth it long to issue forth
From limbs grown old? Is it perchance afraid
To linger, shut within a crumbling frame,
Lest haply its mean house, weathered and worn
With age, fall in and crush it? But no fear
Of danger doth a thing immortal know.

Besides, that souls attend the marriage bed
And birth of beasts, doth seem but laughable;
That souls immortal wait for mortal limbs
In numbers numberless, and hotly strive
Each with another, as to which shall first
And foremost find an entrance, save it be
Perchance they have a compact signed and sealed
That whichsoe'er doth first on wings arrive
Shall first have entry, nor shall any strike
A single blow in strife among themselves!

Again, no tree can in the skies abide
Nor clouds in ocean's deeps, nor in the fields
Can fishes have their home, nor blood reside
In wood, nor sap in stones. Nay, 'tis ordained
And stablished where each thing shall have its place
And prosper. So the nature of the mind
Can ne'er alone without the body come
To birth, nor far from blood and sinews keep
Its life; for could this be, 'twere far more meet
That force of mind itself should find its place
In head, or shoulders, yea, e'en in the heels,
Or in what part soe'er thou wilt, be wont
To be created, so it still remain
Within the single man, aye, still be held
Within the selfsame vessel. But since e'en
In our own body's frame it hath been fixt
And clearly foreordained where soul and mind
Can dwell apart and thrive, so much the more
Must thou perforce deny that set apart
From all the body could they come to birth,
Much less endure. Wherefore, when body's self
Hath passed away, so must thou needs confess
The soul as well hath perished, torn apart
Through all our frame.

               Nay, of a truth, to link
The mortal and the eternal, and to hold
That they can feel as one or suffer aught
In common, were but foolishness. For what
Can be more ill agreed, or more at odds,
Yea, ring more false than this: that what is doomed

To certain death with that which doth abide
Forever deathless, joined in one could thus
Together brave the raging storms of life?

   Besides, if aught eternal doth abide,
It needs must be that, built of solid frame,
It doth all blows repel, nor suffereth aught
To penetrate within which might unloose
Its close-locked parts, e'en as those bodies are
Whose nature I have pictured heretofore;
Or else, mayhap, this is a cause whereby
They can avail through endless time to stand
Unshaken, since exempt from blows they dwell
E'en as the void, which doth remain untouched;
Or else 'twill be because no store of space
Doth stand about, whereunto, as it were,
Their matter might withdraw, and in such wise
Dissolve to naught, e'en as the sum of sums
Doth bide eternal, since it hath no place
Without whereto itself may fly abroad,
Nor bodies are at hand to fall thereon
And with resistless blows bring it to ruin.
But if perchance from this alone the soul
Is to be held immortal, since 'tis kept
Embattled safe against the powers of death,
Whether it be that naught can come to harm
Its life, or haply that which draweth near
Is beaten back and fleeth ere we sense
That it hath brought us hurt—all this, I ween,
With sound and sober truth can scarce accord.

For not alone doth soul with body's ills
Fall ailing, but there oft will come as well
Dark thoughts that torture with their auguries
Of things to come, and keep it ill at ease
With fears, and wear it out with weary cares;
Yea, when its evil deeds are past and done
The memory of its sins will gnaw it still.
Add unto these the frenzy which the mind
At times doth know, and dark forgetfulness
Of all the past; add, too, that it doth sink
Deep in the waters of black lethargy.

So death is naught to us,[7] nay, not one jot
Doth it concern us, since the soul doth wear
A mortal nature; and as in those days
Long gone we felt no ill when all around
The Punic hordes were gathering for the fray,
And all the world with war's wild tumult torn
Did reel and shudder neath the dome of heaven,
Till no man knew which way the stroke must fall
That should allot or here and there control
Of human fortunes on both land and sea,
So when this life of ours shall be no more,
When soul and body part, wherefrom ourselves
Are knit in one, then surely naught can bring
Distress to us, who have no being, nor stir

wwwwwwwwwwwwwwwwwwwwww

[7] After the long and labored "proofs" of the mortal nature of the soul,
we turn with a feeling of relief to the "Triumph Song over Death",
which closes the third book. Here Lucretius probably rises to his loftiest
heights.

Our sense to feeling, nay, not even should earth
Be mingled with the sea, and sea with sky.

And if mind's nature and the life that lieth
Within the soul still hath the power to feel
When sundered from the body, yet e'en this
Is naught to us, who have our being joined
Of soul and body wedded and made one.
And yet, when once our life hath reached its close,
Should time our substance gather, and once more
Remold it to its wonted form, and thus
Again the light of life to us be given,
No whit to us would matter even this,
When once the links of memory's golden chain
Are snapt asunder. So e'en now no heed
We give unto those other selves who were
Before, nor any pain doth gnaw our hearts
At thought of them. For when thou dost survey
All the long lapse of unrecorded time
Now past and gone, and to thy mind doth come
The thought of matter's motions, how diverse
And manifold they are, 'tis easy then
This to believe as well,—that these same seeds
Whereof we now are formed, ofttimes before
In this same pattern have been set as that
Wherein we now do find them placed. But this
Our memory's reach will ne'er avail to grasp;
For dark between doth lie the break of life,
And all the former motions wander far
Apart from sense But if perchance we hold
That pain and grief will be, then, too, forsooth,

There must at that same moment be a self
To whom these ills can happen. But since death
Such chance doth ban, and doth cut off from being
That self on whom these troubles may be fixt,
So may we know that there is naught in death
We need to fear, nor can one wretched be
Who hath no being; nay, 'twould matter not
If he had ne'er been born, when mortal life
By death immortal hath been swallowed up.

And so, when thou shalt see a man bewail
His lot, and groan that after death his fate
Must be to rot away, his body laid
In earth, or waste with flames or neath the jaws
Of savage beasts, so mayst thou know his words
Sound not with ring of sober truth, but deep
Within his heart doth lie some secret sting,
Though stoutly as thou wilt he may himself
Deny he doth believe that aught of sense
Will still remain to him when cold in death.
For, as I think, he doth refuse to grant
The whither and the wherefore of his creed;
Nor doth he boldly tear the deep-grown roots
That bind him unto life, and cast them forth,
But fancieth, witless wight, that somewhat still
Of self doth linger on. For when in life
Each man doth picture to himself his fate,
That birds and beasts will mangle him in death,
It is himself he pitieth. For ne'er
Doth he distinguish from that loathsome thing
His living self, nor hold himself aloof

Far from that outcast corpse, but fancieth still
That it is he, and as he standeth by
Doth color it with feelings of his own.
'Tis hence that he doth mourn his mortal birth,
Nor seeth that death will brook no other self
To live and weep his loss, and standing by
Its stricken fellow feel the stab of pain
That he is torn or burned. For if in death
'Tis torture to be mauled by teeth and jaws
Of savage beasts, I cannot see, forsooth,
Why 'tis not bitter to be laid on fires
And burned with scorching flames, or gasp for breath
Close packed in stifling honey, or grow stiff
With cold on some chill rocky bed, or e'en
Be crushed and ground by weight of earth above.

   'Thee now no more thy happy home shall greet,[8]
Or gentle spouse and loving children run
In eager haste to be the first to snatch
The kiss of welcome from thy lips, and touch
Thy heart with silent rapture. Now no more
Shalt thou be prospered in thy ways, or stand
A bulwark to thine own. But woefully,
Poor woeful one,' men say, 'one dreadful day
Hath snatched from out thy hands life's every prize!'
Yet this they do not add: 'Nor any more

---

[8] Cf. Thomas Gray's "Elegy Written in a Country Churchyard":
    For thee no more the blazing hearth shall burn,
      Or busy housewife ply her evening care;
    No children run to lisp their sire's return,
      Or climb his knee the envied kiss to share.

Shall yearning for all these abide with thee.'
But should men write this truth upon their hearts
And with their tongues proclaim it, all the load
Of fear and anguish from their minds would fall.
'Yea, thou, indeed, as thou art lulled to sleep
In death, so shalt thou be through all the length
Of time to come, released from every pain
And bitter sorrow; but 'tis we who wept,
Nor would be comforted, to see thy form
Melting to ashes on the dreadful pyre;
'Tis we who bear the blight of endless grief
No day shall ever take from out our hearts.'
But this of such an one we fain would ask:
'What is so passing bitter, if at last
All is but sleep and rest, that one should choose
To waste away in never-ending grief?'

   This, too, men oft will do, when, gathered round
The board, their cups they hold and shade their brows
With garlands, as from out their hearts they say:
'Brief is this joy for us poor mortals here;
Soon 'twill be past, nor e'er can be recalled.'
As if, forsooth, in death their crown of ills
Will be to feel their wretched throats parched dry
With burning thirst, or yearn for aught besides.
Yet none himself or his own life doth miss
When lulled to quiet slumber lie alike
Body and mind; for sleep may have no end
And we heed not, nor yearning for ourselves
Doth e'er beset us. Yet throughout our limbs
These first beginnings then but little way

From sense-begetting motions turn aside
Their wandering paths, since roused with sudden start
A man will spring from sleep with sense alert.
Death, then, to us should seem a lesser thing,
If less can be that what we see is naught;
For death doth bring a wider scattering
Of our disordered matter, and one e'er
Doth wake and rise from that long sleep, whose foot
Hath once been stayed at death's chill halting-place.

   Again, should nature on a sudden lift
Her voice, and thus some one of us should chide:
'What doth so ail thee, mortal, to give way
To sickly lamentation? Why dost groan
And weep at death? For if thy life that lieth
Behind thee hath its meed of pleasure brought,
And all thy joys have not, like water, poured
Into a leaky vessel, dript away
And perished without use, why dost thou not
Like one who riseth from a festal board [9]
Depart, full-fed with life, thou fool, and take
With mind serene a rest that knoweth no care?
But if whate'er was thine to be enjoyed
Hath all been spent and lost, and life doth bring
Naught but vexation, why then seek to add

[9] Cf. William Cullen Bryant's "Thanatopsis":
      Thou go not like the quarry slave at night
      Scourged to his dungeon, but sustained and soothed
      By an unfaltering trust, approach thy grave
      Like one who wraps the drapery of his couch
      About him, and lies down to pleasant dreams.

Still more that will but end in wretchedness
And barren loss? Why not the rather make
An end to life, and so thy troubles close?
For naught can I discover or contrive
To please thee more; all things are still the same.
But if not yet thy body worn with years
Doth waste, thy limbs grown weak and weary, still
All things remain the same, wert thou to live
Far past thy wonted span, yea, even more,
Wert thou never to die';—what shall we say
In answer, save that nature doth present
A just indictment and an honest plea?

But now if one weighed down and bowed with years
Should make lament, and with unseemly moans
Bewail his going forth, would she not e'en
More justly chide him with sharp stinging words?
'Take hence thy tears, thou fool, thy whinings cease.
Filled with life's every blessing thou dost sink
Into thy grave; but since thou gapest e'er
For what thou lackst, and scornest what is thine,
Joyless and unfulfilled thy life hath slipt
From out thy grasp, and ere thou art aware
Death at thy head hath ta'en his stand, or e'er
Thou canst depart sated and filled with things.
But come, relinquish now all that thy years
Have known not how to use, and calm of heart
Yield up thy place to those of nobler stuff,
For so thou must'—justly, I ween, would fall
Her plea, justly her words of bitter scorn.

For old doth e'er give way, thrust out by new,
And from one life another's life is born;
Nor e'er to Tartarus' black pit is sent
A single mortal creature: nay, thy stuff
Must needs be left, that those who take thy place
May grow and thrive. Yet all of these, when once
Their little life is done, shall follow thee;
Yea, like thyself have passed in days gone by
Their generations, and again will pass.
So one thing from another ne'er shall cease
To spring, and no man hath the grant of life
In freehold, but each one in tenantry.
Look back once more, and see how all the lapse
Of everlasting time before our birth
Was naught to us. Herein doth nature hold
Before our eyes a mirror of that time
That is to come when we are dead and gone.
Seest thou aught there to dread? or aught of gloom?
Is it not all more calm than any sleep?

Yea, be assured, those storied horrors set
In the black depths of Acheron are here,
Here in our very life. No Tantalus [10]

---

[10] Tantalus: king of Sipylus, in Phrygia, son of Zeus. As punishment for
his overbearing and insulting treatment of the gods, who had invited him
to their deliberations and banquets, he was condemned to everlasting
punishment in the lower world. According to the more usual tradition,
followed by Homer, his "tantalizing" punishment consisted in his being
immersed in water to the chin, while a branch of the choicest fruits hung
just over his head. Whenever he opened his mouth to enjoy a feast, the
water receded and the branch sprang out of reach. Lucretius follows another version of the story: that Tantalus himself was suspended in the air,

There is, who, numbed with fruitless dread—for so
Doth run the tale—doth cringe with fear to see
A mighty rock poised in the air above;
But rather here in life doth idle fear
Of gods hang over men, and each doth dread
The falling of the stroke that chance may deal.
Nor into Tityos' vitals [11] as he lieth
In Acheron do vultures bore their way,
Nor can they find, forsooth, e'en in the depths
Of that huge breast, aught to reward their search
Through endless time. Yea, howe'er vast of bulk
His prostrate body, were it e'en to fill
With sprawling limbs not acres nine alone
But all the world besides, yet can he not
Forever bear the torturing pain, nor yield
From his own body food forever. Nay,
Our Tityos is he who on the bed
Of love doth lie, while birds of passion tear
His breast, yea, aching anguish at his heart
Doth gnaw, and lust-born cares thrust deep their wounds.
A Sisyphus [12] as well our life doth hold

while above his head hung a huge rock which was ever threatening to fall
and crush him.

[11] Tityos: a giant of Euboea, who, having offered violence to Latona, was
killed by the arrows of the latter's children, Apollo and Diana. As a pen-
alty for this outrage, his body lay stretched over nine acres in the lower
world, while two vultures perpetually pecked at his liver.

[12] Sisyphus was the traditional builder of Corinth, and is called by
Homer "the slyest of men". For an offense the nature of which cannot
now be determined, he was condemned to punishment in the lower world
by being forced to roll a huge boulder to the top of a steep hill, only to
see it roll down to the valley, and to start the hopeless task again.

To view of all in him who is athirst
To win from suffrage of the crowd the gift
Of rods and cruel axes, to return
Each time a beaten and a sadder man.
For seeking power, which is but emptiness,
And ne'er is truly given, and in the quest
Bearing for aye the weight of grinding toil—
This is the agony of sweat and strain
That up some rugged mountain side would thrust
A massive rock, which but a moment poised
Upon the peak, doth pause, then start once more
Its downward course, and swiftly gathering speed
Roll crashing to the level plain below.
And then to feed alway a thankless mind,
Yea, fill it brimming full with goodly gifts
Yet satisfy it not; e'en as for us
The changing seasons in their yearly round
Pour forth their store of fruits with varied charm,
And yet we ne'er are filled with life's delights—
This is, I ween, the meaning of the tale
Of those unhappy maidens, [13] who perforce
Through all their years of youthful bloom must pour

wwwwwwwwwwwwwwwwwwwww

[13] Reference is here made to the fifty daughters of Danaus, king of Egypt, who with their father were driven out of Egypt by their uncle, Aegyptus, twin brother of Danaus, and made their way to Argos, in Greece. There they were pursued by the fifty sons of Aegyptus, who forced Danaus to give them his daughters in marriage. At their father's command the unwilling brides, with a single exception, killed their husbands at night, and buried their heads in the valley of Lerna. The forty-nine murderesses atoned for their bloody deed in the regions below by being condemned for ever to pour water into vessels full of holes.

Their draughts of water into leaking jars
Which yet are destined never to be filled.
So, too, it is, forsooth, with idle tales
Of Cerberus,[14] and Furies, and the realms
Of sunless gloom, where Tartarus doth belch
From gaping jaws his fearsome fires. All these
Nowhere exist, nor verily can be.
But in our life 'tis fear of punishment
For deeds ill-done, grave as the deeds are grave,
And thoughts of that last debt that guilt must pay—
The dungeon, or the ghastly hurtling fall
From the grim Rock,[15] the lash, the torch, the rack,
The hangman, burning pitch, the grid—all these,
Though they be with us not, the guilty mind,
Fearful e'en now for its misdeeds, doth wield
As torturing whips that sear with fiery lash,
Nor seeth the while what end its ills may find,
Or where at last will be a limit set
To punishment, and so doth fear lest these
Increase in death. Thus here on earth the life
Of fools doth prove withal an Acheron.

This, too, thou mayst at times say to thyself:
'E'en the good Ancus [16] saw the light of day
Fade from his eyes—a better man than thou

~~~~~~~~~~~~~~~~~~~~~~~~~~~~~~~~~~

14 Cerberus, in Greek mythology, was the three-headed dog which
guarded the entrance to the lower world.
15 Reference is probably to the Tarpeian Rock on the Capitoline Hill in
Rome, from which condemned criminals were often thrown.
16 Ancus Marcius was the fourth of the seven kings of Rome.

By many times, thou knave; and after him
An endless line of potentates and kings
Who held their sway o'er mighty nations, all
Have gone their way. E'en he [17] who once did lay
A road upon the raging sea, and gave
His hosts a path that they might cross the deep,
Yea, taught their feet to spurn the watery wastes,
And with his prancing chargers laughed to scorn
The roaring of the main—yet reft of life
Breathed forth his soul from out his dying frame.
The Scipios' noble son, dread thunderbolt
Of war, terror of Carthage, yielded up
His bones to earth, e'en as the meanest slave.
Yea, count with these those who were first to find
The truths of science and the charms of art.
Count, too, the comrades of the sisterhood
Of Helicon,—midst whom, enthroned alone,
Hath Homer won the scepter—yet he lieth
In his last slumber like to all the rest.
Nay, e'en Democritus, when ripe old age
Gave sign that memory's nimble movements now
Were feebler growing, of his own free will
Laid down his head upon the lap of death.
So passed our Epicurus, when the light

vvvvvvvvvvvvvvvvvvvvvvvvvvvvvvvv

[17] Xerxes, king of Persia, in preparation for his invasion of Greece, built
a pontoon bridge across the Hellespont (Dardanelles). It is interesting to
note that as late as the 19th century school copybooks in this country,
under the letter X, made use, for practice purposes, of a sentiment similar
to that of Lucretius:

>   Xerxes the Great did die,
>   And so must you and I.

Of life was spent, he who hath far outstript
Mankind in understanding, yea, outshone
All others, as the rising sun the stars.
And thou, forsooth, wilt falter, and bewail
Thy doom, whose life e'en now is all but dead,
Though thou dost live and look upon the light!
Thou, who dost waste in sleep the better part
Of thine existence, snoring while awake,
Nor e'er dost cease from day-dreams! Thou, whose heart
Is stirred with fruitless fears, nor canst thou find
The cause of thy distress, when like one drunk
With wine thou art beset on every side
With countless cares, and drifting here and there
Dost reel and stagger with uncertain mind!

But if, e'en as they seem to feel their minds
Weighed down and wearied by a crushing load,
Mankind could only know the cause as well,
Whence come these ills that like a millstone lie
On their uneasy breasts, they would not live
Their lives as now we oft do see them, each
Not knowing his own wants, and seeking e'er
To change his place, as though he thus might lay
His burden down. So, oft, when home doth irk,
One from his stately house doth walk abroad,
And then straightway return, as who doth feel
No more at ease outside; or, urging on
His ponies at a gallop, he is off
To seek his country-place, like one in haste
To save a house on fire. But once his feet
Have touched the threshhold, straightway he will yawn,

Or sinking in a sodden sleep will seek
Forgetfulness, or in the same hot haste
Will make once more for town. Thus each doth strive
To flee that self, which ne'er, in sober truth,
Can he escape; yet in his own despite
He still doth cling to it and hate it, since,
Though ill, he knoweth not the cause thereof.
But if they saw it clearly, men would leave
All else behind, and strive with zeal to know
The nature of all things, since 'tis their state
Not for one little hour that is in doubt,
But for that everlasting time wherein
Each mortal creature needs must spend the years
That stretch in endless length beyond our death.

And finally, what craven lust of life
Doth urge thee so, to spend thy troubled days
In doubt and danger? For no less that hour
Awaiteth us, nor shall we fail to meet
Our doom. Yet never doth our narrow round
Of life beyond the selfsame eddy move,
Nor doth our living forge one new delight;
But that which doth elude our gaping mouths
Doth seem to top all else; but once 'tis ours,
We gape at something new, and equal thirst
Of life doth keep us ever open-mouthed.
We know not what of fortune time to come
Will bring, what cast of chance be ours, or what
The issue that awaiteth. Nor, forsooth,
By living on can we one jot abate
Of death's unending interlude, nor aught

That in our power doth lie can e'er subtract
One single instant from its sum, that so
We might mayhap a lesser time remain
In nothingness. Yea, though thou wert to reap
The harvest of unnumbered centuries,
Yet will that death eternal none the less
Await thee; nor will he less long be reft
Of being who with this morning's light hath closed
His mortal life, than he whose sun hath set
These many months, yea, many years ago.

BOOK FOUR

BOOK FOUR

With wandering feet I thread dim pathless haunts
Of the Pierides, ne'er trod before
By foot of man. My joy it is to seek
Springs yet untasted, and to drink my fill.
I long to pluck fresh flowers, and crave to win
A glorious coronal to crown my head
Whence heretofore the holy sisterhood
Hath never wreathed the brows of mortal man;
First, since I teach of great and wondrous things,
And haste to free the mind from close-knit bonds
Of superstition; then because I shed
On darksome ways verses so full of light,
Touching all things with music's magic charm,
Since this, I ween, with reason doth accord.
For even as healers, when they would essay
To give to ailing children bitter draughts
Of loathsome wormwood, first will overlay
The cup's rim round with the sweet golden dew
Of honey, that thereby the trustful age
Of childish innocence may be beguiled
To ope the portal of the lips, and all
Unwitting swallow down the nauseous draught
Of wormwood, thus deceived though not betrayed,
But rather by such means may be restored
And once again made strong; so now do I,

Since these my teachings oft too bitter seem
To those who have not known their taste, and since
The common herd doth shrink therefrom in dread.
For I have chosen in sweet-tongued melody
The Muses know to frame my reasoning
For thy delight, and as it were to touch
My theme with honey'd sweets of poesy,
If so perchance I might avail to hold
Thy mind upon my verses, till thou come
To grasp the nature of the world entire
And make the lesson of its use thine own.

And now, since I have taught thee heretofore
What nature the beginnings of all things
Display, and how with widely varying shapes,
Each as it will, they take their random flight
With ceaseless movement driven, and how therefrom
Each several thing can be begot; and since
I have revealed to thee what nature hath
The mind, yea, what may be the frame wherewith
It hath been built, to share the body's life,
And in what wise, when all asunder torn,
Into its primal bodies once again
It doth return; henceforth my task shall be
To broach for thee a theme which mightily
Thereto doth hold, that there exist as well
Those natures which we term the images
Of things, which like unto a membrane stript
From off the surface of all bodies, flit
Hither and yon throughout the air, and ranged
Before us in our wakeful hours, bring dread

Into our minds; nay, e'en in sleep we seem
Oft to behold strange shapes, and forms of those
Who have been reft of light, which as we lie
Relaxed in slumber rouse us broad awake
With sudden terror. Yet we must not think
That souls escape from Acheron, or shades
Among the living flit, nor aught be left
Of our own selves beyond our death, when once
Body and mind dissevered, each hath sunk
In dissolution to its elements.

So then, I say that likenesses and shapes
Of slender mold are by all bodies cast
From off their outmost zone, which one might term
A film or husk, since that the counterfeit
Doth bear a mien and form like that wherefrom
It hath been shed and wandereth abroad.
This thou mayst learn, however dull of heart,
From what doth follow: yea, since e'en of things
Held plain to view full many a one will cast
Bodies from off itself, now thin and rare,
As oaken logs will give forth smoke and flame
And heat; or now bodies more closely woven
And more condensed, as oft in summer's prime
Locusts put off their glossy gowns, or calves
At birth will shed a caul from off their frame,
Or as a sleek and supple snake will doff
Her coat among the thorns; for oft we see
The brambles laden with her wind-blown spoils.
Since thus it doth befall, it needs must be
That from the surface of each thing is cast

A slender film. For wherefore these I named
But now should fall away and part from things
With greater ease than those of slenderer mold
No man can ope his mouth to tell; still more
Since many and minute these bodies are
Which gather on the crust of things, that so
They may be shed in order like to that
They knew, and keep the outlines of their form;
Yea, and with greater speed, since few in count
And in the forefront set, they meet with less
Of hindrance. For in truth we oft descry
Full many a thing to pour abroad its dole
Of bodies, not alone from deep within,
As I before have taught, but e'en at times
From off the surface, as doth come to pass
When colors fly abroad. For so ofttimes
Will bright-hued awnings, yellow, red and blue,
Be seen to act, as spread across the expanse
Of some vast theater, stretched from mast and spar,
They flap and flutter, tingeing all below,
Benches and pit, and all the brave array
Of Fathers gathered there, till all doth float
With wave on wave of color. And the more
The hoardings round about are covered o'er,
So much the more all things that are within
Will smile o'erspread with charm, as day's clear light
Is straitened. Therefore, since these awnings shed
Bright colors from their surface, so likewise
Must all things else give off thin likenesses,
Since from the outmost rim in either case
The bodies stream. There are, then, traces clear

Of outlines, dowered with textures fine, which here
And there do fly about, nor can be seen
Set by themselves apart. Again, all scent
And smoke and heat, and all things else which show
A nature similar, whenas they stream
From bodies, are diffused abroad because,
Rising from deep within, as they go forth
Along their winding roadways, they are rent,
Nor can they find unbroken paths wherethrough
To rise and issue forth. But otherwise
It is when slender films of color fly
From off the surface, for that naught is there
Which can disperse them, since in readiness
They lie, and stationed in the foremost rank.

And last, whate'er of likenesses appear
To us in mirrors, or in water, yea,
In any shining object, these must needs,
Since they are dowered with semblance like to things,
Consist of images from bodies cast.

There are, then, slender forms and likenesses
Of things, the which, though singly none can e'er
Their forms discern, yet driven back amain
With swift and unremitting thrust, return
To us an image from the mirror's face;
Nor else, 'tis clear, can they be kept entire
To render shapes so like each several thing.

And now give heed and learn how thin the mold
Whereof is shaped this image. First of all,

Since primal bodies lie so deep beneath
Our senses' ken, and smaller far must be
Than that whence first our eyes would fain withhold
Their sight, come let me give you further proof;
And thou from these few words discern how fine
The mold of first beginnings of all things.
First, there are living creatures so minute
That no third part thereof could e'er be seen.
What then in such an one must be the size
Of any inward part? What of its round
Of heart, or eye? What of its limbs, its joints?
What tiny things they are! And then besides,
The several first beginnings whence must needs
Be formed their souls and minds, seest not how fine
And how minute are these? Or, once again,
Whate'er from out its substance doth exhale
A pungent odor, as the panacea,
Or noisome wormwood, or the acrid strength
Of southernwood, or noxious centaury:
Of these shouldst chance to press which one thou wilt
Betwixt two fingers lightly, so wouldst find
The scent will linger, though the herb hath long
Been cast aside, and naught to sight or touch
Is manifest. Thus thou mayst know how fine
The nature of the first beginnings whence
The scent of things is formed; so, then, think not
That these I term the images of things,
Being formed of texture passing fine, stand not
Among the ranks of body; but the more
Shouldst thou believe that images of things

Many in count, in many ways, speed on
Knowing no touch and ever stolen from view.

   But lest thou deem these images alone
To roam abroad which pass away from things,
Know there are others too, born of themselves
And self-created, in the firmament
We term the air. These, formed in various wise,
Are borne on high, nor ever cease to shift
And change their aspect, as now here, now there,
They mold the fitful outline of their forms;
E'en as at times we see white drifting clouds
Pile high their billowy heaps, and in a trice
Stain all the sky's calm countenance, the while
They touch the lingering airs with soft caress.
For oft we mark strange giant faces float
And trail a shadow far and wide; or now
Vast mountain shapes, and crags from mountains torn
Are seen to tower before the sun and drift
Athwart his face, or some huge beast will pass
Yoked in a stately chariot of cloud.

   Now in how facile and how swift a wise
These images are born, and ebb from things
With ceaseless flow, I shall forthwith explain.
For ever from each several thing doth stream
A store of films which it may send abroad;
And when these meet with certain things, straightway
They pass therethrough, as readiest of all
Through glass; but when they come to rugged rock
Or solid wood, there in a trice their form

Is rent, that so no image may they yield.
Yet when there have been set athwart their path
Objects both hard and bright, whereof doth stand
In foremost rank a mirror, so will naught
Of this befall; for neither, as through glass,
Can they a passage find, nor yet indeed
Be rent, since that bright smoothness doth give heed
Their safety to ensure; and thus it is
That images of these will greet our view.
And howe'er suddenly at any time
Thou'lt set a thing before a mirror's face,
Its image will appear. Thus thou mayst know
That from the surface of each thing doth stream
A never slackening tide of slender webs
And shapes imponderable. Thus, then, 'tis clear
That many images in one brief space
Are bred, that so with judgment sound their birth
Is instantaneous deemed. And as the sun
In one brief breath unnumbered rays of light
Must needs send forth that all the world may lie
Forever filled with brightness, so likewise
By reasoning similar we may be sure
That many images are cast from things
In but a point of time to every side;
Since toward whatever side of things we turn
Our mirror, there the things will give reply
In shape and color like unto themselves.
Again, although but now the sky's bright face
Hath been of purest blue, how suddenly
'Tis fouled with blackness, till thou wouldst believe
That all the gloom of Acheron, let loose

From every side, hath filled the vasty deeps
Of hollow heaven, so darkly o'er our heads,
Rising from out the cloud-born midnight, lower
Dread faces of black fear. Of these how small
A part an image is, no man can say,
Nor frame thereof in words a concept clear.

   And now, give heed, and learn how swift the flight
Wherewith are borne these idols, and what speed
Hath been thereto assigned, as through the airs
They cleave their way, that so an ample space
Is compassed in a fleeting hour, as each
With diverse impulse toward its goal doth fly,
The while my theme in verses sweet but few
I shall unfold; e'en as the swan's brief song
Is sweeter than the long-drawn clamorous cries
Of southward-winging cranes far-heard among
The airy clouds. First, since we see full oft
That things endowed with little weight, and formed
Of tiny particles, are swift to move;
Whereof the sun's clear light doth give us proof,
Yea, and his heat as well; for that they stand
Composed of primal elements of mold
Exceeding small, which smiting each on each
With ne'er a pause speed through the parted airs
Urged by pursuing blows. For light by light
Incessant is supplied, and gleam by gleam
As by a harnessed mate is goaded on.
So then in manner like it needs must be
That in a moment images avail
To sweep through realms of space incalculable.

First, since a cause, though slight and far behind,
Doth start and drive them forward, as is meet
In things that thus on wings of lightness ride;
And next, since they are shed abroad endowed
With texture passing fine, that so with ease
They can avail to penetrate within
Bodies of various kinds, and as it were
To filter through the intervening air.

Again, if bodies sent from deep within
The heart of things, as light and heat are shed
From out the sun, in but an instant's space
Are seen to fall and sweep across the expanse
Of heaven's wide dome, aye, fly o'er sea and lands
And flood the sky, what then of those which stand
Ready to hand and in the foremost rank
When they are cast abroad, and naught is there
To bar their going forth? So then, seest not
That swifter and more far they must be borne,
Yea, even many times the tract of space
They must traverse in that brief moment while
The sun's bright flaming beams run o'er the sky?
Or this besides doth fitly seem to mark
How swift the pace at which these idols speed:
For soon as e'er beneath a starlit sky
Is spread a shining pool of water, straight
Upon the instant answer one for one
Within its depths the calm bright stars of heaven.
Dost thou not, therefore, see how brief the space
Wherein doth fall their image from the coasts
Of heaven e'en unto the coasts of earth?

Wherefore I say once more, thou must confess
That wondrous is the speed wherewith do fly
The idols through the trackless deeps of space.

   And now give ear, and learn what doth remain.
These images it is whereby our eyes
Avail to sense the form of things. For ne'er
Do idols cease to stream abroad, but fly
Amain to every side; nor is it strange,
Since from all things of whatsoever kind
Matter doth ever flow; so some will shed
Bodies that strike the eye and stir our sight,
The while from others ebb unceasing streams
Of scent, e'en as from rivers cold will flow,
Or heat from out the sun, or briny spray
Upriseth from the billows of the main
To gnaw the walls that line some rock-bound shore
So too do voices diverse in their sound
Fly ever through the air; or now the tang
Of salty moisture lingereth on our lips
As by the sea we wander; or 'twill chance
That quite in other wise as we behold
A draught of wormwood mixt with water, straight
There riseth in the mouth a bitter taste.
With flow so unremitting from each thing
Is borne its flux appropriate, shed abroad
To every quarter from each side; nor aught
Of pause or respite to this flow is given,
Since constant is our feeling, and 'tis ours
To grasp alway sight, scent and sound of things.

Again, since any shape felt by our hands
In darkness is perceived to be at one
With that discerned in day's clear brilliance, so
It needs must be that touch and sight are roused
By common cause. If then an object square
We touch, and in the darkness it doth stir
Our sense, what, pray, can come to meet our sight
As square, if it be not its image? Thus
In images, 'tis clear, doth lie the cause
Of all our seeing, nor apart from these
Can any thing unto our sight appear.

Now what I term the images of things
Are everywhere dispersed, and cast abroad
To every side; but since with eyes alone
We have the power to see, so doth befall
That toward whichever place our sight we turn
There all things meet it with their form and hue;
And e'en how far away from us doth lie
Each object 'tis the image doth empower
Us to descry, and our appraisement seal.
For once an image is cast off, straightway
'Twill thrust and drive before it all the air
That hath its place betwixt it and our eyes,
And thus the stream of air entire doth glide
Into our eyes, and sweeping, as it were,
On through the pupils passeth on its way.
And thus it is we see how far removed
Each object standeth. And the more of air
Is driven before it, and the more doth stretch

In length the draught that sweepeth through our eyes,
So much the more remote will seem to stand
The object. Clearly, then, they speed at pace
Surpassing swift, since we at once discern
The object's nature and its distance mark.

Herein by no means must it seem a cause
Of wonder, that whenas we cannot view
Each idol singly that doth strike our eyes,
The object's self can be perceived. For e'en
As when with gust on gust a wind doth beat
Upon us, or when piercing cold doth flow
About our frame, 'tis not our wont to feel
Each separate portion of the wind and cold,
But rather all in one; and we perceive
That blows then fall upon our bodies, e'en
As if somewhat did lash us and give rise
To feeling of its substance from without.
Again, if with our finger tips we tap
Upon a stone, we touch its outmost rind
Of surface color, yet no sense of hue
Our touch will give us; rather do we feel
Naught save the stony hardness deep within.

Now list, and learn why images are seen
Beyond a mirror, for in sooth they seem
Set far within. E'en as beyond a door
Objects are truly seen, when e'er thrown wide
The opened door will grant unhindered view.
And from the house will many a thing disclose

Which lieth without. For this perception too
Is brought to pass by twinned and doubled airs.
For first, in such a case, is seen the air
Betwixt us and the doorway, then straightway
Follow the doors themselves, on right and left,
And next the light beyond will sweep its way
Into our eyes, and last a second air
And whatsoe'er is truly seen outside.
And so when first hath cast itself abroad
The image from a mirror, as it flieth
Unto our pupils, it doth thrust and drive
Before it all the air which hath its place
Betwixt it and our eyes, and thus vouchsafe
That we avail to sense this air entire
Ere we behold the mirror. But when once
We have perceived the mirror's self as well,
Straightway the image, borne from us, will pass
Thereto, and once again cast back, retrace
Its path unto our eyes, as it the while
Doth roll and drive before it another air,
Which thus it doth contrive to make us see
Before we sense itself; thus then it is
The image will appear to stand removed
An equal distance from the mirror's face.

Wherefore I say once more, no slightest need
There is to marvel that such aspects rise
Of objects seen through doors and those as well
Which from a mirror's surface seem to yield
A phantom image, since in either case

'Tis the twinned airs wherefrom the effect doth spring.
And thus it chanceth that the limbs that hold
Their place upon the right appear instead,
When imaged in a mirror, leftward turned,
For that the likeness, soon as it doth meet
The mirrored surface, turneth not about
Unchanged, but backward straight is dashed, as when,
Ere it be dry, a plaster mask were flung
Against a beam or pillar, and straightway
It were to keep its wonted shape, but turned
Straight round to meet us, and to mold once more
Its battered features; thus 'twill come to pass
The eye that erst was right will left appear,
And left in turn show right. Then too, 'twill chance
That mirror unto mirror may hand on
A single image, till e'en multiplied
Five or six-fold the likeness will appear;
For whatsoe'er will lurk, deep hid within
The inmost corners of a room, may yet,
However far removed by tortuous paths,
Be brought from out its hiding-place by ways
That wind and twist, and with the effectual aid
Of many mirrors stand revealed to all
Within the house. So with unerring truth
From mirror unto mirror doth reflect
The restless image; and if so it be
A left hand is presented, so 'twill prove
Transferred to right, then shifting once again
Return unto its wonted place. Again,
When flank-curved mirrors, with their surface bent

Like to our bodies' contour, give us back
Right-handed images, the cause doth lie
In this: from plane to mirrored plane doth shift
The image, whence 'tis dashed back twice amain
And flieth toward us; or mayhap 'twill come
Sheer twisted round, since by the mirror's shape
'Tis taught, as 'twere, to ape our very selves.
Then too thou mightst believe these idols move
In time with us, and lift their feet as we,
Yea, ape our very gait, since wheresoe'er
Thou chancest to step back and leave a part
Of a mirror's face, from that same part forthwith
No image can be given; for nature e'er
All things constraineth to be backward driven,
Yea, each from each to glance and leap, impelled
At equal angles by her changeless law.

Bright things, again, the eyes avoid, and shrink
From looking on. So doth the blazing sun
Blind thee if thou wouldst seek to raise thine eyes
To meet him, for that great his power doth stand
In its own might, and through the lucent airs
His idols stream, and sinking ever down
Through deeps of space, strike full upon the eyes
Disordering their texture. So will oft
Some other piercing brightness sear our eyes,
Since it doth hold abundant seeds of fire
That entering the eye give birth to pain.
Again, whate'er the jaundiced look upon
Doth turn a sickly yellow, since from out

Their frames stream many seeds of saffron hue
To meet the idols; many, too, are mixt
Within the eyes, which with their taint will tinge
All things with their own sicklied cast. So too,
From out the darkness we behold these things
That stand in light, since, when the nearer air
Of dusky gloom hath entered and once seized
Upon the open eyes, there followeth straight
A bright air full of light which, as it were,
Doth cleanse the eyes, and scattereth all abroad
The dusky shadows of the former air.
For nimbler far this air, aye, many times
More subtile and more potent. And when once
It hath with light filled all the devious ways
Within the eyes, and oped those darkened aisles
But now beset by air of darkness, straight
There follow idols of those things that lie
Full in the light, and rouse our eyes to see.
But this in manner opposite, from light
To darkness, we can ne'er achieve, since now
In quick succession there doth follow on
A denser air of gloom, that filleth all
The channels, and doth so beset the ways
Our eyes have known that ne'er an idol cast
From aught may reach and stir them. And at times
When from afar we see the square-built towers
Of some high town, 'tis from this cause that
They will appear as rounded, since when seen
Remotely, every angle is perceived
As blunted, nay, 'tis rather not descried

At all, its impact lost, nor doth its stroke
Fall full upon the eye, since through wide space
Of air its images are borne, the while
The airs by frequent buffetings constrain
The whole to lose its sharpness. So when all
As one each angle thus hath 'scaped our sense,
'Twill chance these stone-reared piles take on the form
Of giant pillars shaped in some vast lathe;
Yet seem they not like objects truly round
To present view, but faintly picturing forth
Their shape like some dim shadow. So likewise
Our shadow in the sun's clear light will seem
To move with us, and dog our footsteps, aye,
Copy our very gait; if so it be
Thou wilt believe that air bereft of light
Can walk, and ape men's movements and their tread.
For naught save air devoid of light can be
That we are wont to name a shadow—nay,
In very truth 'tis but that here and there
In certain spots in order due, the ground
Is reft of sunlight wheresoe'er ourselves
As we proceed obstruct it; and likewise
That part which we have left again is filled.
Thus doth it come to pass that what was now
Our body's shadow evermore doth seem
To follow at our heels unchanged. For e'er
New rays of light stream forth, the while the old
Perish like wool in flame. And thus with ease
The ground is robbed of light, and, filled once more,
Its sable shadow-stains doth wash away.

And yet we grant not that therein the eyes
Are in the least deceived.[1] For theirs it is
To see where'er may linger light and shade;
But if that light may be the same or no,
Or if it be one shadow which was here
And now doth yonder pass, or if so be
That rather hath befallen which we but now
Have said, herein the reasoning of the mind
Alone must judge, nor can the eyes, I ween,
Avail to know the nature of all things.
So then forbear to fasten on the eyes
The fault which is the mind's. For as a ship
Whereon we sail doth move, e'en though it seem
To stand at rest; another, anchored fast,
Is thought to pass us by. So hills and plains
Past which we fly with skimming sail, appear
To flee astern. The starry host, fast set
Within the vault of heaven, seem motionless,
Yet all in ceaseless movement wheel, since each
Doth rise, and journeyeth on to seek once more
Its distant setting, as its gleaming orb
Hath measured all the tract of heaven. So sun
And moon appear in manner like to bide
Each in his wonted place, yet fact itself
Doth show they move. And mountains, rising high
Amidst the distant waters, oft will leave

[1] Lucretius, true Epicurean that he is, refuses to hold the senses responsible for optical illusions, holding that these are rather due to false interpretations of sense perception by the mind. However faulty may be his general theory of optics, his discussion of optical illusions has much of interest and value.

A free wide passageway for ships, yet seem
To blend in one and form a single isle.
E'en children at their play, when they have ceased
To whirl themselves about are prone to feel
The halls spin round them and the pillars race
In dizzying circles, till they all but fear
The very roof will fall upon their heads.
Again, when nature first doth lift on high
Above the mountain tops her morning beam
Ruddy with shifting flame, those very heights
Whereon the sun doth seem to stand, as close
In his own fiery mantle he doth wrap
Their glowing crests, are distant from us scarce
Two thousand arrow-flights, nay, often less
Than half a thousand spear-casts; but there lie
Betwixt them and the sun the vasty plains
Of ocean, strewn beneath the far-spread coasts
Of heaven; yea, set between are lands
In thousands upon thousands, wherein dwell
Races diverse, and beasts of many a breed.
And yet a pool of water that doth lie
No deeper than a single finger-breadth
Between the flagstones of a paven street
Will yield a view beneath the earth as deep
As heaven's high vault doth stretch above our heads,
That thou wilt seem to scan the very clouds
And stars of heaven, hid in wondrous wise
In a new sky deep down beneath the earth.

   And when our eager steed full in mid-stream
Hath halted, and we cast our eyes straight down

Into the hurrying waters, so their force,
E'en though he standeth still, athwart the stream,
Will seem to sweep his body on, and e'en
Against the current drive him back amain;
And wheresoe'er we turn our eyes, all things
Seem rushing onward, e'en as we ourselves.
Then too, a colonnade, though it be built
In straight-drawn lines throughout its length, and set
With rows of well-matched columns, yet when viewed
In its whole range from the topmost end, will seem
To narrow bit by bit, till it doth shrink
To but a straitened pointed cone, with roof
Conjoined with floor, and all the rightward side
Meeting with left, till all at last converge
Into the vanished apex of the cone.
To mariners at sea 'twill seem the sun
Doth rise from out the waves, and once again
Beneath the waves doth set and hide his light,
For that they see naught else save sea and sky.
But folk strange unto sea ways seem to mark
Ships in the harbor crippled, as they ride
With broken stern the waves; for straight doth stand
The portion of the oars that doth o'ertop
The salt sea-spray, and straight above doth stand
The rudder; but whate'er is sunk beneath
The water will appear as snapt in twain
And backward bent, aye, upward turned again
And all but floating on the water's top.
And when across the heavens the winds of night
Drive on the scattered clouds, then it will seem

The twinkling stars speed full athwart the clouds
And ride on high toward another goal
Than that they truly seek. But if perchance
A hand beneath one eye should lightly press
The eyeball, 'twill befall its wonted sense
Is changed, and whatsoe'er we gaze upon
Will twinned appear unto our sight; for twinned
The flower-flamed light of burning lamps; twinned too
Is all the household gear, and twinned we see
Men's features and their bodies multiplied.
Again, when sleep hath bound our weary limbs
In soothing rest, and all our frame doth lie
At utter peace, yet then we feel ourselves
To be awake, and move our limbs, and e'en
In night's blind gloom we think to see the sun
And light of day; and from our close-walled room
We seem to pass to unknown skies, strange seas,
New streams and mountains, or to plant our feet
On distant plains; or haply seem to hear
The sound of voices, e'en though all about
Doth brood the solemn stillness of the night,
Yea, e'en to answer, though our lips be numb.
And many a thing of kindred kind we see
To rouse our wonder, all whereof conspire
To spoil the trust we place in sense; but all
Without avail, since far the greater part
Thereof do trick us through the exercise
Of our own mind's opinion, which ourselves
We add thereto, that so those things unseen
To sense are counted seen. For naught, 'tis sure,
Is harder than to sift things manifest

From things uncertain, which the active mind
Forthwith doth add from out its own full store.

Again, if one doth hold that naught is known,
No surety hath he that this very thing
Can e'en be known, since by his own avowal
He knoweth naught. With him, then, I refrain
From joining issue who doth plant himself
With head in place of heels. And yet were I
To grant he hath this knowledge too, yet this
I fain would ask: since he ere now hath seen
No truth in things, whence doth he grasp, I pray,
What knowing is, or knowing not, in turn?
Or what is it which hath in him begot
The notion of the true and false? What, pray,
Hath proved the doubtful differeth from the sure?
Nay, thou wilt find the concept of the true
Doth first from out the senses rise, nor e'er
Can senses be gainsaid. For past all doubt
Somewhat must needs be found wherein to place
Our major trust, somewhat which of itself
May vanquish falsehood with the test of truth,
And what than sense can win our greater trust?
Will reason, sprung from senses false, avail
To witness 'gainst sensation, when itself
Ariseth wholly from our senses? Nay
If they be void of truth, all reason, too,
Must stand as false. Or will the ears avail
To sit in judgment on the eyes, or touch
On ears? Or will the mouth by taste refute
This touch? Or nose or eyes declare it false?

Not so, I ween; for to each sense is given
A power apart, a function of its own;
And thus it needs must be that what is soft,
Or cold, or hot, we grasp by sense distinct
From that whereby the varied hues of things
Fall neath our ken, and whatsoe'er doth wait
On color. So likewise its separate use
Hath taste within our mouth; in one wise scents,
In other, sounds are known. So it must be
Sense cannot sit in judgment upon sense;
Nor, further, can they e'er convict themselves,
Since equal trust must aye be placed therein.
True, then, is what doth seem in every case
To them as true. And if the reason fail
To solve the cause, wherefore these things which, viewed
From close at hand, were square, when far removed
Are seen as round, still 'twere more meet through lack
Of reasoning to spell awry the cause
Of either shape than suffer things clear seen
To slip from out our grasp, and to assail
The groundwork of belief, yea, e'en to wreck
The whole foundation whereupon doth rest
Our life's security. For not alone
Would reason totter, but e'en life itself
Must straightway sink to utter ruin, except
Thou dare to trust the senses, and avoid
The treacherous spots, and all else of that ilk
Which should be shunned, and seek the other path.
Know thou, therefore, that this is naught but store
Of idle words, tricked out in brave array
And marshaled 'gainst the senses. And, in fine,

As in a building, if at first the rule
Be bent awry, or square be out of true,
Or if the level sag e'en but a whit
In all its length, so will our structure prove
Built faulty and askew, as here or there
'Twill bulge, or lean this way or that, and stand
All out of line, as one or other part
Doth seem forthwith to long to fall, yea, e'en
Will fall, betrayed by first false reckonings;
E'en so that reasoning of thine must prove
False and awry, when sprung from senses false.

And now it doth remain to tell the tale
Of how the other senses grasp those things
Suited to each; nor stony is my path.

First, every sound and voice is heard, when once
It hath found entry to the ears and struck
By virtue of its body on our sense.
For bodily, thou must confess, are voice
And sound, since they have power to beat
Upon the senses. Or again, the voice
Will ofttimes scrape the throat, and shouting bring
A roughness in the windpipe, as abroad
It issueth, because, we may be sure,
The first beginnings of the voice have risen
In throng too great through the sore-straitened path
Whence now they issue forth, and as they crowd
Scrape e'en the doorway of the harassed mouth.
So, past all doubt, voices and words are formed
Of elements corporeal, since they tend

To give us pain; nor doth it 'scape thy ken
How body's store is lessened, yea, how weak
Grow e'en men's strength and thews, when without pause
They speak from flush of rising dawn till fall
Of night's dark shadows, most of all when strained
At topmost pitch. Voice, then, must be endowed
With form corporeal, since they who make
Much use of speaking lose perforce a part
From their own frames. Now roughness in the voice
From roughness in its elements doth spring,
And likewise from their smoothness is begot
Its own smooth quality. Nor like in form
Do first beginnings pierce the ear, when deep
With muffled moan soundeth the trumpet blast,
Or roused to bellowing wrath doth belch abroad
Its barbarous blare, and when from the cool slopes
Of distant Helicon the sad-voiced swans
Lift through the night their liquid elegies.

These voices, therefore, when from deep within
Our frame we drive them forth, and send them on
Straight through the gateway of the mouth, forthwith
The nimble tongue, artificer of words,
Doth shape apart, and in their turn the lips
By molding give them form. So, when not long
The interval wherefrom doth take its rise
And reach our ear each several utterance,
It needs must be the words themselves as well
Are clearly heard, distinguished sound by sound;
For each doth keep its semblance and its form.
But if the space be greater than is meet

That lieth between, so must the words perforce
In passing through much store of air be tossed
Together, and their utterance all deranged
While on the winds it flieth. Thus 'twill chance
Thou canst perceive the sound, and yet will grasp
No meaning from the words; so utterly
Confused and tangled do their accents fall.
Again, one single syllable bawled forth
From a crier's mouth will oft arouse the ears
Of all the gathered multitude of folk.
One voice therefore doth straightway fly apart
To many voices, since to separate ears
It doth itself disperse, and stamp thereon
Each word's peculiar form and clear-marked sound
But whate'er part of voices falleth not
Straight on the ears, forthwith is onward borne
And lost, dispersed upon the empty air.
Or haply some there be which, flung against
A solid object, from its face recoil
And give us back the sound, yea, e'en at times
Will mock us with the specter of a word.
When this thou seest clear, so to thyself
And unto others thou canst give account
Of how in lonely regions rocks will oft
Give back our very words in order due,
When, wandering mid the dusky hills, we seek
Our straying comrades, and with loud halloo
We fain would rally them. Nay, I have seen
Places yield cries six-fold, or, seven, when one
Alone was voiced. So clear did hill to hill
Fling back afresh the patient syllables.

Such haunts the fancy of the neighbor folk
Doth fill with goat-hoofed satyrs and with bands
Of shy wood-nymphs; and 'tis the fauns, they say,
By whose wild clamor, trailing through the night
In sportive rout, the hushed wide silences
Are ofttimes shattered, and anon is heard
The sound of strings and the sad, sweet lament
The pipe doth breathe, stopt by the finger tips
Of players; and the peasant folk, they say,
List far and wide, as Pan, his half-wild head
Agog beneath its piny crown, doth run
With curling lip over the open reeds,
That so his pipe cease not to breathe the charm
Of woodland melody. And much besides
Of kindred marvels and of signs they tell,
Lest haply they be deemed to dwell apart
In lonely wastes, deserted e'en by gods.
'Tis thus these wonders in their speech they boast,
Or led by other fancy; for, I ween,
All human kind hath e'er an itching ear.

As for the rest, no cause for wonderment
It is, that oftentimes through paths whereby
The eyes will fail to view things clearly, there
Voices will pass and rouse the ears. So, oft,
Despite unopened doors, we see men speak
And make reply, because, we may be sure,
Though voice may pass unharmed through winding pores
In things, yet images demur; for these
Are rent asunder, save it be they stream
Through passages unbent, as those of glass

Wherethrough all idols speed their wingéd flight.
Then too, a voice to many sides is cleft
Apart, since sounds and voices are begot
One of another, when, once issued forth,
One voice is sundered into many, e'en
As oft a single spark of fire is wont
To strew itself into its several fires.
And so will spots hid far from view be filled
With voices, till each nook thereof will seethe
And stir with sound. But idols everywhere
Press on their paths unswerving, soon as once
They have been sent abroad upon their ways.
And thus it is that none, while pent within
A walled enclosure, can behold whate'er
Doth lie without, yet haply may perceive
The sound of voices; yet this very voice
In passing through the walls is dulled, and all
Confused it entereth the ears, that so
We seem, in lieu of words, to hear a sound.

Nor do those instruments whereby we grasp
Savor in things, the tongue and palate, crave
A longer quest, or claim our greater toil.
For savor in the mouth we first perceive
Whene'er by chewing from our food 'tis prest;
As one perchance should squeeze within his hand
A sponge well filled with water, and essay
To wring it dry. Then all abroad is spread
The moisture, laving all the palate's pores
And all the tongue's wide winding ways. And thus,
When smooth the drops of flowing savor, so

With soft and soothing touch they sweetly woo
All the moist vault about the tongue. But quite
In other wise, the more each several thing
Is touched with roughness, so will it assail
All in its path, and stab with rending pain.
And last of all, the savor's pleasantness
Doth gain the palate's rim; but soon as e'er
Down through the throat it hasteneth on its way,
So is all pleasure lost, as through the frame
'Tis spread abroad. Nor mattereth a whit
The food whereon our body doth subsist,
If that we take can be absorbed, and spread
Abroad through all the limbs, and if so be
The stomach's wonted humors we maintain.

And now, that we may see how various breeds
Of creatures have their proper sustenance,
Each in his kind, 'tis mine to tell; or why
That which to some is harsh and bitter, yet
Can seem to others sweet; so wide herein
Is set the gulf between, that what to one
Is sustenance to other breeds will prove
A bitter poison; e'en as there is found
A certain serpent [2] which, when once 'tis touched
By human spittle, straightway perisheth,
Devouring its own body. So to us
Is hellebore rank poison, yet thereon
Will goats and quail grow fat and thrive apace.

---

[2] Pliny the Elder, in his *Natural History*, 7, 15, refers to a similar phe-
nomenon.

If thou wouldst learn wherefore this doth befall,
'Twere well to hold first in thy mind a truth
We have ere now proclaimed: that many seeds
Are held in things, conjoined in many ways.
Again, all living creatures which subsist
On food, e'en as to outward view they show
A varied aspect, and a form diverse
Doth mold the outward contour of their limbs,
Each in his kind, so too they are composed
Of seeds of varying shape. Now since the seeds
Are formed unlike, so must their intervals
And so those passageways we term the pores
Differ in all their limbs, yea, in the mouth
And palate too. Hence it were meet that some
Be lesser, some more great, while these will show
A shape three-cornered, those a square, or round,
Or e'en with many angles set in ways
Diverse; for as the ordering of their shapes
And movements doth prescribe, so must the form
Of openings between abide diverse,
And varied all the ways, proportionate
Unto the texture which doth hem them in.
Wherefore, when what is sweet to one doth turn
To bitter in another's mouth, for him
To whom 'tis sweet, bodies exceeding smooth
Must needs find entry to the palate's pores
And give it feeling; but in other wise
To those who find the same things sour within
We can be sure 'tis bodies rough and hooked
Which make their way into the passages;
Nay, to the selfsame mouth the liquid sweets

Of honey oft will harsh and bitter prove.
And yet from what doth follow we may learn
With ease the cause of both. For whensoe'er
A fever seizeth on a man, or taint
Of some distemper roused in other wise,
Disordered lieth all the frame, and all
The pattern of the first beginnings changed;
So will it chance that bodies meet but now
Unto his taste no longer suit, while those
Of other kind more apt can win their way
Within, and in the mouth beget a taste
Of sourness; for that both commingled lie
In honey's savor, as I oft have shown.

Now list, while I unfold the mode wherein
The assault of smell is wont to win its way
Unto our nostrils. First, there needs must be
Great store of things wherefrom a varying **stream**
Of scents doth flow in rolling tide; then too,
We must recall that in abundant streams
'Tis cast abroad and scattered far and wide.
Yet will there be one scent more favorable
To certain living creatures, and again
Another unto others, since unlike
Abide the shapes whereof they stand composed.
And so will bees through endless tracts of air
Be lured by honey's fragrance, while the reek
Of rotting corpses summoneth the breed
Of carrion fowl. So too the keen-nosed scent
Of dogs sent on before will lead the way
Whither the wild game's cloven hoof hath left

Its well-marked track; and e'en the milk-white goose,
Deliverer of the sons of Romulus,[3]
Doth sense afar the scent of man. 'Tis thus
To diverse creatures scents diverse assigned
Will lead them on, each to his proper meat,
Constraining them the while to fly afar
From noisome poisons;•thus o'er all the earth
Preserved from harm is every breed of beasts.

Yet not alone in scents doth this befall,
And in the field of savors, but no less
Will forms and hues of things at times refuse
To yield the selfsame aspect to the sense
Of all beholders; but that some will prove
Too piercing for the sight of certain breeds.
Nay, e'en the lion's ravening race doth shrink
To face with steadfast gaze the cock,[4] whose wont
It is with clapping wings to banish night
And greet with clarion cry the dawn; so prone
Are they to yield themselves forthwith to flight,
Because, no doubt, the cock hath certain seeds
Within his body which, when cast abroad
Into the eyes of lions, straightway stab
Their way into the pupils and therein
Will bring to birth sharp pangs of piercing pain,
That so, all fierceness lost, they cannot brook

wwwwwwwwwwwwwwwwwwwwwwwww

[3] Reference is to the well-known story of the sacred geese, kept in the Temple of Juno on the Capitoline Hill in Rome, whose cackling roused the sleeping sentinels just in time to ward off a surprise attack by a band of Gauls who had been encamped below.
[4] Echoes of this curious notion are found in a number of ancient writers.

To stand against him. Yet unto our eyes
These things can bring no harm, whether it be
They cannot enter, or, once entered, find
Free issue from our eyes, lest lingering on
They may contrive some part thereof to hurt.

   This very odor, then, when it doth stir
The nostrils, haply may be cast abroad
Now farther, now less far; yet none thereof
So far is borne as sound, or voice, to make
No mention of these things which strike upon
The pupil of the eye and stir the sight.
For smell doth stray abroad, and come but late,
Yea, all too soon it perisheth, dispersed
By bit and fragile bit upon the breeze.
First, since from deep within and grudgingly
'Tis yielded from each object; for that smells
Stream off and fly abroad from things deep down
Beneath their surfaces, clear fact doth prove,
Since all things are perceived to manifest
A keener scent when broken, or when crushed,
Or conquered in a flame. Again, 'tis clear
That scent of larger elements than voice
Is fashioned, since it findeth not a path
Through walls of stone, wherethrough both voice **and**
    sound
Will often pass. Hence, too, no easy task
It is, as thou wilt find, to trace the spot
Wherein doth lie whate'er a scent doth shed.
For cool doth grow its force, as through the air
It lingereth, nor hotly to our sense

It hasteth with its tidings of the world
That lieth without. And thus it is that dogs
Oft go astray, and seek in vain the trail.

  Now list, and hear what bodies stir the mind,
And in brief discourse learn whence come those things
Which touch our understanding. First of all,
This I repeat: that many images
Of things in many ways do flit about
To every quarter and on every side,
Yea, idols passing fine, the which with ease
Are linked together through the airs, whene'er
They cross each other's path, as spider's web
And leaves of beaten gold. For slenderer far
In sooth they are in texture than those things
Which fill the eyes and rouse our sight, since these
E'en through the body's pores will pierce, and wake
The subtile nature of the mind within,
And rouse its feeling. Hence it is we see
Centaurs, and limbs of Scyllas, dog-faced shapes
Of Cerberus, aye, forms of those long dead
Whose bones the earth doth hold in her embrace.
For images of every kind are borne
To every side, whereof some part are formed
At their own instance in the very airs,
And others born of shapes of these conjoined.
For in good sooth 'tis from no living thing
Doth come the Centaur's image, for that ne'er
Had living creature such a nature; nay,
'Tis when chance images of man and horse
Have met, and straightway joined in one, they cling

With readiness together, as but now
We have proclaimed, being formed of texture fine
And slender fabric. In the selfsame wise
Are fashioned all things of this ilk besides;
And since so nimbly on their airy flight
They speed, as I have shown, so any one
Such subtle idol will arouse our mind.
For fine and passing swift is mind itself.

 That this befalleth e'en as I relate
Thou mayst hereby with ease discern. Since like,
Each unto each, are images that mind
And eye observe, so too in manner like
Must both be brought to pass. Since, then, I see
A lion perchance, as I have shown, by aid
Of idols which assail the eyes, 'tis clear
That in the selfsame wise is moved the mind,
In that through images it doth perceive
A lion, or aught else, no more, no less
Than do the eyes, save that it can discern
Idols more subtle. Nor from other cause,
When sleep hath loosed the limbs, still broad awake
Doth watch the mind's intelligence, but that
E'en then these very idols stir our minds
As when awake, that so in very truth
We seem to see e'en one whom, reft of life,
Death and the earth have taken for their own.
And this by nature's will doth come to pass,
Since all our body's senses, checked and lulled
To rest throughout the limbs, no more avail
To rout false things by true. And memory, too,

Drowned deep in slumber, lieth all at rest,
Nor doth protest that he our mind would fain
Believe to be alive hath long ago
Laid hold on death and doom. And furthermore,
No marvel is it that these idols move
And toss in rhythmic measure arms and all
Their limbs (for oft in dreams 'twill come to pass
An image thus will seem to do); since soon
As e'er the first hath perished, straight doth come
Another in its place, and thus 'twill seem
The first hath changed its gesture. Clearly, too,
In quick succession must we deem this shift
To come to pass. But such the speed, so great
The store of things, so great the multitude
Of idol-particles in any space
Of time we mark, that never may they fail.

Herein will many a question rise, and much
Must we make clear, if we would fain set forth
The truth in terms explicit. First of all
Doth rise this query: Why, when there doth come
To one the whim to think on this or that,
Straightway his mind unto that very thing
Will turn its thought. Or haply may it be
The idols set a watch upon our will,
And soon as e'er the whim doth take us, straight
An image riseth, whether it be sea,
Or earth, or e'en the heaven itself which hath
Our fancy caught? So too, with crowds of folk,
Processions, banquets, battles, all of these
Doth nature at a word create and set

In use? Albeit within the selfsame place
And spot, the mind of others doth give thought
To things of nature all at variance.
Then what of this, when in our dreams we see
Idols that move in measure, as they lift
Their lissome limbs, weaving now here, now there,
The rhythmic pattern of their arms, or now
With feet attuned make answering gesture? Aye,
In sooth, idols are steeped in art and trained
To prowl about in midnight mummery!
Or is more truth in this, since in the space
Of one brief instant which our sense will grasp,
(Such time, that is, as one short syllable
Would mark in utterance) many 'times' lie hid
Which reason can discover, hence it is
That howe'er brief a space of time there wait
Ready to hand the several images
In every place? For such their speed, so great
The store of things. Therefore, so soon
As e'er the first hath perished, straight doth come
Another in its place, and thus 'twill seem
The first hath changed its gesture. And since fine
Their texture is, none can the mind discern
Thereof with sharpness, saving those whereon
It straineth to attend. Hence all besides
Will pass away, save those alone whereto
The mind hath set itself. For mind in truth
Itself prepareth, and doth hope for that
To come to pass whereby it may discern
What followeth on each act; and hence 'tis done.
And seest not how the eyes, when they would fain

Perceive things small, will strain and set themselves
In readiness, else ne'er could we avail
To see things sharply? And yet e'en in things
Held plain in view, thou mayst take note withal
That save thou turn thereto thy mind, 'twere e'en
As all the time the thing were set apart
And far removed. What marvel is it, then,
If mind doth lose all else save that whereto
It hath itself applied? Then too, from signs
Minute great inferences we draw, and thus
In toils of self-deceit ourselves we snare.

   Nay, 'twill befall at times that there will rise
An image of a different kind, that so
What now was woman doth before our eyes
Seem to become a man; or haply face
Will follow upon face, or age on age;
Yet that our wonder be not roused thereby
'Tis sleep and dark forgetfulness ensure.

   Herein I sorely yearn to have thee shun
This fault, and as with deep felt dread avoid
A general error: lest perchance thou deem
The eye's bright orb hath with design been framed
That we might look before us; or, to ensure
Our power to move with stately tread, for this
The slender length of calves and thighs, well-joined
To steady feet, can bend; or, once again,
That pliant wrists firm linked to sturdy arms,
And hands, those faithful servants, have been given
On either side that we might meet therewith

The needs of life. And all else of this ilk
Which men proclaim, with reasoning all awry,
Doth set effect for cause, since naught was born
In all our body to be used, but what
Hath once been born doth its own use create.
Nor seeing had existence ere the light
Of eyes was born, nor yet to plead in words
Before the tongue had been created; nay,
Rather did birth of tongue by far precede
The use of discourse, and the ears were formed
Long ere a sound was heard; and so, I ween,
Did all the limbs have being ere their use
Was brought to light. Ne'er, then, can they have grown
With eye to use. But, on the other side,
With hands unarmed to join in deadly strife
Of battle, yea, to rend the limbs, and stain
With gore the body of the foe; all these
Men knew long ere there flew abroad a rain
Of gleaming darts; and nature's self would prompt
Avoidance of a wounding blow ere yet
The left arm, trained by art, would interpose
A shield's defense. So too, we may be sure,
Far older is the wont to lay to rest
The weary body than the pillowed ease
Of soft-strewn couches; and to slake the thirst
Rose long ere cups were fashioned. These things, then,
Devised to meet life's needs, might well be deemed
Invented for their use; but all the rest
Whereof I speak do lie apart, since first
Themselves were born, and tardily revealed
The notion of their use. Whereof we see

Senses and limbs to stand in foremost rank.
Wherefore I say once more, 'tis past belief
They could be formed to serve the ends of use.

Likewise in this no cause for wonderment
Need lie, that bodies of all living things
By their own nature seek for food. For well
Have I revealed that many bodies ebb
And pass away from things in many ways;
But most from living creatures needs must pass,
Since oft, sore tried by movement, from the mouth
Is breathed much store of matter, as they pant
In weariness; much too from deep within
Is poured abroad in sweat. Wherefore the frame
Doth thinner grow, and all the strength thereof
Is undermined, and straight there followeth pain.
'Tis therefore food is taken, that once more
It may support the failing limbs, and, spread
Within, renew their strength, as through the veins
And members it doth stop the gaping mouth
Of hunger. Likewise moisture is dispersed
To every place that wanteth moisture. Thus
The many gathered seeds of heat which bring
A burning to the stomach are dispersed
By advent of the moisture, and like flame
Are quenched, that so no more the parching heat
May rage. Thus from our frame the panting thirst
Is laved, and thus the craving hunger stilled.

Next, how it doth befall that we contrive,
Whene'er we will, to tread with stately pace,

Or how 'tis given to move in various ways
Our limbs, and what the force which hath the wont
To thrust our body forward, e'en despite
Its solid bulk, I shall relate; and thou
Give heed unto my words. First, I affirm,
Idols of motion strike and stir the mind,
As I ere now have shown. Next doth arise
The will to move; for none can undertake
The slightest act until mind hath foreseen
What it doth will to do. Now what the mind
Thus seeth in advance can be naught else
Than image of that act. Thus, when the mind
Hath so bestirred itself that it would fain
Step forth and walk, straightway it doth arouse
The force of soul, dispersed through all the frame
In every limb and member. And with ease
It thus may do, since close therewith 'tis linked.
Next doth the soul in turn proceed to strike
The body, till by bit and bit its mass
Entire is forward thrust, and all is roused
To active movement. Rarer, too, doth grow
The body at such times, and floods of air,
In keeping with its nimble nature, stream
Through all the opened spaces, and invade
Its passageways, till to each smallest part
Of all the frame 'tis spread. Thus doth befall
That by a double cause, in double wise,
Is moved the body, as a ship is borne
By sails and wind. Nor yet is need herein
For wonderment that bodies so minute
Can turn about so huge a frame, and sway

Our mass entire; for in like wise a wind,
Fine wrought of subtile body, yet will drive
Amain a mighty ship of ponderous bulk;
Yea, and whate'er its speed, a single hand
May guide it, twisting wheresoe'er it will
A single helm. So will an engine move
With winch and pulley many a solid mass,
And lift its ponderous weight with utmost ease.

　　Now in what wise that sleep we know doth flood
O'er all our limbs its calm repose, and loose
The mind-born cares from out the weary breast,
My task shall be in verses sweet but few
To demonstrate; e'en as the swan's brief song
Is sweeter than the long-drawn clamorous cries
Of southward winging cranes, far-heard among
The airy clouds. And thou, lend heedful ear
And mind alert, lest haply thou deny
That what I say can be, and with a breast
Stubborn to words of truth mayst go thy way,
When thou thyself dost stray, and canst not see.
First, sleep doth come to pass, when shed abroad
Among the limbs doth lie the potency
Of soul, or haply part hath fled, cast out
Upon the air, and part, thrust back, hath shrunk
Still deeper in the frame; for then at length
The limbs are loosed and slackened. For, past doubt,
'Tis soul that doth in us this sense beget,
That so when sleep its nature doth erase
'Tis then the soul we needs must deem disturbed
And scattered; yet not all: for then would lie

Our body wrapt in everlasting chill
Of death. For surely, when no part remained
Of soul, hid in the limbs, as fire is hid
Buried beneath a heap of ashes, whence
Could feeling on a sudden spring once more
Rekindled through the limbs, even as flame
Can rise again from out a slumbering fire?

But by what means this new estate doth rise,
And whence the soul can be disturbed, the frame
Grow slack, I shall unfold; and thou, look well
That I strew not my words upon the winds.
First, then, the body on its outward side,
Since close 'tis prest by breezes of the air,
By frequent blows thereof must needs be thumped
And buffeted; and for this cause it is
That well-nigh all things by an outer hide
Or shell, or rind, or bark, are covered o'er.
Again, as creatures breathe, this selfsame air
Doth smite the inner side, when it is drawn
And once again breathed forth. Hence, since alike
From either side the body is assailed,
And since the blows pass on, and make their way
Through all the body's slender pores, and down
To simplest parts and primal elements
Within our frame, there followeth, as it were,
A crumbling in the limbs, for all deranged
The order of the body's elements
And seeds of mind. And hence it doth befall
That banished is a portion of the soul,
And part doth yield and hide itself within;

Part, too, asunder torn throughout the limbs,
Cannot avail to rally to itself
Nor rouse its mutual movements, since, in truth,
Nature doth all its ways and meetings bar.
And so, its motions altered, deep within
Doth sense withdraw; and since naught is at hand
To prop, as 'twere, its members, so the frame
Doth feeble grow, and slackened all the limbs;
The arms and eyelids droop, and e'en as thou
Dost seek thy couch, the knees will oft give way,
Their strength relaxed. Likewise ofttimes will sleep
Ensue on food, since food one selfsame state
Doth bring with air, as through the body's pores
It is dispersed. And heavier far will prove
That slumber thou dost take when filled with food
Or weary, for that then a greater throng
Of bodies is disordered, bruised and torn
With mighty effort. And in selfsame wise
There doth ensue a deeper refluence
Of soul, and wider is it flung abroad,
While finer it is cleft and torn within.

Then too, 'twill chance most oft that those pursuits
Whereto each man from chains of use doth cling,
Or tasks whereat we long have labored, aye,
Till mind therein was strained beyond its wont,
'Tis these in sleep we seem most oft to meet.
Jurists will plead their cases, frame their laws,
While generals fight their battles o'er and o'er;
Sailors live o'er their conflicts waged with winds;
Ourselves will ply our task, searching for aye

The nature of all things, and when 'tis ours,
Set forth in native verse the truths we find.
And most of all will all pursuits and arts
Of men besides appear in sleep to hold
Their minds in error's toils. And whensoe'er
For many days on end have men bestowed
Unflagging zeal upon the games, we oft
Will see that e'en when they have ceased
To grasp them with the senses, yet remain
Wide opened ways within the mind, whereby
The selfsame images may enter in.
And so for many days the wonted scenes
Will pass before their eyes, that e'en awake
They seem to see the dancers flinging wide
Their supple limbs, while in their ears still ring
The lyre's melodious strains and singing strings;
Aye, e'en to view the selfsame throng, and scan
The varied glories of the stage, that shine
In bright-hued charm; so great the potency
Of zeal and pleasure, and those tasks whereto
Not men alone are wont to give their strength,
But every living creature. For in truth
Oft wilt thou see strong horses, when their limbs
Are laid to rest, yet in their sleep break forth
In sweat, and pant for breath, and strain each nerve
As for the prize, or, as when open fly
The barriers, snort their challenge. So ofttimes
Will hunters' dogs upon a sudden toss
E'en in soft sleep their limbs, and all at once
Give tongue, as ever and anon they sniff
With nostrils keen the air, as following close

The trail of game; yea, e'en from slumber roused
They oft will chase vain phantom images
Of stags, as though they held in certain view
The quarry in full flight, until at length,
The illusion shattered, they return once more
Unto themselves. But pups, that winsome breed,
Wonted to household ways, will in a trice
Body a-quiver, spring from off the ground
As though they viewed a stranger's form and face.
Yea, and the more untamed the breed, the more
In sleep it needs must toss and fume with rage.
So in the night will birds of various breeds
Take sudden flight, and with a whir of wings
Mar all the stillness of the sacred groves,
If haply in their quiet sleep have come
Visions of swift-winged hawks that in pursuit
Bring strife and battle. And the minds of men
Will oft in sleep those mighty deeds achieve
Which in their waking hours they do and dare:
Captains will storm a fortress, yield themselves
To capture, rush into the fray, or raise
A cry as from a mortal wound, yet stir
No whit from where they lie. And many a man
Will fight for life, and groan with pain, and e'en
As torn by jaws of panther or the teeth
Of savage lion, fill the region round
With mighty outcries. Many will discourse
In sleep on lofty themes, yea, oft have been
Their own accusers. Some stand face to face
With death. Many as from a mountain's height
Flung bodily to earth, are numbed with fear.

And e'en when roused from sleep, as though bereft
Of reason, scarce can gain their wits, deranged
By turmoil of the body. So by stream
Or pleasant spring will sit a man athirst
And down his throat gulp well-nigh all its flood.

And oft, in slumber bound, an artless child
As though by pool or earthen jar, will seem
To lift his garment, and forthwith will pour
A flood of gathered moisture from his frame,
Till drenched are all the sumptuous coverings.
So too, when first the vital seed hath crept
Into the veins of youth, when ripening age
Hath formed it in the frame, there oft will come
From some fair form without, sweet images
To tell of lovely face or beauteous hue
That so do stir and rouse the limbs, inflamed
By seed abundant, that as though love's rites
Were fully done, the copious flooding tide
Is poured abroad, and all the raiment stained.

This seed whereof I speak is stirred in us
When first the ripening age of youth doth bring
Full vigor to our frame. For roused and moved
By cause appropriate is each several thing;
But human seed from man by human cause
Alone is summoned. And when once 'tis stirred,
And from its wonted place doth issue forth,
Straightway through every limb and member, aye,
Through all the body doth it pass, and packed
Into the special parts doth rouse forthwith

The generative regions of our frame,
The which, inflamed, swell high with seed, and straight
There doth ensue a rage to cast it forth
Whither the dread desire is bent, and seek
That body whence the mind is sick with love.
For men most often fall upon their wound,
And blood will spurt toward him who gave the blow;
So, if he be at hand, the crimson tide
Will strike full on the foe. So he who once
Is smitten by the shafts of love, forth cast
By some unbearded boy with melting limbs
Or by a woman who from all her frame
Doth shower the darts of love, so doth he long
To join therewith; and cast into that frame
The humor drawn from out his own; for so
Doth mute desire give presage of delight.

'Tis this we know as Venus; this wherefrom
Doth spring the name of love; this whence hath first
Distilled into our hearts that honey'd drop
Of Venus' sweetness, soon to be replaced
By chilling care. For e'en though that thou lov'st
Be absent, yet its image hovereth near
Before thine eyes, yea, e'en its very name
Doth linger sweetly in thine ears. But meet
It were to rout such images, and put to flight
That which doth feed thy love, yea, elsewhere turn
Thy mind, and into random frames project
Thy gathered passion, and not hold it fast
Set once for all upon the love of one,
And earn thyself thereby great store of care

And certain anguish. For the sore doth spread
And fester with fomenting; day by day
The madness groweth, and graver is its weight
Of misery, unless thou put to rout
With new attack the early wounds, and, ere
They deepen, heal their hurt with wandering down
The wanton way of Venus, or mayhap
Canst elsewhere turn the motions of thy mind.

Nor wanteth Venus' fruits who hath foresworn
Love's passion; rather doth he choose those joys
Which bring no pain. For surely to the whole
Of heart the joys thereof are purer far
Than to the love-sick. For e'en on the verge
Of consummation, with a vague unrest
Doth shift the lovers' passion, as they doubt
What first with hands or eyes they should enjoy.
What they have grasped they tightly press, and e'en
Give pain unto its body, and ofttimes
Clash teeth on lips as mouth on mouth they crush,
Since tainted is their pleasure, and beneath
Lie secret stings, that goad them on to hurt
The very thing, whate'er it be, whence spring
These germs of madness. Yet amid the heat
Of love doth Venus gently quell their pains,
And tinge of bland desire the bites doth curb.
For ever doth arise a haunting hope
That from the selfsame body whence hath sprung
The passion's fire, its flame may eke be quenched;
Yet nature doth protest all will befall
In manner opposite; for this will prove

The one thing that is ours whereof the more
We have, the hotter with a fierce desire
Will burn our breast. For meat and drink, I ween,
Are drawn within our members, and since these
In parts appropriate can find abode,
With readiness thereby can be assuaged
Craving for water and for bread. But naught
From human face and beauteous bloom is given
Unto our body's pleasure, save alone
Their shadowy images—poor empty hope,
That oft doth vanish on the vagrant breeze!
E'en as in dreams one parched with thirst will seek
To drink, but ne'er a cooling draught is found
To soothe the burning in his limbs, but e'er
He panteth after phantom streams, and all
In vain he striveth, still athirst, though plunged
Full in mid-flood he seem to drink his fill;
So in the toils of love doth Venus mock
With images the lovers, nor avail
Their bodies' selves to sate them, as with gaze
Deep rapt they strain with all their eyes; nor aught
From off those tender limbs can they abrade
With restless hands that shift o'er all the frame.
And when at last with twining limbs they taste
The flower of youth, when now their bodies feel
A foretaste of delight, and Venus hath
The man in act to sow the female soil,
E'en then frame unto frame they wildly lock,
Mingling the moisture of their mouths, and e'en
Draw in each other's breath, as teeth on lips
They madly press; yet all in vain, since naught

Can they remove therefrom, nor penetrate
Body in body, and thus merge in one.
For this they seem at times to crave, and strive
To do; so eagerly in Venus' toils
They cling, while melt their very limbs, o'ercome.
By violence of delight. But when at length
The gathered passion from their limbs hath burst,
There followeth for a space a little pause
In their impassioned ardor. Then once more
The madness doth return, and the old rage
Again doth torture them, while torn with doubt
They ask what it can be they fain would have,
And find no remedy to heal their ills;
So, wavering e'er, they waste with secret wound.

Add that their strength they waste, and sick with care
Are worn to naught; add that their life is spent
Beneath another's sway. Meanwhile their wealth
Doth ebb away, dispersed on coverlets
Of Babylonian purple; slack doth grow
All duty's prompting, and their once fair name
Doth faint and sicken, while the mistress' feet
Twinkle in gay Sicyonian slippers—yea,
Huge emeralds set in gold flash their green light,
The while from constant wear her sea-hued gown
Is worn to rags and stained with reeking sweat.
Thus into ribands and tiaras melt
The hard-earned riches of their sires, or now
'Tis turned to cloaks or Alidensian robes
Or Chian tissues. Banquets, too, are set
With choicest linens and with costliest foods;

Games, countless goblets, perfumes, garlands, crowns,
Nothing doth lack. But all to no avail,
Since e'en from out this fountain of delights
Doth rise some bitter taste, to strangle them
Among the very flowers, whenas the mind
Neath sting of guilt doth feel the gnawing tooth
Of keen remorse at life misspent in sloth
Or squandered in indulgence; or mayhap
'Twill be she hath let fall some idle word
That left its sense in doubt, and buried deep
Within his jealous heart, it groweth there
Like hidden flame; or haply he may deem
Her glances over-free, as she doth look
Upon another; or may think to see
Some trace of mocking laughter on her lips.

And these the ills that in a love secure
And fortunate are found; but when 'tis crossed
And hopeless, so its woes are plain to grasp
E'en with unopened eyes, yea, numberless.
So that 'twere better far to keep thy guard
Beforehand, e'en as I have taught, and watch
Lest thou be trapped. For easier 'tis, I ween,
To shun the toils of love than, once enmeshed,
To escape the net, and break the powerful bonds
Of Venus. Yet thou mayst, e'en caught therein
And prisoned, flee the danger, if so be
Thou hinder not thyself, nor from the first
O'erlook each fault of body or of mind
In her thou seekest for thine own. For men
Are often passion-blinded, and ascribe

To those they love ideal excellencies
Not truly theirs. And so we oft will see
Some creature maimed and ugly dearly loved
And prospering in high favor. And one man
Will laugh to scorn another, urging him
To soften Venus' wrath, since he is plagued
With an untoward passion, nor, ofttimes,
Doth sense, poor wretch, his own most piteous plight.
The black is 'honey-dark', the unkempt and foul
'Hath such a careless grace'; this green-eyed jade
Is 'Pallas' self'; that one, all skin and bone,
Is a 'gazelle', the dwarfed 'a pet', 'a grace',
'A pinch of unadulterated salt';
One huge and bulky 'grand', and 'distinguée'.
This cannot speak from stammering—she 'hath
A charming lisp', the dumb is 'circumspect';
The hateful spitfire is 'a blazing torch'.
'A slender amourette' doth she become
Who scarce can live from wasting, while the fat
Big-breasted one is 'Ceres' self, fresh risen
From birth of Bacchus'; and yon splay-nosed ape
Is dubbed 'Silenus' sister', 'satyress';
Her thick-lipped twin is 'an incarnate kiss'.

But more of this were tale too long to tell.
Yet grant she be however fair of face,
Breathing the charm of love from every limb,
Yet others too there be, 'tis sure, as fair,
And we, 'tis sure, have somehow lived till now
Without her; yea, 'tis sure she doth perform
The selfsame ritual—and well we know

She doth it—as the ugliest of her kind,
And with rich scents doth all her person drench,
Poor creature, till her handmaids flee afar
And shake with secret laughter. But in tears
The excluded lover doth her threshold heap
With flowers and garlands, or with perfumed oil
Her haughty doorposts doth anoint, the while
His wretched kisses rain upon her doors;
Yet, once admitted, should a single breath
Salute his entry, forthwith would he seek
Some honest pretext to be gone; his plaint,
Deep-drawn and long rehearsed, would die away,
And straightway would he curse his witlessness,
Knowing full well he had ascribed to her
More than a mortal's due. And this, I ween
Our queens of love take note on, that the more
They are at utmost pains themselves to hide
The back-stage scenes of life from those they scheme
To hold close bound in love; but all in vain,
Since thou in thought canst none the less bring all
To light of day, and search into the cause
Of all this laughter; and if she be fair
Of mind, nor spiteful, thou mayst in thy turn
O'erlook her faults, her human ways condone.

Nor always with a feignéd love doth sigh
The woman who in locked embrace doth join
Her body to the man's, and hold him close,
With dewy kisses pressing lip on lip;
For oft 'tis from her heart she thus will do,
And seeking mutual joys will lead him on

To run love's race unto the goal. Nor else
Would birds and wild things, nor the farm-bred kine
Nor ewes and mares submit to bear their mates,
Save that their natures too conceived the flame,
And glowing with its heat gave back with joy
The lusty ardors of the covering male.
And seest not oft how creatures bound in bonds
Of mutual pleasure by their common chains
Are held in torment? So at cross-roads oft
Will dogs, in frantic struggle to disjoin,
Pull eagerly in diverse ways amain,
While yet they cling in Venus' powerful toils.
But this they ne'er would do, did they not know
Those mutual joys that lure them to their hurt
And hold them prisoned. Hence it is I say
Again, as I have said, the joy is shared.

And when, in mingling of the seed, perchance
The female potency hath suddenly
O'ermastered and usurped the virile force,
Then of the mother's seed are offspring born
Like to the mother; e'en as those wherein
Prevail the father's seed are like their sire.
But those thou seest both parents to recall,
With features like to each, these are begot
Of father's substance and of mother's blood,
When mutual ardor hath in consonance
The seeds together brought, roused through the limbs
By goads of Venus, as nor this nor that
Or mastereth or is mastered. And at times
It will befall that children are begot

In likeness to grandparents, or recall
The features of their great-grandsires; since oft
Do parents hide within their frames a store
Of first beginnings mixt in many ways,
Which, traced from early parent stock, will sire
Hand on to sire; and thence by varied chance
Doth Venus draw this shape or that, and mold
Mien, voice, or hair of generations past.
For these no less from seed assured are bred
Than features, forms, and limbs. Then too, from seed
Of father female issue well may spring,
Or males come forth formed of the mother's frame;
For ever of twinned seed is offspring shaped,
And whichsoe'er that which is born doth more
Resemble, of that parent it hath more
Than equal share; as thou thyself canst see,
Be it a man-child or a female birth.

And ne'er doth will divine deny a man
A fruitful sowing, that he ne'er may hear
The name of father from sweet childish lips,
But pass in barren wedlock all his years;
For so do many hold, and sadly drench
With offerings of blood the holy shrines
And kindle with rich gifts their altar fires,
That thus with seed abundant they may make
Their wives to teem; but all in vain they tire
The powers divine and holy oracles.
For some men are unfruitful from a seed
Too thick, or liquid beyond wont, and thin;
Since seed too thin cannot avail to cling

Unto the proper places, but forthwith
Will melt and fall abortive, summoned back
From fruitful union; whereas others spend
Seed heavier than is meet, that so 'twill chance
It either flieth forth with cast too short,
Or cannot penetrate its proper fields;
Or, if it chance to penetrate, 'tis loth
To mingle with the woman's seed. For wide,
I ween, are variances in love's accord;
For some men will impregnate certain wives
More readily than others, while from some
Will wives receive their burden, and conceive
With greater ease. So many wives who proved
In previous unions barren, at length have found
A mate by whom they could avail to bear
A brood of children, blessing all their house
With goodly offspring. And for men as well
Whose wives, though erstwhile fruitful in the house
Of others, could not bear, there have been found
Natures harmonious, enabling them
To prop their waning years with goodly sons.
So much importeth, in the fruitful blend
Of seed with proper seed, if solid mix
With liquid, liquid with the dense. Then, too,
Importeth much herein the food whereon
Life doth subsist; for by some foods the seed
Within our frame is clotted, while again
From others it will grow more thin and rare.

Then, too, the mode wherein the bland delight
Itself is practised hath an import great;

For 'tis a wide belief that in the style
Of wild things' couplings and the four-foot breeds
Our wives will best conceive, since, postured thus,
Breast down and loins upraised, the fruitful ground
Can best receive the seed. But naught avail
In wives unbridled motions; for 'twill thwart
Her own conceiving if an honest wife
With unbecoming zeal will lend herself
To wanton acts. For movements such as these
Will throw the furrow from the plowshare's track,
And from its proper ground will turn aside
The cast of seed. And thus in furtherance
Of their own ends are strumpets wont to move,
Lest often they be filled and brought to bed,
And likewise that the union to their men
May give the more of pleasure—wanton arts
Whereof our own good wives have naught of need.

And sometimes it befalleth that apart
From heaven-born gifts and charms by Venus lent,
A woman is beloved, though sparely blest
With dower of beauty; for ofttimes herself
By her demeanor, by her gracious ways,
Her person trimly kept, will she with ease
Win thee to spend with her thy quiet days
In deep content. And use, when all is said,
May breed affection. For whate'er is struck,
However lightly, by repeated blows,
Will yet give way and yield with lapse of time.
Seest not how drops of moisture, dripping slow
Upon a rock, at length will pierce the stone?

BOOK FIVE

Proemium, 1-54.

Argument of the book, and new proemium against the teleological concept, 55-234.

Origin of the world and of life, 235-1457.

BOOK FIVE

Who can avail with heart upraised to build
A lofty lay to match the majesty
Of truth and these discoveries? Or who
Hath tongue fitly to shape a song of praise
To suit the worth of him who hath bequeathed
To us such store of treasure, sought and found
In his own heart? It will be none, I ween,
Of mortal frame begot. For could we speak
As doth befit the matchless majesty
Of truth to us revealed, a god was he,
Yea, e'en a god, good Memmius, who was first
To find that way of life which now we term
Philosophy, and by his skill did bring
Our life from stormy seas and darkness drear
To quiet waters and to light serene.
For match herewith those heaven-sent bounties found
By others' hands in days of old; for corn,
'Tis said, was Ceres' gift to man, the boon
Of vine-born juice did Liber's grace bestow;
And yet cut off from these could life have gone
Upon its way, as even now 'tis told
Some races live. Yet could no life be lived
In worthy wise without a well-purged heart.
Wherefore the more with reason doth he seem
A god to us, from whose great heart have spread

To mighty nations those sweet solaces
Of life that still have power to soothe men's minds.
But if perchance thou'lt deem the mighty deeds
Of Hercules this boon transcend, the more
From reasoning sure wilt thou be cast adrift.
For what to us now those huge wide-gaping jaws
Of Nemea's lion? [1] or the bristling boar
Of Arcady? What power to harm would bide
In Cretan bull, or Lerna's ancient curse,
The hydra, hedged with venomous serpents? What
Could now avail the triple-breasted might
Of threefold Geryon? Or those birds that dwelt
In the Stymphalian fens—could they have wrought
Such hurt to us? Yea, and those steeds as well
Of Thracian Diomedes, snorting fire
From quivering nostrils hard by Ismara
In far Bistonian climes? That dragon, too,
Grim warder of the gleaming golden fruit
Of Hesperus' daughters, as with eyes aflame
He wrapt the trunk in mighty coils—what harm
Could he have wrought by the Atlantean shore
And Ocean's untamed wastes, where ne'er a man
Of us doth come, nor stranger ventureth near?
Yea, and all monsters of this ilk besides,
Foredone to death, e'en had they ne'er been quelled,
What harm, forsooth, could they have wrought alive?
No whit, I trow; for so doth earth e'en now
Teem with its savage creatures, yea, is filled

wwwwwwwwwwwwwwwwwwwwwwww

1 In this passage Lucretius enumerates a number of the traditional twelve
labors of Hercules.

Brimful with shuddering terrors, that beset
Wood, mighty mountain and deep wilderness;
But yet the power is ours most oft to shun
These regions. But unless the heart be cleansed
What battles and what perils must be ours,
Yea, e'en against our will! What piercing pangs
Of passion then will rend the troubled soul,
Yea, and what fears besides! What shall we say
Of pride, and filthiness, and wantonness?
What havoc do they wreak! And what of sloth
And luxury? He, then, who hath subdued
All these, and swept them from our hearts by force
Of words, not arms, were it not meet that he
Be ranked among the gods? And most of all
Since 'twas his wont in fair and godlike words
To make much discourse on the deathless gods
Themselves, and in his sayings to reveal
To men the nature of all things that be.

　　So in his steps I plant my feet, the while
His doctrines I pursue, and in plain words
Set forth the laws whereby all things are framed,
And how they needs must hold thereto, nor e'er
Can break the ancient rock-bound laws that rule
Their being; as in foremost rank whereof,
Mind's nature hath been found to be begot
And shaped beyond all else besides with frame
That knoweth birth; nor can its life abide
Unharmed through endless years, but images
It is that in our sleep at times are wont
To trick our minds, when that we seem to view

The form of one whom light of life hath left.
As for the rest, the order of my theme
Hath brought me now to this, that I must give
Account of how the world entire is framed
Of mortal body, yea, hath come to birth; [2]
And in what fashion too that gathering
Of matter hath established earth, sky, sea,
Stars, sun, and orb of moon; then next what breeds
Of living creatures sprang from earth, and what
Could ne'er at any time have come to birth;
And how the race of men first reaped the fruit
Of interchange of varied sounds of speech
By giving names to things; and in what wise
There crept into their hearts that ancient fear
Of gods, which keepeth still in holy awe
Shrines, lakes, groves, altars, images divine.
And next my theme shall be the power whereby
Nature with hand on helm the wandering ways
Of sun and moon doth guide, that so perchance
We fancy not 'tis of themselves they run
Their yearly round 'twixt earth and sky, to bless
With large increase the fruits of earth and breeds
Of living creatures, or mayhap should deem
'Tis by some providence divine they roll
Upon their destined track. For who hath writ
Deep in his heart that gods a life must lead
Free from all care, yet if from time to time
He chance to marvel at the power whereby

~~~~~~~~~~~~~~~~~~~~~~~~~~~~~~~~

[2] Lucretius here briefly summarizes the content of the latter half of Book
V.

All things in order move, and most of all
Whate'er above our heads in heaven's high realms
Is seen to glide, so doth he drift once more
Back to religion's ancient creeds, and take
Unto himself stern masters, whom he fain
Would think, poor wretch, unmeasured power can wield,
For that he knoweth not what things can be
And what can not, and in what wise the power
Of things is limited, and how for each is marked
On every side its deep-set boundary.

   Now for the rest, lest I delay thee more
With promises, consider first of all
Seas, lands and sky; those threefold essences,
Those bodies three, those threefold forms diverse,
Those triple textures vast, one single day,
Good Memmius, shall hurl to ruin, aye,
This solid form and fabric of the world,
For countless years upheld, shall plunge headlong
To utter chaos. Nor doth 'scape my mind
How new and strange the force wherewith must strike
This thought upon our reason, that one day
Heaven and our earth shall pass away, aye, e'en
How hard a task it is in my discourse
To prove its truth beyond dispute; for thus
It ever doth befall when thou wouldst bring
To ears of men somewhat till now unknown,
And yet thou canst not set it plain to view
Before their eyes, nor lay thereon thy hands;
For these the ways whereby doth straightest lead
The high-road of belief into the heart

Of man and to the temple of his mind.
Yet will I speak; and haply it may be
The fact itself will lend a warranty
Unto my words, and thou shalt see ere long
The earth rise up and tremble, and all things
To reel and shudder neath a mighty shock.
Yet may our guiding fortune steer afar
From us these terrors, and may reason's power
Rather than fact itself rouse our belief
That all our world can fall in ruin, rent
With awful thundering crash.

                    Yet ere I move
To read herein the scroll of destiny
In holier wise, with wisdom far more sure
Than ever Pythian priestess spake her rede
From Phoebus' laureled tripod, 'twill be mine
Full many a solace to impart to thee
In learned lore; lest haply neath the curb
Of superstition thou mayst hold that earth,
Sun, sky, sea, stars, and moon must needs abide
For all eternity, endowed with frame
Divine, and hence shouldst deem it right that, e'en
As did the giants,[3] so all men must pay
The price, as for a crime unspeakable,
Who by their reasoning shake the very walls

[3] Ephialtes and Otus, sons of Poseidon, were giants who attempted to storm the heights of heaven by piling Mt. Pelion upon Mt. Ossa. According to Homer, they were slain by the arrows of Apollo, and condemned to everlasting punishment in the lower world.

That ring our world, yea, and who fain would quench
The glorious sun in heaven, naming with names
That smack of death things that shall never die.
Yet these are things which stand so wide aloof
From will divine, so far unworthy prove
To dwell with gods, that rather are they deemed
Well framed to give a notion of whate'er
Is in its nature far removed from sense
And vital movement. For in very truth
It cannot be we should suppose that linked
With each and every frame there needs must dwell
Nature of mind and reason's potency,
E'en as no tree can in the skies abide,
Nor clouds in ocean's brine, nor in the fields
Can fishes have their home, nor blood reside
In wood, nor sap in stones. Nay, 'tis ordained
And stablished where each thing can have its place
And prosper. So the nature of the mind
Can ne'er apart from blood and sinews keep
Its life. For could this be, 'twere far more meet
That force of mind itself should find its place
In head, or shoulders, yea, e'en in the heels,
Or in what part soe'er thou wilt, be wont
To be created, so it still remain
Within the single man, aye, still be held
Within the selfsame vessel. But since e'en
In our own body's frame it hath been fixt
And clearly foreordained where soul and mind
Can dwell apart and thrive, so much the more
Must thou perforce deny that set apart
From all the body and the living form

It could last on in crumbling clods of earth,
Or fire of sun, or water, or in heights
Of heaven itself. Wherefore they are not blest
With dower of heaven-born feeling, since no whit
Can they be quickened with the sense of life.

  This too thou canst not find it in thine heart
To hold as truth, that anywhere abide
In all this world of ours the hallowed homes
Of gods. For subtile is their essence, far
Removed from human sense, yea, scarce is grasped
E'en by the understanding of the mind;
And since it lieth far beneath all touch
Or grasp of hand, so must itself touch not
Aught which is touched of us. For naught can touch
Which may not in itself be touched in turn.
Wherefore e'en their abodes must needs be found
Unlike to ours, of nature passing fine
E'en as their bodies, as my task shall be
Ere long to prove to thee in ample words.
To say, moreover, that in man's behoof
They did vouchsafe to rear the wondrous frame
Of this our world, and for this cause 'twere meet
To laud with worthy praise their handiwork
And deem it shall through endless time abide
Immortal, aye, and hold 'twere sacrilege
To stir by any force from its firm seat
What once by ancient wisdom of the gods
Hath for all time been stablished for the race
Of men, or e'er with argument assail
And overthrow its structure, top from base—

Error on foolish error thus to heap,
Good Memmius, were but madness. For what boon
Could all our thanks bestow upon those beings,
Deathless and blest, that they in our behoof
Should venture aught? Or what strange circumstance
Could lure in latter days those who erstwhile
Abode in quiet rest to crave to change
Their former way of life? For clear it is
That he would fain find joy in new delights
Whom old do irk; but he who naught of ill
Hath known in days gone by, when life was passed
In deep content, what, pray, in such an one
Could fan to flame this passion for the new?
Yea, wrapt in darkness and in grief, forsooth,
Their life did lie till dawned upon their sight
The first birth-morning of the world! And we,
What ill had been to us if we had lain
Fore'er unshaped? For who hath once been born
Belike will cling to life while yet the lure
Of sweet delight doth bind him. But who ne'er
The love of life hath tasted, nor hath once
Been numbered with the living, what to him
Were it of evil had he ne'er been born?
Again, how first was planted in the minds
Of gods a pattern for the fashioning
Of things, or whence a concept did they gain
Of man, that they might know and clearly set
Before their minds what they would fain create?
Or in what wise was ever learned the power
Of primal seeds, or what they might achieve
With order interchanged, save nature's self

Gave pattern of creation? For so vast
A store of first beginnings, driven in paths
Diverse from time untold till now, and moved
By their own weight, have gone their wonted ways,
Mingling in motley unions, venturing this
Or that which by their mutual confluence
They might perchance create, that 'tis not strange
If they at last into such mold have fallen
And to such movements passed as those whereby
This sum of things doth live and is renewed.

But howe'er scant may be my little lore
Of what the first beginnings are, yet this
From heaven's own workings would I dare affirm
And prove with many an argument besides—
That in no wise the nature of the world
Was made for us by will divine; for oh
How great the faults wherewith it is beset!
For first, of all the earth whereo'er doth arch
The broad expanse of heaven, one half is seized
By mountains and beast-haunted woods, or claimed
By rocks and marshy wastes, or by the sea
That sundereth far the shores of men's domains;
Besides, well nigh two thirds have burning heat
And ceaseless fall of frost from mortals stolen.
Nay, all the plow-lands that remain, e'en these
Would nature of her own exuberance choke
With brambles, did not men with straining toil
Resist her, doomed for aye in quest of life
To groan above the heavy hoe, and cleave
With deep-pressed plow the stubborn soil of earth.

Nay, were it not that turning with the share
The fertile clods, and taming to our will
The soil of earth, we summon them to being,
Ne'er of themselves could goodly fruits arise
Into the limpid airs. E'en now at times
When scarce through all our fields each tree and plant,
Won by sore toil, hath sprung to leaf and flower,
Straightway the sun in heaven with heat o'er fierce
Will wither them, or sudden rains destroy,
Or frost fall chill, and blasts of boisterous wind
Blight them with wintry breath. And why, withal,
Doth nature cause to grow and multiply
The fearsome tribes of savage beasts, to wreak
Harm to the race of men on land and sea?
Why bring the seasons their distempers? Why
Before his time stalketh grim death abroad?
Then too the child, like sailor tossed ashore
By cruel waves, when nature first hath cast
Him forth by travail from his mother's womb
Upon the coasts of light, naked doth lie
Upon the ground, speechless and stript of all
His life doth crave, and filleth all the place
With woeful wailings, as is meet for one
Whose life must pass through such a flood of ills.
But beasts of flock and herd and wood grow up
With ne'er a need of rattles, nor must hear
Sweet broken baby-talk of some fond nurse,
Nor seek a change of garment for each phase
Of heaven's seasons, nay, nor need have they
Of arms or lofty walls to guard their own,

Since all for all in ample store doth earth
Herself and artful nature e'er provide.

First, then, since earth and moisture, and the breath
Of airy winds, and burning heat, whereof
This sum of things is seen to stand composed,
Are each and all created with a frame
That knoweth birth and death, so must we hold
That with the selfsame nature all our world
Is fashioned; for in truth whate'er we see
Hath parts and limbs that taste of birth and death,
And hence itself as well we must conceive
To share in death and birth. Since, then, I see
The master parts of this our world dissolved
And once again reborn, so may I know
That likewise heaven and earth have seen the hour
Of birth, and shall achieve their day of doom.

Herein lest thou shouldst fancy I have laid
O'erzealous hands upon these proofs, and held
That earth and fire are mortal, yea, nor grudged
To claim that moisture and the airy winds
Alike do perish and once more are born
And find increase, consider first of all
That no mean portion of our earth, when baked
By ceaseless suns, and trampled neath the tread
Of many feet, will breathe forth murky clouds
Of flying dust, which wanton winds disperse
Through all the air. And of its sods as well
A part by flooding rains is yielded back
To soggy marsh-land, and the hungry streams

Gnaw ever at their banks. And whatsoe'er
Doth bless with increase somewhat else, with gain
Proportionate is e'er restored. And since
Beyond all doubt the parent of all things
Is seen herself to be the general tomb
Of all, so mayst thou know that earth doth wane,
And blest with increase once again doth thrive.

    Again, that sea and streams and springs well forth
With moisture ever fresh, nor e'er doth cease
Their unremitting flow, no need is there
Of words to prove, since everywhere the rush
Of mighty waters doth its truth proclaim.
But e'er the foremost moisture is dispersed,
And thus it is that in the sum doth stand
No overplus of moistness, since in part
The stormy winds that sweep across the seas
Cause them to shrink, as doth the sun, high throned
In airy heaven, unweaving with his rays
Its texture; and in part since 'tis dispersed
Hither and yon neath every land. For thus,
Its saltness spent, the moisture floweth back
And gathereth to each spring and river head,
Whence forth o'er all the lands its fresh sweet streams
It poureth, wheresoe'er its tinkling feet
Have wandered down their winding watery way.

    Next I shall tell of air, which countless times
Its body changeth with each single hour,
For ever to the boundless sea of air
Doth pour whate'er doth ebb from things. If, then,

'The air gave not these bodies back to earth,
And so restored its losses, so would all
Long since have been dissolved, and changed to air.
Thus air doth never cease to rise from things,
And back to things returneth, since 'tis clear
That all things shift with ceaseless ebb and flow.

Likewise that bounteous fount of liquid light,
The sun, high throned in heaven, doth flood the sky
With radiance ever new, and with fresh light
At once doth light supply, as beam on beam
His foremost light doth perish, wheresoe'er
It chance to fall, as thou mayst learn from this:
Since soon as once beneath the sun hath passed
A sudden cloud, and sundered, as it were,
His radiant beams, all residue thereof
That lay beneath will on the instant fail,
And earth is shadowed o'er, where'er the cloud
Doth move; so mayst thou know that things have need
Of brightness ever new, and each first shaft
Of radiance perisheth, nor else can aught
In sunlight meet our view, save from the source
And fountain head of all our light doth well
Supply perpetual. Nay, e'en those lights
That through the night an earthlier radiance cast,
The hanging lamps and pitchy torches, bright
With flickering fires amid the murky dark,
These in the selfsame wise are quick to shed
Fresh stores of heat-born radiance, as by beam
On beam they flash incessant, nor doth fail
In any spot their interrupted light;

So speedily by sudden birth of flame
From each earth-fire is hid the death of that
Which passed before. Thus, then, must sun and moon
And stars be deemed to cast their light, with birth
Forever new, and evermore to lose
Their foremost flames; lest haply thou shouldst deem
They dwell with strength for aye inviolate.

   Again, seest not how rocks give way, o'ercome
By lapse of time, and lofty towers sink down
In crumbling ruin, their moldering stones consigned
To lowly dust? Nay, e'en the holy shrines
And images of gods grow weak and worn,
As naught the sacred presence can avail
To extend the bounds of fate, or set at naught
The laws of nature. Aye, and see we not
The moldering monuments of man that fain
Would ask us if, like him, they too in turn
Must wane with age? And flinty crags uptorn
From some great mountain peak come crashing down,
All powerless to withstand the stubborn strength
Of measured time? For scarce would aught be reft
From its firm seat, and fall in headlong haste,
Which from eternal ages had stood fast,
Unscarred by all the artillery of time.

   Again, lift up thine eyes unto this sky
That high o'erhead and all around doth hold
Our earth in its embrace; if from itself,
As some would hold, it doth all things beget,
And at their perishing doth claim once more

Their substance, so it must be formed entire
Of frame that knoweth birth and death. For that
Which from itself doth bring increase and growth
To aught besides must needs be lessened, aye,
And blest with gain when things thereto return.

Then too, if ne'er had dawned the natal day
Of earth and sky, and from eternal time
They have stood fast, why, save for those who sang
The wars of Thebes and doom of Troy, hath ne'er
A bard attuned his lyre to other deeds
In other lands as well? Whither have fled
So oft those ancient glories manifold
Of other men? Why stand they not enshrined
In deathless scrolls of fame? Nay, youthful still
Is this our world, I ween, and new the frame
Of this high firmament, nor long ago
It saw its rising. Wherefore, even now
Do certain arts of men still strive to reach
The fulness of perfection; even now
They grow in stature. To our ships hath much
Of late been added, while but yesterday
Musicians woke their tuneful harmonies.
Again, this theme of mine anent the laws
And works of nature is but newly found,
The while myself have proved the first of men
Whose skill could shape it to our native tongue.
But if perchance thou deem'st that heretofore
All these same things have been, but that the tribes
Of men have perished neath consuming flames,
Or cities sunk in ruin beneath some shock

That rocked the world, or, swollen by ceaseless rains,
Rivers on havoc bent have issued forth
O'er all the lands and swallowed towns from sight—
If this be thy belief, so much the more
Must thou give way and own that there will come
An end unto our earth and sky as well.
For when by such distress, such perils dire,
Things were assailed, were but a deadlier blow
To fall upon them, wide had been their doom
And great their ruin. Nor in other wise
Is seen our mortal state, save that we fall
A common prey to those same ills as they
Whom nature hath cut off from mortal life.

Besides, if naught eternal can abide,
It needs must be that built of solid frame
It doth all blows repel, nor suffereth aught
To penetrate within which might unloose
Its close-locked parts, e'en as those bodies are
Whose nature I have pictured heretofore;
Or else, mayhap, this is the cause whereby
They can avail through endless time to stand
Unshaken, since exempt from blows they dwell
E'en as the void, which doth remain untouched;
Or else 'twill be because no store of space
Doth stand about, whereunto, as it were,
Their matter might withdraw, and in such wise
Dissolve to naught, e'en as the sum of things
Doth bide eternal since it hath no place
Without whereto itself may fly abroad,
Nor bodies are at hand to fall thereon

And with resistless blows bring it to ruin.
But neither with a solid frame doth stand,
As I have shown, the nature of our world,
Since void is mingled in the heart of things;
Nor is it as the void; nor yet do lack
Bodies which mustering from the infinite
Might haply in a mighty whirling blast
Wreck all this sum of things, or bring thereon
Some deadly ruin else. Nor faileth room
Or vast expanse of space whereto the walls
That ring our world may be dispersed abroad,
Or shattered by some violence besides
May meet their doom. And so the gate of death
Is not fast closed on sky or sun or earth
Or ocean's billowy deeps, but opened wide
It standeth, waiting with vast gaping jaws.
Wherefore again thou must perforce confess
That these same things have birth; for past all doubt
Whate'er hath mortal frame would ne'er avail
From boundless time till now to laugh to scorn
The stubborn strength of age immeasurable.

Once more, since all those mighty elements
That shape our world, roused to unholy war,
Are locked in mortal combat, seest thou not
Some end may come unto their age-long strife,
Or when the sun with all his heat hath dried
Earth's general moisture, and his victory won,
Or moisture hath the sun's fierce ardor drowned?
For thus they aim to do, yet up to now
Fruitless hath been their toil; such mighty floods

The rivers pour, while from its vasty deeps
The main doth raise its threat to whelm all things
In one devouring deluge. But in vain,
For that the winds that sweep across the seas
Cause them to shrink, as doth the sun, high throned
In airy heaven, unweaving with his rays
Their fabric, as each boasteth of his power
To parch to dryness all the watery world
Ere moisture can its task achieve. So vast
A discord do they breathe, as blow for blow
In mutual strife their bootless war they wage
For mighty spoils. Yet once hath fire come forth
A victor in the strife; and once, for so
Doth run the tale, hath moisture reigned supreme
O'er all the lands. For fire the mastery won,
And with quick flaming tongues great store of things
Consumed, when far astray through all the expanse
Of heaven and o'er the lands the untamed might
Of Sol's swift coursers whirled in mad career
Young Phaethon.[4] But stung to furious rage,
The all-powerful Father, with a sudden stroke
Of his dread bolt, hurled reeling from his car
To earth the headstrong truant, and anon,
E'en as he fell, full in mid-air the Sun
Caught up the world's eternal lamp, and tamed

[4] Phaethon, son of Helios, the sun-god, demanded of his father the privilege of driving the chariot of the sun for a single day. Being unable to restrain the horses, he allowed the sun to approach so close to heaven and earth that both began to take fire. To save the whole world from destruction, Zeus shattered the young man with his lightning and set the chariot once more upon its proper course.

The unharnessed steeds, as neath the prisoning yoke
Their trembling necks he curbed, then back once more
Upon their wonted track he set their feet,
And so all things restored. For thus in sooth
Once sang the ancient bards of Greece; but far
From truth and reason doth their tale diverge;
For fire belike may conquer when a store
Too great of fiery substance hath arisen
From out the infinite; but in due time
Its strength must wane, in some wise overcome,
Else all would perish neath its scorching breath.
And once had moisture, gathering in a flood,
For so the tale is told,[5] well nigh prevailed,
As many a town of men it had o'erwhelmed;
But when at length its force was turned aside
And went its way, e'en all that from the deeps
Of the illimitable had gathered, so
The rains did cease, the rivers calmed their rage.

But in what fashion that ingathering
Of matter hath established earth and sky,
The depths of ocean, paths of sun and moon,
I shall set forth in order. For in truth
Not with design or reasoning shrewd did all
The first beginnings take their divers posts
Each in his proper place; nor yet, forsooth,
Did they by mutual compact fix upon

wwwwwwwwwwwwwwwwwwwwwwwww

[5] The Greek tradition of a universal flood, which destroyed all mankind
except a single pair, Deucalion and Pyrrha, parallels in many respects the
Hebrew account of the Deluge and the family of Noah.

Their several movements; but in numbers vast
Shifting now here, now there, the primal seeds,
Harried by blows relentless through the course
Of endless time, where'er their tiny weights
Might speed them on, have gone their wonted ways,
Meeting at random, groping sightlessly
For whatsoe'er they haply might create
By meeting; hence it did befall that, tossed
Through age on age, essaying this or that
Of motion and of union, those at last
Did meet which are henceforth to be for aye,
Through their swift union, seeds of mighty things—
Earth, sea and sky, and tribes of living beings.

But then could be discerned no orb of sun,
Wheeling on high with bounteous light, nor stars
In all the mighty firmament, nor sea,
Nor sky; nay, earth itself was not, nor air,
Nor aught besides like to the world we know;
Naught save a vague and seething mass, new formed
Of primal elements of every kind
Whose warring discord wild confusion made
Of spaces, paths, encounters, weights and blows,
Meetings and movements, born of unlike forms
And figures manifold, since scarce could all,
As then, remain together linked, and suit
Their motions each to each. Thus, here and there,
Portions from off the general mass began
To take their flight, and like to join with like,
And thus a world unfold, as part from part
Was sundered, and the mighty elements

Were gathered each unto his place, to mark
High heaven from earth, and by itself the sea,
That it might spread with waters set apart,
And by themselves likewise the fires of heaven
Might dwell apart, unmingled and alone.

For of a surety first those bodies formed
Of earth, heavy and intermeshed, did sink
Together in the midst, and joined in one
Did take the lowest places; and the more
They drew together in a tangled mass,
The more from out their midst did they express
Those bodies which were destined to create
Sea, stars, the sun and moon, yea, e'en the walls
Of our high firmament. For each of these
Is formed of seeds more smooth and round and fine
Than is our earth. Hence, streaming here and there
Through opened pores of earth, there first did rise
The flaming ether, carrying in its flight
Full many a fire, in no far different wise
Than oft we see, when first the golden beams
Of the bright morning sun with ruddy gleam
Tinge all the dew-bejeweled grass, and pools
And ever-living streams breathe forth a mist;
Yea, e'en the earth herself is seen at times
To steam with rising vapors; and when these
High o'er the earth have gathered, formed in clouds
They weave a floating veil beneath the sky.
Thus then, with body gathered into one,
The light and drifting ether spread its wings
High arched o'er all the world, and far abroad

To every side its mantle flinging, wrapt
All else, as now, within its greedy arms.
Then followed next in order due the birth
Of sun and moon, whose wheeling orbs do hang
Midway in air; for earth hath claimed them not
Nor loftiest ether, since they wanted weight
To pull them earthward, nor so light were they
That they could glide along the topmost coasts.
But in mid-space between their paths are set,
That so like living bodies, sweeping on
Along their track, they keep their wonted place
In this great world of ours; as in our frames
Some limbs there are which must abide firm fixt
In their own place, while some are free to move.
So, with these elements withdrawn, forthwith
The earth sank down, where now doth stretch afar
The vast blue belt of ocean, till at length
Each gulf and hollow brimmed with flooding brine.
And day by day, the more the circling tides
Of ether and the sun's strong rays that beat
Incessant on its rim constrained the earth
To greater solidness, that so, assailed
And buffeted, it shrank upon itself,
So much the more, distilled from out its frame,
Oozed forth the briny sweat, to bring increase
To sea and brimming plains, yea, and the more
The many particles of heat and air
Slipt forth and flew abroad, and, far removed
From earth, condensed to form the lofty realms
Of radiant heaven. Then sank the level plains,
And mountains piled their towering heights above

For that their rooted rocks stood fast, nor deigned
To settle downward, nor in every part
In equal measure could the earth subside.

Thus then with body formed the weight of earth
Sank to its place, and, as it were, the slime
Of all the world, like heavy dregs, slipt down
Unto the bottom. Whereupon first sea,
Then air, and last the fiery ether's self
Were left with fluid bodies all unmixt;
For each is lighter than the next beneath,
And ether, lightest and most fluid of all,
Doth float above the breezes of the air,
Nor doth commingle with the warring winds
Its liquid substance; nay, all things below
May seethe with whirling blasts, or brawl with shock
Of shifting storms—it heedeth not, but e'er
Along its sure untroubled course doth glide
Bearing its own pure fires. For that with smooth
Uninterrupted sweep can ether glide
Upon its way, the Pontus [6] doth attest,
That sea that, moving with a changeless tide,
Keepeth for aye its one calm measured flow.

Now let us sing what cause doth move the stars.
First, if that spacious globe we call the sky

[6] The Black Sea. Cf. Shakespeare, *Othello*, 3, 3:

> like to the Pontick sea
> Whose icy current and compulsive course
> Ne'er feels retiring ebb, but keeps due on
> To the Propontick and the Hellespont.

Doth turn about, so must we needs declare
That weight of air upon the pole doth press
On this side and on that, and from without
Doth hold it close, hemmed in on either side;
Whereon, above, another stream of air
Doth flow, striving amain toward that far goal
Whereto have set their course the rolling stars
That twinkle in the deathless firmament;
Or haply other current there may be
Which from beneath in counter wise may drive
The globe of heaven, e'en as our streams we see
Turn slowly round the creaking water-wheels;
Or this perchance may be: that all the sky
May in its place abide, the while the hosts
Of starry signs sweep on, since pent within
Swift seething tides of ether, seeking vent,
Whirl round amain, and drive the flaming orbs
Through all the regions of the midnight sky;
Or, streaming from some other source without,
An alien air may drive their wheeling fires;
Or, haply, of themselves they have the power
Forward to creep each where its sustenance
Doth summon and invite, as wandering o'er
The heavenly plains their living fires they feed.
For hard the task to assign in this our world
This cause or that; but what may come to pass,
Yea, needs must be, throughout the general Whole
In worlds diverse, fashioned in various ways,
'Tis this I teach, and in my discourse strive
To set forth many a cause which through the deeps
Of the great Whole may drive the wandering stars.

Yet one thereof it needs must be which here
In this our world as well doth keep alive
The frame of heavenly bodies. But to seize
On one of these is scarce the task of those
Who step by step proceed toward their goal.

But that our earth may stand at rest midway
In the great world of space, it well may be
Its bulk by slow degrees may thinner grow,
Its weight grow less, and it may have beneath
A second nature, linked and knit in one,
Since time began, with those ethereal parts
Of the great Whole mid which it doth maintain
Its place and hath its being. Hence it is
No burden doth it prove, nor doth its mass
Weigh down the air; e'en as to every man
His limbs ne'er seem a weight, nor is the head
A burden to the neck, nor do we feel
That on the feet doth rest the weight entire
Of our own body. But whate'er of weight
Is laid upon us from a source without
Will bring us pain, e'en though it oft may prove
Smaller by many times. Of such import
The power that doth pervade each several thing.
So, then, our earth is not a body strange
Brought suddenly from elsewhere, and thrust in
Upon an alien air, but 'twas conceived
Together with the world at its first birth
As a fixt part thereof, as were our limbs
For us. And so the earth, when sharply rocked
By violent thunder causeth all above

To shake with its own tremor; yet nowise
Could it thus do had it not been fast bound
To regions of the air and to the sky.
For earth and sky must needs together cling
By common roots, since their beginning joined
And blent in one. Seest thou not, too, how great
The weight of body, which the subtile force
Of soul in us supporteth, since 'tis joined
And blent with it as but a single whole?
Again, what can it be but force of soul
Controlling all our limbs, that hath the power
To lift our bodies in a nimble leap?
So, then, seest not how mightily can strive
A nature subtile, once it hath been linked
With weighty body, e'en as air with earth
Is joined, and with our frame the force of mind?

Nor can the sun's clear orb much greater be
Nor less his brightness than unto our sense
It doth appear. For whatsoe'er the space
Wherefrom our fires can cast their light and breathe
Upon our limbs their genial warmth, no loss
They suffer in the body of their flames
By reason of their distance, nor one whit
Their fire is shrunken to the sight. E'en so,
Since the sun's warmth and his far-spreading light
Do reach our sense and gently warm the lands
Of many a clime, e'en from our earth his form
And bulk may well and truly be perceived,
That so no whit thereto thou mightest add
Of greater or of less. So, too, the moon,

Whether it be her wheeling orb doth shine
With borrowed radiance, as on every hand
Her light she spreadeth, or mayhap doth shed
From her own body beams that are her own—
Howe'er it be, 'tis with no ampler orb
She glideth on than that wherewith our eyes
Seem to endow her. For in truth all things
Which we behold far sundered from ourselves
By spacious tracts of air, will seem to grow
Confused in shape or e'er one whit will shrink
Their seeming bulk. Wherefore it needs must be,
Since she doth hold a shape clear-marked and stand
With outline sharp; the moon must meet our eye
From her calm heights e'en as she is, with rim
Clear-cut and of her proper magnitude.
And last, consider all the heavenly fires
Thou dost behold from earth. For whatsoe'er
We do perceive of earthly brightness, these,
While yet their twinkling light is clear, and still
Their blaze may be perceived, are seen to change
Only by some small jot from time to time
To greater or to less their seeming size
According to their distance; so, be sure,
The fires of heaven, save by the tiniest jot,
Can ne'er be less or greater than they seem.

Nor need this rouse our wonder, in what wise
A sun so small can send such store of light
To fill with radiance every sea and land,
Yea, heaven itself, and with its genial warmth
All things suffuse. For hence it well may be

The one free-flowing fountainhead of light
Of all the world is oped, and forth doth burst
The welling radiance, since the elements
Of heat from every side throughout the world
Are gathered there and in such wise compressed
That from a single fount their blazing light
Doth stream abroad. For seest not how at times
The trickling moisture from a tiny spring
Will spread across the fields, till all the plain
Is filled with watery richness? Or again,
It may befall that from the sun's own fire,
E'en though it be not great, some blazing heat
Doth on the air with fiery ardor seize,
If haply there be air at hand and meet
To be enkindled as by living rays
Of heat 'tis smitten; e'en as we perceive
At times our fields of grain or stubble, caught
From one small spark, leap to a sudden blaze
On every side. Or thus perchance 'twill be:
That high in heaven with rosy torch agleam
The sun doth hold at his command such store
Of fire on every hand whose warmth is hid,
Nor e'er by radiance marked, that, armed alone
With heat, it doth unto his piercing rays
A greater fierceness lend.

              Nor hath been found
A clear and simple tale the cause to tell
Of how from summer's climes the wandering sun
Doth journey toward the winter turning-point
Of Capricorn, and how, receding thence,

He doth return unto his solstice goal
In Cancer's sign; and how the moon is seen
Each single month that course to travel o'er
Wherein the sun doth make his yearly round.
To these, I say, there yet hath been assigned
No single cause. For, first af all, 'tis clear
It may befall e'en as the holy heart
Of our Democritus hath taught, that as
Each several star is nearer to our earth,
Less swiftly by the whirling dome of heaven
'Tis borne along its path. For so his quick
And eager strength doth wane, and lesser grow
Beneath, and thus by bit and bit the sun
Is left behind amid the rearmost signs,
Since lower far is he than all the host
Of heavenly orbs. And even more the moon;
The lower is her course, and far removed
From sky and near to earth, so much the less
Can she avail to strain upon her course
To match the starry signs. For since her path
Is lower than the sun's, and with a whirl
More weak she tosseth, so do all the signs
On every hand o'ertake and pass her by.
Hence doth befall that to each several sign
More speedily she seemeth to return,
Since 'tis themselves which ever and anon
Recross her path and leave her far behind.
Or haply it may be that, risen afar,
In distant quarters of the world that lie
Athwart his path, alternate airs may stream
Each in its proper season, the one more meet

To thrust the sun afar from summer's signs
E'en to his wintry turning-place, beset
With icy frost, and one to hurl him back
From the chill nights of cold e'en to the realms
That teem with heat, and to the burning signs.
So too, in manner like we must suppose
The moon and stars, that through the rolling years
Their circling orbits trace, by airs that blow
In turn from diverse quarters can be moved;
For seest not how at times by diverse winds
Low-lying clouds in counter-wise are driven
To those above? Why, then, should stars the less
Through their wide orbits in the heavens avail
To be impelled by diverse tides of air?

But night doth shroud the earth in darkness vast
Whene'er the sun, his daily journey o'er,
Hath touched the farthest bounds of heaven, and faint
With weariness breathed forth his dying fires,
Sore shaken with the pilgrimage and spent
From copious air; or else the selfsame force
That bore his orb high o'er the lands once more
Constraineth him to sink beneath the earth.

Likewise at season fixt, along the coasts
Of heaven Matuta doth disperse abroad
Her rosy dawn, and spread on every hand
Her morning light, since 'tis the selfsame sun
Once more returning from beneath the earth
That with his rays in eager haste doth seize
Upon the sky he fain would set alight;

Or haply 'tis because the gathering fires
And many seeds of heat at season due
Are wont to stream together, and each morn
A new sun's light they bring again to birth.
E'en so the tale doth run that from the heights
Of Ida's mountains scattered fires are seen
As morn doth rise, then gathering as it were
Into a single mass, a flaming orb
They fashion. Nor, I ween, need this herein
Be cause for wonderment, that thus these seeds
Of fire at season fixt contrive to stream
Together, and the sun's clear light renew;
For many a thing we see to come to pass
In season due in all around us—yea,
Trees bloom at their fixt time, and at a time
Appointed shed their blossoms. So doth age
At proper season make the teeth to fall,
Or bid the face of hairless youth to bloom
With silken down, till both his cheeks are clothed
With manhood's sign. And lastly, thunder, snow,
Rain, clouds, and winds have each their birth at times
Of year not undetermined. For where'er
The primal germ of causes thus hath stood
Since time eternal, and, since first the world
Was molded, things have thus been brought to pass,
So now, each after each in order due,
They make their destined round.

                                And in like wise
It well may be that days will longer grow
While nights decrease, or in its turn the light

Of day will wane while nights an increase find,
Since that the selfsame sun, as he doth trace
His course in arc unequal neath the earth
And in the skies above, doth part the coasts
Of heaven and his own circuit doth divide
In segments disproportioned, and whate'er
From the one part he hath withdrawn, the more,
As he doth make his round, doth he replace
Within the opposing zone, till he hath reached
The heavenly sign whereat the yearly node [7]
Doth mark with equal length the shades of night
And daylight's gleam. For in mid-course between
The north-wind's blast and breath of southern breeze
The sky doth hold his turning-points apart
At distance held in balance, in accord
With all the starry orbit's path, wherein
The wandering sun his yearly course doth trace
With rays aslant illuming earth and sky;
E'en as the scrolls of those reveal whose skill
Hath marked all regions of the sky, adorned
Each with its several signs in order due.
Or haply, since in certain zones is found
A denser air, 'tis thence the trembling ray
Of his bright fire is prisoned neath the earth,
Nor easily can thrust its way and leap
Unto its rising. Hence in winter time

[7] By "node", Lucretius seems to mean the "knot" formed by the crossing
of the equator with the ecliptic. The signs of the Zodiac where this crossing is placed would be Aries at the time of the spring equinox, and Libra
at the autumnal equinox, about March 21 and September 21, respectively.

The long nights drag their weary length, till forth
Doth burst the radiant herald of the day;
Or else it is that in the selfsame wise
In times of year alternate, all the fires
Which from a quarter fixt constrain the sun
To lift his head, more slowly now are wont
To stream together, now more quickly. Hence
It is they seem to speak the truth who claim
That with each day a sun is born anew.

The moon, it well may be, doth shed her light
When struck by rays of sun; and day by day
That light will turn more straightly to our sight
The farther from the sun's bright gleaming orb
She is withdrawn, till full athwart his path
She gloweth with a full and plenteous light
And, as she riseth, from her lofty throne
Doth look upon his setting; then by bit
And bit retiring, she must needs give o'er
As 'twere her light the nearer she doth glide
Unto the sun's bright fire, as she doth trace
From quarter opposite her shining path
Through the great circle of the signs, as they
Would claim who hold the moon is like a ball,
And keepeth to her path beneath the sun.
Then, too, there is a way whereby, endowed
With light that is her own, she yet may roll
Upon her way, and glow with changing forms
Of varied brightness. For there well may be
Some other orb, which, borne along therewith
And gliding close beside her, doth obscure,

Yea, wholly block her light, yet ne'er is seen,
Since reft of light itself doth ever move.
Or she herself may turn, e'en as, belike,
A ball's smooth sphere, with half its surface tinged
With gleaming light; and so by turning round
She showeth changing phases, till at length
Unto our view that face she doth present,
Whiche'er it be, that is endowed with fires;
Thence day by day again she twisteth round
And taketh from our sight that luminous face
Of her round orb; as the Babylonian lore
Of Chaldee seers, denying all the wit
Of our astronomers, would seek to prove
In opposition; e'en as though, forsooth,
What either doth assert may not be truth,
Or cause there were why thou shouldst choose to hold
This less than that. Or why, with every day,
A fresh-born moon could not be framed anew
With order fixt of phases and fixt shapes,
That with each several day her fresh-formed orb
Might pass away, and in its room and place
Another be created, 'tis a task
Not easy to achieve by reasoning
Or prove by words; so many things there be
Which can be brought to birth in order fixt.[8]

So cometh Spring and Venus, while before
Danceth Love's winged harbinger; and now

[8] It is interesting to note Lucretius' unscientific indifference as to which
of the above explanations may be the true one.

Light tripping down the West-wind's track, doth pass
Sweet Mother Flora, strewing all their path
With glorious tints and perfumes. Followeth next
Dry parching Summer, leading in her train
Dust-laden Ceres and the searing blasts
Of withering North-winds. Then with stately tread
Proud Autumn draweth nigh, while at her side
Rejoiceth Euhius Euhan.[9] Now succeed
The storms and winds, Volturnus, thundering high,
And Auster, strong in lightning. Lo! at length
The year's end bringeth snows, and once again
Doth Winter spread his numbing frosts; and last
Of all with chattering teeth doth stalk grim Cold.
Wherefore, 'tis less of marvel if the moon
Be born at time determined, and again
At time determined may be quenched, since things
So manifold at seasons fixt befall.

So too, in manner like we needs must deem
The sun's eclipses, and the furtive veils
That hide the moon, by causes several fold
May be achieved; for whence, I pray, doth come
Unto the moon the power to shut the earth
From out the sun's clear light, and, thrusting high
Her head before him in the path of earth,
Cast her dark orb before his glorious beams,
While side by side therewith 'twere not conceived

~~~~~~~~~~~~~~~~~~~~~~~~~~~~~~~

[9] Another name for Dionysus, or Bacchus, the god of fertility, especially
that of the vine; hence the god of wine. "Euhoe" or "Evoe" was the
ecstatic cry of the participants in Bacchic worship.

That in like wise some other orb may act
Which glideth ever reft of light? Again,
Why, pray, could not the sun at season fixt
Grow faint and lose his fires, and once again
His light renew, when, journeying through the air,
He hath traversed some quarter that doth wage
A deadly warfare on his fires and cause
His flames to fail and perish? Or, again,
Why should the earth in turn avail to rob
The moon of light, and in her high career
Hold all the sun in darkness, while the moon,
Rolling along her monthly track, doth glide
Across the sharp-drawn shadow of the cone,
While yet some other body ne'er can run
Beneath the moon, nor o'er the sun's bright orb
Its path pursue, to interrupt his rays
And hide his far-flung light? Or e'en suppose
The moon to shine with sheen her own; why, pray,
Should not she too grow faint when she must pass
Through regions hostile to her beaming light?

Now to resume my theme: since I have traced
The scheme whereby through all the azure vault
Of our great world each several thing hath birth,
That we might mark the journeyings near and far
Of sun and moon, and what the force and cause
Which give them motion; how with failing light
Their faces they may hide, and in a veil
Of darkness shroud the all unwitting earth,
When as it were they wink, and once again
Will ope their eyes, and scanning every place

Behold all things in their clear rays to shine;
Now to the new-born morning of the world
Do I return, and earth's soft fields, and what
With fresh creative power they first resolved
To raise into the coasts of light, and yield,
A tender charge, unto the wayward winds.

In the beginning, earth did bring to being
Herbage of every kind and verdure bright
Upon the hills and over every plain,
Till all the flowery meadows were agleam
With vesture green, and mongst the various trees
A mighty contest rose, as each did strive
To rise aloft with every rein let loose
Through the soft airs. And e'en as down and hair
And bristles first are formed upon the limbs
Of fourfoot creatures and the bodies too
Of strong-winged fowls, so then the new-born earth
First reared her shrubs and herbage; then in turn
In order due did bring to birth the tribes
Of mortal creatures, risen in many ways
By means diverse. For ne'er could living beings
Have fallen from heaven, nor beasts that roam the earth
Have issued from the briny pools. With right
It followeth then that earth hath won the name
Of Mother, since from earth have all things sprung.
And even now we see full many a breed
Of living creatures rise from out the earth
Begot by rains and by the genial warmth
The sun doth shed. Hence we may marvel less
If then in larger numbers and endowed

With ampler bulk were creatures brought to birth
And reached their prime, since earth and air were new.
First, then, the wingéd tribes and every breed
Of flying fowl did leave their eggs, safe hatched
By springlike warmth, as now, in summer's heat,
Locusts will fain put off their polished shells
In quest of life and living. Then it was
That earth did first give birth to mortal beings.
For all the fields did teem with gentle warmth
And moisture. Hence, where there was at hand
Appropriate place, there grew up wombs, attached
By roots to earth; and when, at time fulfilled,
The tiny creatures' growing age, in flight
From moisture and in search of air, had burst
Their prison, so would nature turn toward each
The pores of earth, and from wide-opened veins
Constrain them to exude a sap most like
To milk, as even now, when she hath borne
A child, each woman's breasts are filled forthwith
With sweet new milk, since thitherward are turned
All the rich humors of her nourishment.
Earth gave these little ones their food, the warmth
A garment, and the soft thick-tufted grass
A downy bed. But since the world was young,
No bitter cold it roused, nor heat o'er fierce,
Nor winds of violent might. For evenly
Do all things wax and reach their full-grown strength.

Wherefore once more I do aver that earth
Hath justly won, and justly doth she keep
The name of Mother, since 'twas she herself

Did in her own fixt time create the race
Of men, and every breed of beast that here
And yon among the mighty mountain tops
Doth hold wild revel; and the flying fowl
Likewise that dwell in air, in all their range
Of forms and hues diverse. But since at length
She needs must reach some end of bearing, so
Did she give o'er, e'en as a woman, worn
With length of lingering years. For time doth change
The mold of all the world, and one estate
Upon another needs must overtake
All things that be, nor aught doth long abide
Like to itself, but all things shift their place;
Yea, nature altereth all, and doth constrain
Each one to change its form. For one doth wane
And, worn with age, doth pine, then somewhat else
Doth rise to take its place and issue forth
From whilom place of scorn. So then did time
Bring change to all the nature of the world,
And one estate upon another seize
Upon the earth, that so what once it bore
It can no longer compass, and can bear
What ne'er it brought to birth in days of old.

And in those days did earth essay to frame
Full many a monster, born with visage strange
And limbs awry, the woman-man, midway
Between the two, yet neither, and apart
From both; and some there were bereft of feet,
Or wanting hands in turn, and some were found
Dumb without mouths, or featureless and blind,

Or chained through all their frame by limbs that clung
One to another, so that power they lacked
To compass aught, or move toward any side,
Or flee from danger, or to gain whate'er
Their needs required. And other monsters, too,
And creatures strange would she create, but all
In vain, since that their nature did forbid
Increase, nor could they reach the envied bloom
Of age, nor gather sustenance, nor join
In Venus' arts; for many a requisite
We see must be fulfilled in living things
Ere they avail to propagate their kind
By generation: first, they must have food,
And then the means whereby from out their frames
Birth-giving seeds may issue, cast abroad
From the appropriate members, so that male
And female may be joined, and each possess
The means whereby to exchange their mutual joys.

And in those far-off days full many a race
Of living things must needs have perished, nay,
Nor aught of offspring could beget and thus
Preserve its kind; for whatsoe'er we see
To breathe the vital air of heaven, 'tis craft,
Or courage, yea, or fleetness [10] that since first
Their life began hath guarded and preserved
Their several breeds. And many too there be
Which by their use commended to our care
Live on, entrusted to our guardianship.

wwwwwwwwwwwwwwwwwwww

[10] There is a suggestion here of the doctrine of the survival of the fittest

First, to the ravening race of lions, that breed
Of savage beasts, 'tis valor hath vouchsafed
A sure protection; in the fox 'tis craft,
The stag, the swiftness of his flying feet;
But otherwise the lightly slumbering minds
Of faithful-hearted dogs, and all the breeds
That spring from seed of burden-bearing beasts
And fleecy flocks withal, and horned herds;
All these, good Memmius, are nursed by care
Of human kind. For eagerly, I ween,
Have they escaped their savage enemies
And sought the quietude and plenteous store
Of sustenance ourselves are pleased to grant
As wage for service rendered. But those breeds
Whereunto none of these advantages
Hath nature granted, so that of themselves
They cannot live, nor render unto us
Some useful service, in return wherefor
We might permit their kind to feed and dwell
Beneath our safe defense, these, thou mayst know,
Did fall a prey and spoil to others, each
Chained by the fateful trammels of its being,
Till nature brought their kind at length to doom.

And yet no Centaurs did arise; nor e'er
At any time, forsooth, can beasts have being
Of twofold nature, and a double frame,
Formed into one from limbs of alien kinds,
That so the power and strength of each, derived
From either parent, can be equal. Nay,
That we may learn, however dul' of heart,

From this: when three full years have rolled their round
The horse doth flourish in the vigorous prime
Of all his eager powers; not so the child;
For oft e'en now in sleep his hands will seek
His mother's milky breasts. But with the years,
Whenas doth wane the horse's sturdy strength
And his stout limbs grow weak with age, as life
Therefrom doth ebb, 'tis then at length that youth
And manhood's bloom do seize upon the boy
And clothe his cheeks with silken down. Therefore,
Think not perchance that Centaurs can be born
Or have existence formed from human kind
And seed of burden-bearing horses. Nay,
Nor Scyllas, with their bastard sea-born bulk
Girt round with ravening dogs, nor other beasts
Of kindred kind, whose limbs can ne'er agree
One with another; for these ne'er will reach
Their prime together, nor together gain
Their body's strength, nor see it fail and wane
With lingering age, nor burn with like desires,
Nor in their ways agree, nor in their frame
Feel equal pleasures. Yea, we oft may see
The breed of bearded goats grow fat and thrive
On hemlock, which to man is deadly bane.
Or, once again, since flames are wont no less
To scorch and burn the lion's tawny frame
Than every kind of flesh and blood beside
That dwelleth on the earth, how could it be
That dread Chimera, triple frame in one,
In front a lion, in the hinder part
A dragon, in the midst her goat-like self,

Forth from her mouth should belch a scorching flame,
Enkindled in her body? Hence, be sure,
He who doth feign that when the earth was young
And sky new-born, such creatures could be brought
To birth, relying on the empty plea
Of youth alone, full many a tale besides
Of import similar may babble forth
With foolish tongue; that so he may proclaim
That in those days did rivers run with gold
O'er all the lands, and trees were wont to bloom
With precious jewels, or that man was born
Of such expanse of limb that he could plant
His steps across the deep sea-floods, or turn
With his own hands all heaven above his head.
For while in truth abundant seeds of things
Lay in the earth what time she first did frame
Her living creatures, scarce will this be proof
That beasts of mingled breed could be begot
Or limbs of diverse beings patched in one,
Since e'en the tribes of herbage, and the crops
And gladsome trees which even now do spring
From earth in great profusion, yet can scarce
Be brought to being commingled each with each,
But one by one, in manner each his own,
They come to birth, and by the unchanging law
Of nature keep the figure of their kind.

But that first race of men that dwelt among
The fields was hardier far, as did befit
A race of hard earth born, compact within
Of larger bones and heavier frame, and knit

With sturdy sinews through their solid flesh,
Whose rugged strength could not with ease by heat
Or cold be sapped, nor by unwonted food
Nor any taint of body. Many a round
Of the great sun revolving through the sky
Their lives dragged on, in mode of beasts that roam
From place to place. And none was there to guide
With sturdy arm the curving plow, and none
Had learned to work the fields with iron, or plant
The earth with tender shoots, or with the knife
To lop the age-worn branches from the trees.
What sun and rains had given, what earth herself
Had borne unasked, such simple boon sufficed
To please their hearts. And mid the fruitful oaks
Their usual wont it was to nurse the needs
Of their rough bodies; and the crimson fruits
Which now in winter season we behold
Grow ripe upon the arbute trees, earth then
Did bear in ampler size and larger store.
And much besides the earth's exuberant youth
Would then afford of foodstuffs rude, but meet
For wretched mortals. But to slake their thirst
Did streams and springs invite, as now a rush
Of flowing stream from some high mountain side
With its clear voice doth call from far and near
The thirsty breeds of beasts. So too, their feet
Would stray into the woodland haunts beloved
Of nymphs, wherefrom they knew that bubbling streams
Of living water in abundant flood
Laved the moist rocks, those cool moist rocks, as down
O'er the green moss it trickled, or anon

Welling from out the grassy mead burst forth
Over the level plain. Nor yet they knew
How fire might prove of service, or to use
The skins of beasts and clothe their limbs in spoils
Of hunted game, but shelter sought in wood
And mountain cave and forest, and would hide
Amid the underwood their shaggy limbs,
Constrained to shun the scourge of wind and rain.
Nor could they look toward aught which had regard
Unto the common weal, or know the use
Of mutual sanctions or of laws. Whate'er
Chance offered unto each he took, well schooled
To live and thrive each for himself alone.
And Venus mid the woods would join the frames
    mating lovers; for each mate was won
By mutual passion, or the male's fierce strength
And reckless lust, or haply by a price,
Wild arbute berries, acorns, gathered pears.
And trusting to their wondrous strength of hand
And foot, they would pursue the forest breeds
Of savage beasts with well-aimed stones or clubs
Of massive weight; and many a one would fall
Before their onslaught, some they needs must shun
By seeking cover; and like bristly boars,
Caught by the night would lay their brutish limbs
Naked upon the ground, and wrapt about
With leaves and branches. Nor was it their wont
With outcries loud to wail the vanished day
And light of sun, in terror o'er their fields
Groping their sightless way through the thick dark;
But hushed and wrapt in slumber they would wait

Till once again the sun with rosy torch
Should light the skies. For, since from childhood's days
They had been wont to note that ever, turn
By turn, darkness and light are brought to birth,
It could not be they e'er should wonder, nay,
Nor feel distrust lest never-ending night
Should seize upon the world, and lost for aye
Should be the sun's bright light. 'Twas rather this
A greater care did prove, that oft the breeds
Of woodland beasts made sleep for wretched men
A thing of dread; and driven forth amain
From out their rocky shelters, they would flee
Before the advent of a foaming boar
Or mighty lion, and in dead of night,
All trembling with affright, would forthwith yield
Their leaf-strewn couches to their savage guests.

   Nor then much more than now would mortal beings
Yield up with many a groan the well-loved light
Of fading life. For then no doubt, more oft
Some luckless wight, caught up and torn by jaws
Of savage beast, would yield thereto his flesh
A living food, and with his wailings fill
Coppice and hill and forest dim, to see
Before his eyes his living flesh interred
Within a living tomb. But they whom flight
Had saved, with mangled bodies, as the hours
Crept slowly by, clasping their trembling hands
Over their ghastly wounds, with fear-struck cries
Would call on Death, until their cruel pains
Reft them of life, knowing no means of cure

Or what their wounds required. And yet, one day
Brought not to doom its many thousands, led
Neath streaming banners, nor did angry waves
Of the wild main dash ships and men alike
Upon the rocks. For then in bootless rage
And blustering impotence the sea would rise
And lightly lay her idle threats aside,
Nor could her calm and crafty harlotry
Lure men to doom beneath her smiling waves.
For all unknown did lie the impious art
Of sailing then. Then, too, 'twas dearth of food
That oft consigned to death their fainting limbs,
While plunged in surfeit now men sink to ruin.
Then in their ignorance men oft would pour
A draught of poison for themselves, which now,
Grown wiser, to another they consign.

But when in time they shaped unto their use
Huts, skins, and fire, and woman joined to man
Retired to common shelter, and the joys
Of wedded life were known, and they beheld
Sweet offspring of themselves begot, then first
Mankind began to soften. For 'twas fire
Did make their shivering bodies less inured
To bear the cold beneath the open sky;
And Venus sapped their strength, and children too
With all their winsome ways with ease did break
The haughty spirit of their sires. 'Twas then
That neighbors eagerly began to join
In mutual pact to do no violence
Nor suffer harm, and to the general care

Did trust their children and their womenfolk,
The while with gesture and with faltering speech
They made it known 'twas just for all to show
Compassion on the weak. Yet full accord
Could not be won, e'en though a goodly part,
Yea, far the greater, loyally would hold
Unto their compacts; else the human race
E'en then would all have perished, nor have left
One single scion to preserve his kind
In line unbroken from that time till now.

But divers sounds of tongue did nature first
Lead men to utter, and 'twas use that shaped
The names of things, in no far different wise
Than very speechlessness of tongue is seen
To prompt to gesture those of tender age,
Whenas their innocence it doth constrain
To mark with pointing finger whatsoe'er
Is set before them. For each living being
Doth sense the end whereto each several power
He may employ. E'en ere his horns appear
And from his forehead sprout, a calf will butt
Therewith in ire, and thrust as in a rage.
But panthers' cubs and whelps of lions with foot
And claw and tooth will fight, when scarce their teeth
And claws are formed. Again, the breed entire
Of flying fowl we see to trust their weight
Unto their wings, and from their pinions seek
A dubious aid. But yet to hold that one
Did in those days assign to things their names,
And thence men learned their earliest syllables,

Is utter foolishness. For why, I ask,
Could he alone note every thing by name
And utter diverse sounds of tongue, and yet
None else be deemed this virtue to possess?
Besides, if other men had not made use
Of sounds of voice, whence, pray, in him was fixt
The notion of their use? And whence to him
Was first assigned this power to know and frame
Within his mind what he might wish to do?
Nor e'er could one the many force, or tame
Unto his will, that they be fain to learn
His names for things. (For 'tis no easy task
In any wise to teach the deaf, and urge
What must be done.) For nowise would they brook
Nor suffer more at any cost the strange
Unmeaning sounds to beat upon their ears.
And last, what is so marvelous herein,
If human kind, in whom the tongue and voice
Are strong, should things denote with diverse sounds
For diverse feelings, when dumb cattle, yea,
And e'en the beasts of savage breeds are wont
To utter sounds unlike and manifold,
In fear, or pain, or when their joys swell high?
Yea, this thou well mayst know from facts clear proven.
Whene'er in sudden snarl the long loose lips
Of great Molossian hounds,[11] drawn back in rage,
Lay bare their strong white teeth, their warning voice

----

[11] Molossian dogs, originating in Molossus, in Epirus, were much esteemed by the Romans as watch dogs. In appearance they seem to have
resembled our bloodhounds.

Hath sound far other than the noise wherewith
They bark, and fill the air with clamorous din;
And when with fondling tongue they will essay
To lick their whelps, or now with playful feet
Will roll them o'er, or with wide opened jaws
Make at each one, and harmless bitings feign,
In quite another wise with gentle growls
They fondle them than when, confined alone
Within the house, they bay, or when they whine
With cringing body as they shrink from blows.
Again, is not the sound of neighing seen
To differ likewise, when in lusty prime
Of vigorous youth a stallion runneth wild
Among the mares, sharp goaded by the spur
Of wingéd love, and when with nostrils wide
He snorteth for the fray, or stricken sore
In all his trembling limbs doth scream with fright?
And last, the divers tribes of flying fowl,
Hawks, ospreys, and the circling gulls that haunt
The ocean's billows, seeking in the brine
Their life and livelihood, will cry at times
With sound far other than the raucous notes
They voice when fighting for their sustenance
Or struggling with their prey. And e'en at times
With shift of weather certain birds will change
Their harsh shrill cries, as do the long-lived tribes
Of crows and flocks of ravens, when, 'tis said,
They call for rain and moisture, or anon
Summon the winds and breezes. Clearly, then,
If even speechless brutes are thus constrained
By feelings manifold to utter cries

Diverse in sound, how much the more 'twere meet
That mortals then should have the power to mark
With varied utterance things all unlike!

And next, lest haply thou shouldst chance to ask
In silent questioning, 'twas lightning first
Brought fire to earth for mortals, and therefrom
Hath spread on every hand the heat of flames.
For many a thing we see, touched by the fire
Of heaven, burst into flame, whenas a stroke
Sent from the sky hath brought its gift of heat.
Or yet again, when some tall branching tree,
Rocked by the wind, swaying this way and that,
Doth rub upon some neighboring trunk, 'twill chance
That, with the constant rubbing, fire will oft
Be struck from out its substance, and anon
A tongue of flame will glow, as branch and trunk
Are worn by mutual contact. This or that
May first have brought to man the gift of fire.
And then to cook his food and make it soft
By heat of flames the sun did teach; for here
And there among the fields did they behold
Full many a thing grow ripe and mellow, tamed
By his fierce heat and lashing of his rays.

And day by day those who were keen of wit
And strong of heart did teach them more and more
To change their former life and livelihood
By new-found ways, and by the boon of fire.
Then kings began to build unto themselves
Strong cities, and to rear therein the walls

Of mighty citadels, that they might have
A stronghold and a refuge; and to each
They gave his dole of cattle and of lands
According to his beauty, or his strength,
Or to his wit. For then of much avail
Was comeliness, and strength of body stood
In high esteem. Thereafter were devised
The rights of property, and gold was found,
The which with ease did rob the strong and fair
Of all their honor; for most oft 'tis true
That howe'er strong of body men are born,
Or fair of form, they follow in the train
Of him who hath the more. And yet if one
Would guide his life by reasoning true and sound,
'Tis greatest riches to a man to live
In simple modesty with heart content;
For where a little is, there is no lack.
But men did yearn for fame and power, that so
On sure foundation might their fortunes rest,
The while themselves might pass their quiet days
In peace and plenty; but alas! in vain,
Since in their eagerness to rise to heights
Of power and fame they made the way of life
A way of peril; and, in spite of all,
From their high vantage envy, like a bolt
From heaven, anon doth cast men down in scorn
To bitter Tartarus. For envy 'tis
That like the lightning oft will set ablaze
The topmost pinnacles, yea, whatsoe'er
Doth lift its head above all else; wherefore
'Twere better far in quietude to bow

The servile knee than yearn to rule the world
With kingly power, and sit upon a throne.
So let men sweat their very life-blood, worn
With fruitless toil, as up the narrow way
Of pride they struggle on, since they have learned
But from another's lips, and sought for truth
From hearsay rather than from evidence
Of their own senses; and as this hath been,
So is it now, and evermore shall be.

So kings did fall, and all the ancient pride
Of lordly thrones and haughty scepters lay
O'erturned in lowly dust; and stained with blood
The glorious diadem of kingly heads
Beneath the feet of swarming mobs did mourn
Its once great honor; for whate'er was once
Dreaded o'ermuch, with greater eagerness
Is trampled underfoot. So things returned
To lowest dregs of dire confusion—aye,
When each man for himself did seek to win
The place of highest lordship. Then it was
That some did teach their fellows how to choose
A magistrate, and frame good laws, that men
Might of their own accord submit themselves
To regulations; for the human race,
Worn with a life of violence, lay faint
From many feuds. Wherefore they yearned the more
Of their own will to yield to ordinances
And binding laws. For since ere now in wrath
Each man would undertake to avenge himself
More fiercely than is suffered now by laws

Made just for all, on this account had men
Grown weary of a life of violence.
Hence is begot that fear of punishment
That tainteth every prize of life. For hurt
And violence take each man in their toils
And fall most oft upon the guilty head
Of him whence they have risen. Nor easily
Can he live out his days in quiet peace
Who by his deeds doth break the common pact
Of peaceful living. For e'en though unmarked
By gods and men, yet must he needs distrust
His guilt may lie forever hid; for oft
Have men, 'tis said, loosing their tongues in sleep,
Or fever-crazed, themselves betrayed, and brought
Misdeeds long hid from sight to light of day.

Now what the cause which spread through all the tribes
Of mighty lands those presences divine,
Yea, filled with altars all the towns of men,
And taught the folk, as seasons rolled their round,
Those rites of pious worship which e'en now
At solemn time and place swell high with praise,
Whence still in mortal breasts is planted deep
A shuddering dread, which o'er all the world
Doth raise new shrines of gods and summon men
To flock thereto on festal days—of this
'Tis no hard task to give account in words.
For even then were mortal beings wont
With wakeful minds to view the glorious forms
Of presences divine, and e'en more oft
In sleep would they behold their shapes, endowed

With wondrous growth of body. Hence to these
They granted life and sense, since they were seen
To move their limbs, and utter haughty words
As did befit their majesty of mien
And ample strength. And everlasting life
They gave to them, since never did they fail,
Nor e'er their forms did change; yea, more than all,
Since they would fain believe that beings blest
With powers so great could scarce be overcome
By any earthly force. They fancied too
That for this cause they far excelled in bliss,
For that no one of them by fear of death
Was troubled, and likewise because in sleep
They would behold them compass many a feat
Of wondrous prowess, yet themselves derive
No weariness therefrom. And they would see
Besides the workings of the heavens o'erhead
In order fixt, the changing seasons come
And go, nor could they spell the cause thereof.
Therefore all these they made good shift to lay
To charge of gods, and hold that by their nod
All was controlled. And in the skies they set
The gods' abiding-place, since through the skies
Night and the moon were seen to wander—aye,
Moon, day and night, and night's slow solemn signs,
Night-roving brands of heaven, and flying flames,
Clouds, sun and rains, snow, lightnings, winds and hail,
The sudden crash, and long deep-muttering growl.

O hapless human kind, when unto gods
Such deeds it hath assigned, and to their charge

Hath laid such bitter wrath! What groans they drew
Upon themselves! To us what grievous wounds
They have bequeathed! What heritage of tears
Unto our children's children! For, I ween,
No piety it is, in sight of men
With veiléd head to turn toward a stone
And pause by many an altar, nor to lie
Prone on the ground, and stretch forth suppliant hands
Before the shrines of gods, nor drench with blood
Of fourfoot beasts their altars, nay, nor join
Vow unto linkéd vow—'Tis rather this:
To view all things with heart and mind at peace.
For when we lift our eyes unto the dome
Of heaven's great firmament, and nigh o'erhead
The spacious sky set with its twinkling stars,
And to our mind there come the wandering ways
Of sun and moon, then doth this fear, till now
By other ills crushed deep within our hearts,
Begin to lift anew its wakened head:
Lest haply it may be a power divine
We cannot span, that in their several paths
Doth turn the glittering stars. For 'tis a want
Of reason doth assail our minds, in doubt
Whether the world hath known a day of birth,
And if likewise some end is set, whereto
Its walls can bear this ceaseless grinding strain
Of restless motion, or if so it be,
By will of gods with everlasting life
Endowed, they may avail to go their way
Down time's unending track, and set at naught

The stern unyielding strength of endless years.
Again, who doth not feel his very soul
To shrink with dread, as neath the shuddering shock
Of sudden lightning-stroke, all the parched earth
Doth rock, as peal on peal through the wide heaven
Rolleth the thunder blast? Aye, tremble not,
Peoples and nations, and the kings of earth
In all their pride, sore struck with fear of gods,
Feel every limb to shrink, lest for some deed
Ill done, or word of boastful pride, the hour
Of heavy reckoning be at hand at last?
Or, once again, when o'er the stormy main
In its full fury flung, a wild whirlwind
Doth sweep at will across the watery waste
The master of the fleet, his legions, yea,
And elephants withal, doth he not seek
With many a vow for peace from powers divine,
And mad with terror crave in prayer a calm
From winds, and favoring breezes? But in vain,
Since oft, caught by the tempest, he is driven
For all his prayers upon the shoals of death.
So doth some secret power crush to the earth
The schemes of men, yea, e'en is seen to tread
Beneath its heel and hold in mockery
Proud rods and cruel axes. And, e'en more,
When all the earth doth reel beneath our feet,
And cities shake and fall, or on the brink
Of tottering ruin stand, what wonder then
If mortal men themselves despise, and leave
The world to sovereign might and wondrous strength
Of powers divine, whose hand doth all things guide?

Then for the rest, copper and gold and iron
Were first discovered, and therewith the weight
Of silver, and the homely worth of lead,
When on some mighty mountain side a fire
With its devouring heat had burned vast tracts
Of forest land,—whether a bolt from heaven
Was hurled thereon, or, waging forest-war
Against each other, they themselves had brought
The threat of fire upon their foes, to strike
Their hearts with terror; or perchance, allured
By richness of the soil, 'twas their intent
To clear the fertile fields, and tame the expanse
Of wild waste land to pastures, or to slay
The savage beasts, and win their wealth of spoils.
For hunting game with pit and fire arose
Long ere men learned with nets to fence a grove,
And rouse the prey with dogs.—Howe'er it be,
And from whatever cause the flaming heat
With hideous roar had licked the forests clean,
E'en to their deepest roots, and baked the earth
Into a smoldering mass, in molten veins
There trickled streams of silver and of gold,
Of copper and of lead, that here and there
Would gather into hollows in the earth.
And when in after time they chanced to find
These hardened shapes that lay upon the ground
All bright and shining, they would lift them up,
Pleased with their smooth bright fairness, and they saw
That each was shaped with outline like to that
Its hollowed footprints had but now displayed.
And then it slowly dawned upon their minds

That these same metals, melted by the power
Of heat, to various forms and shapes of things
Might e'en be molded, and by beating formed
To points and edges howe'er sharp and fine,
That they might fashion weapons for their use
And tools to fell the forests, and to hew
Timber for houses, smooth the rough-hewn beams,
Yea, and to bore and punch and drill withal.
Nor less with silver and with gold at first
They set themselves unto these various tasks
Than with the sturdy strength of stubborn bronze;
But all in vain, since, vanquished all their powers,
They yielded, nor, as harder substances,
Could bear the strain of toil. And then it was
That bronze was held in high esteem, and gold
Lay scorned by reason of its uselessness,
Grown dull with blunted edge. But now 'tis bronze
That is despised, while gold hath risen to take
The place of highest honor. So doth time
In his revolving round bring many a change
Unto the season of each several thing.
What was but now of worth in turn is held
Of no repute; then riseth in its room
Some bauble else, leaving its place of scorn,
And day by day with greater zeal 'tis sought,
And, brought to light, it doth wax high in praise
And stand in wondrous honor among men.

Now in what wise was found the natural use
Of iron, 'tis no hard task for thee to learn,
Good Memmius. Men's arms of old were hands,

And nails and teeth, or stones, and branches torn
From trees, and flame and fire, when once their use
Was known. Then in good time the strength of iron
And bronze was brought to light. And use of bronze
Was learned ere that of iron; for easier far
Its nature was to work, and greater store
Thereof was found. And 'twas with bronze they tilled
The soil of earth, with bronze they joined in strife
Of shifting combat, dealt their weltering wounds,
And plundered flocks and fields. For every foe
Naked and weaponless would forthwith yield
To those equipped with arms. Then by degrees
The sword of iron came forth, and turned to scorn
Became the crude bronze sickle; and with iron
They now began to plow the soil of earth;
And war's uncertain odds were equal made,
And 'twas the warrior's wont to climb full-armed
Upon a horse's flanks, and with the rein
Guide him to battle, and with good right arm
Do many a deed of valor, ere men learned
To tempt war's fortunes with a well-matched pair
Of yokéd steeds; and training to the yoke
A single pair arose before the art
Of harnessing twice twain, and ere they learned
To mount full-armed the scythe-shod car of war.
And 'twas the Poeni who were first to train
The wild Lucanian kine,[12] with towering bulk,

[12] The Romans first became acquainted with the use of elephants in war
when Pyrrhus, king of Epirus, brought twenty of these beasts into Lu-
cania, in lower Italy, for use in his campaigns. In the Second Punic war
the Carthaginian general, Hannibal, also used these predecessors of the
modern "tank" as a part of his military forces.

Grim shapes, with snaky hands, to bear the wounds
Of warfare, and confound the hosts of Mars.
So one thing from another dire discord
Would e'er beget, to bring its meed of dread
To men in arms, and ever day by day
Give increase to the wildering woes of war.

Bulls too they tried in war's emprise, and boars
Of savage breed they would essay to send
Against the foe. And some drove on before
Great lions with well-armed trainers and a band
Of cruel masters who might curb their rage
And hold them chained. In vain, since in the heat
Of slaughter and confusion they would show
Their untamed nature, and on all the hosts
Wreak deadly havoc, friend and foe alike,
Tossing on every side the fearsome manes
Upon their heads; nor could the riders soothe
The hearts of their own horses, sore dismayed
By all the fearful din, or with the rein
Turn them against the foe. With furious bounds
To every side would lionesses launch
Their blood-mad bodies, clawing at the face
Of all who came against them, or anon
Would strike them down, unwitting, from behind,
And crouching low, by dint of massive jaws
And crooked claws would pin to earth their prey,
Foredone with wounds. And bulls besides would toss
Their own allies, trampling their prostrate forms
Beneath their feet, or with their horns would rip
The horses' flanks and bellies from beneath,

And tear the ground with threatening brow. So too,
The maddened boars with their stout tusks would rend
Their masters, splashing with their own life-blood
The splintered spears that pierced them, and would deal
A general ruin to both horse and foot.
For oft the chargers, eager to avoid
The thrust of angry tusks, would swerve aside,
Or rear and paw the air; but all in vain,
Since one would see them reel, with tendons slashed,
And crashing down lie huddled on the ground.
Yea, whate'er beasts they fancied ere the event
Had been well tamed at home, they would behold
Grow mad with rage in thick of battle, crazed
By wounds and shouting, by the sudden flight,
The panic and the din; nor one thereof
Could they contrive to rally to the fray.
For all the various breeds of savage beasts
Would scatter far and wide, as oft, e'en now,
Sore wounded by the steel, Lucanian kine
Will turn and flee, whenas full meed of hurt
Have they availed to deal unto their own.
(If so indeed they e'er would do; but scarce
Am I persuaded to believe that ere
Such dire disaster should befall alike
Both friend and foe, they could not in advance
Foresee and picture what must come to pass.
And rather shouldst thou hold this might have been
Somewhere in all the various worlds, begot
In ways diverse, than on one certain earth.
Nay, such the means they might be fain to use
In final cast of chance, and less in hope

Of victory than of dealing to the foe
A cause for groans, resolved themselves to die,
Distrustful of their hosts and wanting arms.)

And knotted garments came before the use
Of woven raiment. Nor till iron was found
Could weaving come to birth. For 'tis with iron
That looms are fashioned, nor in other wise
Can be devised the fair smooth-polished grace
Of heddles, spindles, shuttles, and the strength
Of clattering yarn-beams. And the menfolk first
Did nature prompt to spin and weave, ere yet
Had women learned their uses; for the male
Doth far excel the female sex in skill,
And hath much more of cunning; till at length
The sturdy husbandmen made scorn thereof,
And fain would leave such chores to women's hands,
The while themselves in sterner tasks would share
And harden hands and limbs in hardy toil.

But nature's self, creatress of all things,
Was pattern for their sowing, and likewise
The source of grafting, since in season due
Berries and acorns, falling from the trees,
Put forth rich growth of tender shoots beneath;
And hence it took their fancy to ingraft
Fresh scions unto branches, and to plant
Young saplings in the ground throughout their fields.
And one by one new ways they would essay
To till their smiling garden-plots, and saw
Earth's bitter fruits grow sweet, with loving care

And patient tending. And from day to day
They would constrain the forests to retreat
Yet farther up the mountain sides, and yield
The land below to tilth, that they might have
Meads, pools and streams, cornfields and vineyards glad
O'er every hill and plain, and, set between
To mark their bounds, gray files of olive trees
Might spread o'er knoll and hollow and champaign;
As now we see the countryside clear marked
With varied beauty, where men lend it charm
With pleasant checkered orchards, or set round
With fruitful shrubs will hold their broad domains.

But with the lips to feign the liquid notes
Of birds prevailed long ere men had the skill
To frame in melody the sweet-tongued songs
That charm the ear. And 'twas the zephyr's breath,
Soft whispering through the hollow reeds, that first
Did teach the rustic folk how they might blow
Through hollowed stalks of hemlock. Then by bit
And bit they learned the sweet lament
The pipe doth utter, stopt by fingers deft
Of practised players, the haunting strains that rose
From out the pathless forests, woods, and glades
In shepherds' lonely haunts, in their blest hours
Of sweet repose. With these they soothed their minds
And cheered their hearts when filled with food; for then
Are all things sweet. And oft in friendly wise
On some soft bank of verdure they would lie
Flung at their length in careless ease beside

A running stream, or neath the sheltering arms
Of some tall tree, and with delight would take
From nature's bounty all their bodies craved;
And most of all when Springtime's smiling face
Painted the greening grass with flowers. Then jest
And talk and many a merry laugh were wont
To rise; for strong was then the rustic muse.
And joyous mirth would prompt to wreathe their heads
And shoulders with fresh garlands, twined of flowers
And foliage, and with loutish steps to move
Their clumsy limbs, reckless of time and tune,
Beating their mother earth with heavy tread;
Whence smiles and merry laughter rose; for then
All things were fresh and fair and wonderful.
And hence unto the wakeful there would come
Solace for loss of sleep, as they would sound
The modulations of a song, or run
With curling lip over the oaten reed.
Thus even now are watchmen wont to hold
This heritage, as they have learned to keep
The measure of a song; and yet withal
No whit more pleasure do they win therefrom
Than that rough race of earth-born men of old.
For what is close at hand, had we not known
Somewhat more sweet before, doth give us joy
Beyond all else, and seemeth to excel;
But oft is found some thing of greater charm
Which doth the first destroy and change our love
For all the old. So then began to rise
Hatred of acorns, and abandoned lay

Those erstwhile couches, strewn with grass and leaves;
A thing of scorn likewise became the coat
Of wild beast hides, the which, I ween, was found
Mid such a storm of envy that the first
To wear it was waylaid and slain; and yet,
Torn into shreds in bloody strife, 'twas lost
Among the crowd, nor could be turned to use.
So in those days 'twas skins, but now 'tis gold
And purple that do vex men's life with cares
And weary them with war; wherefore, I ween,
The greater fault doth lie with us. For cold
Would rack those naked shivering sons of earth
For want of skins; but us it hurteth not
To lack a purple garment, richly dight
With gold, if but a common sack be ours
To fend the winter's chill. So doth the race
Of men forever run its fruitless round
Of ill-spent toil, and waste its little life
In idle cares, because in sooth e'en now
It hath not learned what limit hath been set
To man's possessing, and nowise doth grasp
How far true pleasure may increase. And this
It is that inch by creeping inch hath thrust
Man's life out on the deep, and hath aroused
From unplumbed depths the mighty tides of war.

But sun and moon, that scan with sleepless eye
The vast revolving vault of heaven, gave sign
To men of how the seasons come and go
In yearly round, and how in certain course
And order due each thing doth come to pass.

And now, ringed round with mighty towers, they spent
Their days and prospered, and each man's demesne
Was parceled out and marked with bounds; and now
The sea was bright with flying sails; now pacts
Were drawn, that they at need might have the aid
Of strong allies, when poets first began
To tell men's deeds in song; nor long before
Were letters first devised; [13] and thus it is
Our age can never scan that ancient page
Of past achievements, save where reason's hand
Doth point the way. Then slowly, step by step,
The sailor's craft, the tilling of the soil,
Walls, laws and arms, roads, dress, and all their ilk,
Yea, all life's prizes and its dear delights
As well, songs, painted pictures, and the art
Of carved and polished images, 'twas use
And the bold urge of tireless minds withal
That taught them bit by bit, as they progressed
With stumbling feet along the upward path.
So hour by hour doth time bring forth to view
Each several thing, and reason lift it up
Into the coasts of light. For in their hearts
Would they behold one thing to catch the gleam
From that which went before, until at last
They reached the topmost pinnacle of art.

[13] Lucretius is incorrect in his assumption that writing necessarily preceded literature. He leaves entirely out of account the oral transmission of songs and legends.

BOOK SIX

BOOK SIX

'Twas Athens once of glorious name that first
'Mongst weary mortals spread the precious boon
Of fruitful corn, and shaped men's life anew,
And gave them laws and statutes—she who brought
To life its first sweet solace, when she bore
That golden-hearted one who poured of old
From lips prophetic such great store of truth.
Yea, e'en though long ago his light was quenched,
Yet still his ancient glory, noised abroad
From his divine discoveries, doth soar
Unto the very heavens. For when he saw
That mortals had by now well nigh attained
Whate'er their daily needs did crave, with lives,
So far as might be, stablished and secure;
That men through wealth and station and repute
Were rich in power, and mighty in the name
Of goodly sons, and yet not one withal
That bore within his house a heart less vext
With anguished dread, but sick at heart would fret
Through weary days, nor find surcease, and e'er
Must needs make bitter plaint—'twas then he knew
That 'twas the vessel's self was fouled, and thence
Was all within corrupted with its taint;
Yea, whatsoe'er was gathered from without,
E'en that which fain would bless; for that in part

He saw 'twas full of yawning holes, nor e'er
In any wise could it be filled; and part,
Since he perceived itself did basely foul
As with a noisome savor whatsoe'er
It had received within. And so he spake,
And by his words of truth did purge men's hearts,
And set a bound to their desires and fears,
And showed withal what is the highest good
Toward which we all do strive, and with his hand
Marked plain the path whereby our wandering feet
May walk aright that narrow upward way;
Yea, his the task to show what host of ills
In mortal life doth everywhere abound,
Born under many a guise, and flung abroad,
Be it by nature's hazard or her spite,
Since she had willed it thus; then what the gates
Wherefrom we needs must sally forth to meet
Each several ill, he marked, and likewise proved
That in large measure 'tis in vain that men
Stir in their hearts the gloomy tides of care.
For e'en as children tremble with affright
At darkness' unseen terrors, so at times
Do we ourselves in broad daylight have fear
Of things which we in truth should dread no more
Than those vain fancies children in the dark
Do tremble at, and fear will come alive.
This terror, then, this gloom that doth enshroud
Our troubled minds, not piercing rays of sun
Nor day's bright shining beams must needs dispel,
But nature's outward mien and inward law.

Wherefore the more I now must haste to weave
In my discourse the task I have begun.

   And now, since I have shown that mortal stand
The walls of our great firmament, and formed
With frame that hath known birth the very heavens,
And much besides of all the tangled skein
Of that which doth befall therein, yea, all
That must perforce befall, I have unwoven,
Give ear to that which doth remain to tell.
For once I have made bold to set my foot
Upon the glorious car whose high-reared track
Doth top the heavens, 'twill be my task to tell
How stormy winds arise, and how once more,
Their anger past, all things are changed to calm;
And many a thing besides, which mortal eyes
In earth and sky behold to come to pass,
When oft with fear-struck minds they hang in doubt
And feel their hearts shrink with a shuddering dread
Of powers divine, as groveling on the earth
They cast their prostrate limbs, since 'tis a want
Of understanding of the cause thereof
That doth constrain them to assign all things
To sovereignty of gods, and own their sway.
For they whose hearts have come to learn aright
That gods live through their tranquil days apart
From care and fear, yet if from time to time
They chance to wonder what the means whereby
All things can run their round, and most of all
Whate'er above our heads is seen to move
Along the coasts of heaven, so are they borne

Once more unto religion's ancient creeds,
And take unto themselves stern overlords,
That in their wretched plight they would believe
Can all things compass, since they fail to grasp
What can, what cannot be, yea, in what wise
Each body's power is limited, and how
For each is marked its deep-set boundary;
Wherefore the more they wander, led astray
By reasoning blind. And thou, if thou spew not
All this from out thy mind, nor banish far
Thoughts all unworthy of the blessed gods
And alien to their peace, so will those powers
Divine, for thy dispraise, oft do thee harm.
Not that the gods' high majesty by act
Of thine can be abased, that so in wrath
They thirst to wreak sharp vengeance, but that thou
Of thine own self wilt fancy that those beings
Who dwell in tranquil peace may set astir
Their mighty tides of wrath, nor with a heart
Serene wilt thou approach their holy shrines,
Nor yet avail with calm untroubled mind
To greet those idols which from forms divine
Go forth to herald to the minds of men
Their holy presences. And thence what cast
Of life will follow, thou mayst well perceive.
And that the truest reasoning may dispel
All this afar from us; though much ere now
Hath passed my lips, yet much doth still remain
To be adorned in polished verse: we needs
Must grasp the outward mien and inner law
Of all the heavens; and we must sing as well

Of storms and flashing lightnings, what their ways,
And from what cause upon their several paths
They speed amain; lest haply thou shouldst mark
The regions of the sky, and in mad haste
Shouldst ask whence came this wingéd flash, or which
The quarter whither it hath sped, or how
E'en walled enclosures it hath breached, and thence,
Its reign of outrage o'er, hath gone it way.
And now, as toward the last white mark I speed,
Trace thou the track before me, wisdom's muse,
Calliope, sweet solace unto men
And dear delight of gods, that led by thee
Mid high acclaim I may attain the crown.

Now, first of all, the sky's pure azure deeps
Are set a-tremble neath the thunder's shock
Whenas high scudding clouds clash each on each
Before the warring winds. For ne'er doth fall
The sound from regions of the heavens that bide
Serene and clear; but in what part soe'er
The clouds in denser host are massed, 'tis thence
More oft will come the deep loud-rumbling roar.
(Nor e'er can clouds be formed of body dense,
As stocks and stones, nor yet so rare as mist
And flying smoke; else they were bound to fall,
Dragged down like stones by their dead helpless weight,
Or haply, e'en as smoke, they scarce could hold
Their mass together, or imprison within
Chill snow and showers of hail.) Again, at times
Across the spreading plains of heaven they give
A sound as when an awning, stretched above

Some spacious theater, will whip and toss
Amongst the masts and spars; or now, perchance,
Rent in the midst by wanton winds, 'twill crack
With sound of tearing parchment; for, I ween,
A sound akin thereto thou well mayst mark
In thunder; or as when in fitful gusts
The winds will catch a garment spread to dry,
Or flying papers, and with many a flap
And flutter whirl them hurtling through the air.
For so 'twill come to pass from time to time
That clouds cannot so much avail to clash
Each full on each, but rather flankwards pass,
And as they move in paths diverse will touch,
Close grazing mass on mass, whence on our ears
Doth grate that long-drawn rasping, till at length
From their close contact they have passed once more.

And in this wise as well will all things seem
Ofttimes to tremble neath the shuddering shock
Of thunder, and the mighty walls that ring
The spacious firmament with sudden crash
Appear to leap asunder, as anon
A strong swift-gathered storm of rushing wind
Hath bored its way within the clouds, and there,
Pent with its whirling eddy deep within
The cloud-mass, doth constrain it more and more
On every side to hollow out, with crust
Grown thicker on its outward side, till worn
And spent by the wind's fierce onslaught, 'twill give way,
Rent wide apart with fearful shuddering crash.
Nor is it strange, since, burst with sudden blow,

A tiny air-filled bladder oft will sound
With loud report.

And other way besides
There is, when winds blow through the clouds, whereby
They may give forth a sound. For oft we see
Clouds borne aloft with branches manifold,
And rough in outline; as in kindred wise,
When through dense forests sweep the northern blasts,
Loud roar the leaves, the straining branches crash.
Then too 'twill come to pass at times, that roused
To wrath the might of raging wind will drive
Straight through a cloud, and with a front attack
Rend it asunder. For what havoc there
A blast can wreak is manifest from things
Held clear in view among us here on earth,
Where winds, though gentler, yet at times will tear
Tall trees from out the ground, and drag them forth
E'en from their deepest roots. And waves besides
There are, that rolling through the clouds will make
As 'twere a dull deep sound of breaking, e'en
As in deep rivers or the vasty sea
Doth break the rolling tide. 'Twill happen too
Whenas the lightning's fiery force from cloud
To cloud doth fall, if haply into deeps
Of moisture hath the cloud received the flame,
With scream of rage it slayeth it forthwith;
E'en as at times, fresh from the fiery forge,
A glowing iron, plunged quickly in a trough
Of icy water, will give forth a sound
Of hissing. But if drier be the cloud

That hath received the flame, forthwith 'tis fired,
And with a mighty roar doth burn, as when
Across some laureled height a spreading flame
Fanned by the eddying winds will range abroad
Consuming all in one vast sweep. (For naught
Besides, I ween, with sound more dread is burned
By crackling flames than Phoebus' Delphic bay.)
Oft too within the massy clouds on high
Will ceaseless snap of ice and fall of hail
Give forth a rending sound. For once the wind
Hath packed them close, ofttimes asunder burst
The high-piled mountain-shapes of storm cloud, chilled
To icy solidness and mixt with hail.

So too, is lightning formed, when cloud on cloud
Hath clashed amain, and cast full many a seed
Of fire abroad, e'en as when stone doth strike
On stone, or iron; for then likewise a flash
Will fly afar and scatter sparks of fire.
But thus it chanceth that upon our ears
Doth fall the thunder's sound some little space
After our eyes have caught the flash, since e'er
Do things move toward our ears at slower pace
Than those which stir the eyes. That thou mayst learn
From this as well; for shouldst thou chance to see
A far-off woodsman hew with twin-edged axe
Some giant tree-trunk, so 'twill come to pass
Thou'lt see the stroke ere yet the sound hath fallen
Upon thine ear; e'en so it is we see
The lightning ere we hear the thunder's crash,
Though on the very instant 'tis let loose

With the bright flash, and by a single cause
Engendered, yea, born of the selfsame shock.

   And in this wise as well the clouds will bathe
In swift-winged light all things below, as here
Or there with flash on flash the gathering storm
Leapeth in fitful onslaught. For when once
A wind hath swept within, and eddying round
With ceaseless whirl, as I ere now have shown,
Doth make the hollow cloud grow dense, 'twill catch
A glow of heat from its own movement, e'en
As thou wilt see all things grow hot and burn
Through motion, yea, as e'en a leaden ball
Whirling upon its far-flung course, will melt.
And so, when through and through this fiery wind
Hath rent the murky cloud, to every side
It scattereth seeds of fire, which, as it were,
Struck on a sudden by some force within,
Give birth forthwith to flashing tongues of flame;
Thereon the sound doth follow, borne at pace
More slow unto our ears than things which fall
Upon the sight. And this, beyond all doubt,
Doth come to pass in clouds at once condensed
And piled in wondrous masses, each on each;
Lest haply thou shouldst err, since from below
We see how broad their span, nor mark how high
Their towering piles are reared. For look, when next
The winds will lift athwart the air great clouds
In counterfeit of mountains, or perchance
When thou dost see them billowing each on each
Along some mighty mountain range, and there

Hang motionless above, each at his post,
When winds on every side lie hushed in sleep;
Then canst thou mark their mighty mass, and scan
Their high-reared caverns, as of hanging rock;
And when, mid rising storms, the winds have filled
Those hollowed caves, with deep-mouthed roar they chafe,
Prisoned within the clouds, and like caged beasts
Mutter their angry menace, as now here,
Now there, across the reaches of the cloud
They hurl their wrathful roaring, and anon,
Seeking an outlet, round and round they race.
And, catching in their eddy seeds of fire
From out the clouds, many thereof they drive
Into a mass, and set awhirl within
The hollow furnaces the gathered flame
Till all the cloud is rent in twain, and forth
With sudden blaze burst the imprisoned fires.

From this cause too it oft will come to pass
That down to earth doth fly the swift gold gleam
Of liquid flame, for that the clouds themselves
Must needs hold many a seed of fire; for when
In truth no trace of moisture do they hold,
'Tis then most oft their hue is bright, and tinged
With roseate flame. Yea, and 'twere meet besides
That from the sun's bright glow they will conceive
Much store of fire, that so with right they gleam
With ruddy brightness, and anon pour forth
Their hues of flame. Thus, when a harrying gale,
Jostling and thrusting, hath confined them close

Within a straitened space, so will they yield
And pour abroad the seeds wherefrom are born
The flashing hues of flame. Then too, at times
'Twill lighten when the clouds of heaven grow rare.
For when perchance, e'en as they move, a wind
Doth lightly draw asunder and unweave
Their texture, all unbid the seeds that form
The flash will fall. Then with no direful din
And shock of dread doth fall the soundless flame.

For what remaineth, with what nature dowered
Are lightning bolts, doth clearly come to view
In their swift stroke and deep-charred footprints left
By scorching heat, aye, and their brands that breathe
A noisome reek of sulphur. For all these
Are marks of fire, nor wait on wind or rain.
And oft besides they set ablaze the roofs
Of houses, and in one swift swirl of flame
Do work their will through all the halls within.
This fire, thou mayst be sure, hath nature formed
Most subtile of all subtile fires that be,
Fashioned of bodies small and swift to move,
Nor aught can bar its way. For straight through walls
Of houses can the strong bolt pass, as shouts
And cries, yea, e'en through stone, through molded shapes
Of bronze, and in a single instant melt
Hard brass and gold; and likewise in a trice
It maketh wine to vanish, though the jar
Remain unharmed, for that, we may be sure,
Its heat upon its coming doth with ease
Loose all the texture of the vessel's clay

And make it rare, and straightway entering in
With one swift movement doth dissolve and cast
Abroad the first beginnings of the wine.
Yet this, 'tis clear, the sun's fierce heat can scarce
Throughout a lifetime bring to pass, though dowered
In his bright blaze with such exceeding strength.
So much more swift this force, and clothed with might.

Now in what wise they are conceived, and framed
With powers so great that with a single stroke
They can avail to rend strong towers in twain,
Make wreck of houses, pluck up planks and beams,
And shatter and confound the works of men,
Rob men of life, lay low on every side
The pastured flocks; yea, what the force whereby
They can avail to compass all things else
Of kindred nature, will I now set forth,
Nor keep thee waiting on my promise more.

First we must mark that lightning bolts are formed
From dense cloud-masses piled on high; for none
Is e'er hurled forth from skies serene, or clouds
Of slender texture. For beyond all doubt
Clear facts will show this doth befall; for then
With mass on mass the towering cloud-shapes rise
Through all the air, till we would fain believe
That all the gloom of Acheron, let loose
From every side, hath filled the vasty deeps
Of hollow heaven, so darkly o'er our heads
Rising from out the cloud-born midnight lower
Dread faces of black fear, what time the storm

Doth gird himself to forge his thunder-bolts.
And oft above the sea a black storm-cloud,
Like to a murky stream of pitch let down
From out the sky, will fall upon the waves,
And, crammed with distant darkness, in its wake
Will drag amain a glowering tempest, big
With lightning and with gales, while more than all
Itself is filled with fires and winds, till e'en
Upon the land folk shudder and in haste
Seek out a shelter. So we needs must hold
That high above our heads doth mount the storm;
For verily clouds scarce would shroud in gloom
So vast the lands, were they not builded high
And piled in billowing heaps till all the sun
Is stolen away; nor yet could they avail,
As on they sweep, to drown the sodden lands
With floods of rain that make the swollen streams
To top their banks, and all the fields to swim
With moisture, save that all the air were filled
With high-reared clouds. 'Tis thus that all doth teem
With fires and winds; hence burst on every side
The dazzling and the din.

                                For I, in truth,
Ere now have shown that hollow clouds do hold
Great store of seeds of heat, and many too
They needs must gather from the sun's bright beams
And their warm glow. Thus, when the selfsame wind
Which haply to a single spot doth herd
Their scattered ranks, forth from their midst hath driven
Full many a seed of heat, and with their fire

Hath its own substance mingled, swift within
Doth bore a seething eddy, and anon
Whirling about its narrow prison doth forge
The bolt in glowing furnaces within.
For 'tis in twofold wise its burning flame
Is kindled: both when it doth gather heat
From its own movement, and from touch of fire.
Thereafter when the wind's own might hath grown
Exceeding hot, and all the fire's fierce strength
Hath entered in, 'tis then the thunderbolt,
Like brand full-forged, doth on a sudden rend
The cloud asunder, and in one swift leap
Range far abroad, flooding all regions round
With blazing light. Then followeth in its train
A heavy crash, till all the broad expanse
Of heaven above our heads doth seem to burst
Its walls upon the instant and to crush
All things in general ruin. Then doth seize
Upon the earth a trembling vast, while far
Across the high-flung arch of heaven do run
Deep distant rumblings. For 'tis then the storm,
Shaken unto its utmost depths, is set
A-tremble, and loud roarings move abroad.
And from the shock anon there followeth rain
In drenching floods, till all the air doth seem
A sea of gathered moisture that would fain
With headlong fall summon the earth once more
To watery wilderness; so vast a shower
Is loosed with rending of the cloud, and storm
Of raging wind, as forth with searing stroke
Leapeth the levin bolt. Then, too, ofttimes

A mighty wind roused from without will fall
Upon the cloud, hot with its fresh-forged brand;
And when its force hath rent the mass, straightway
Doth fall therefrom that fiery dart we name
With name our fathers gave, the thunderbolt.
But oft to other sides as well the stroke
Will fly abroad where'er its force may tend.
Likewise it chanceth that at times the might
Of wind, sent forth devoid of heat, may yet
In its long wandering course burst forth
In flame e'en as it moveth, since 'twill lose
Along its path some coarser particles,
Which cannot make their way with equal ease
Through the wide air; and gathering other store
Of smaller bodies from the air itself,
'Twill sweep them on, till mingling with its stream,
E'en as they fly, they shape the stuff of fire,
In no far different wise than oft a ball
Of lead in its swift flight will glow with heat,
As, losing many a mass of stiffening cold,
It catcheth fire in air. And oft besides
It will befall that fire may e'en be roused
From impact of the blow, whenas the might
Of rushing wind, though cold and void of heat
When first 'tis loosed, hath reached its mark; for then,
We may be sure, when with resistless blow
It hath struck home, small particles of heat
Can stream together from the wind itself
And from whate'er doth on the instant meet
The impact of its blow; as when on stone
We strike with iron, there floweth forth amain

A stream of fire, nor aught the less will seeds
Of burning brightness muster at the blow
Since cold the iron's nature. Even so
A thing must needs be kindled by the bolt
Of lightning if so be it is itself
Of nature formed and meet for flame. And yet
We must not idly hold that wind is framed
With nature wholly cold, when with a force
So violent it hath been loosed on high;
But rather should we deem that though when first
It doth set forth 'tis kindled not with fire,
Yet as it flieth 'tis warmed and mixt with heat.

And hence withal doth spring the swift-winged stroke
Of lightning, and its shattering blast (for e'er
With swift descent unto their goal its bolts
Do speed); since, first of all, its force is launched
By impulse of its own, and from its lair
Within the cloud it gathereth all its strength
Into one mighty effort for its leap;
And when the cloud no longer hath the strength
To stem its rising onslaught, so its force
Is loosed and in hot haste doth fly abroad,
E'en as swift missiles on a sudden hurled
From war's grim engines. Yea, and what is more,
'Tis formed of bodies small and smooth, and naught
With ease such nature can withstand; for deep
Within all textures doth it find forthwith
Its furtive way, and through their hollowed paths
Doth force a passage. Hence it meeteth not
With let or hindrance from whate'er would bar

Its onward way, and thus doth fly amain
On its swift gliding course. Again, since true
Unto their nature bodies dowered with weight
Will downward tend, but when a blow as well
Hath been applied thereto, so will their speed
Be doubled, and a stronger impulse given,
That so with greater violence and pace
Grown swifter will it scatter with its blow
Whate'er would stay its course, and, lingering not,
Continue on its way. Or, once again,
Since with a lasting impulse it doth move,
It needs must gather ever more and more
Of flying swiftness, which doth grow apace
E'en as it doth proceed, and bring increase
Unto its stubborn might, and arm its stroke
With giant strength. For it doth bring to pass
That all the seeds thereof in file direct
Are borne as toward one goal, their whirling hosts
Sped each and all along the selfsame road.
Or haply it may be that in its flight
It gathereth even from the air some store
Of bodies which by virtue of the force
Of their own violent impact kindle there
An added swiftness. Often, too, 'twill pass
Through objects without harm, yea, many a thing
'Twill pierce straight through, nor leave a trace behind,
For that its liquid flame doth make its way
Along the opened pores. And many, too,
'Twill enter, since its fiery bodies fall
E'en where the bodies of the object meet
In patterned texture. And cold bronze with ease

'Twill liquefy, and gold in one brief breath
'Twill cause to seethe and boil, for that its force
Is finely fashioned, framed of bodies small
And elements smooth-shapen, which with ease
Can make their way within, and, entered there,
Forthwith loose every knot and break each bond.

And most in autumn is the house of heaven,
Set round with twinkling stars, constrained to shake
On every hand, and all the earth as well,
Or when the springtime first doth fling abroad
Her flowery mantle. For the times of cold
Are marked by dearth of fires, while in the heat
Winds fail, nor with so dense a body rise
The gathering clouds. And so, when midway stand
The seasons of the sky, then doth converge
Each several cause to shape the thunderbolt.
For now the straitened channel that doth mark
The changing of the year doth of itself
Commingle heat and cold, of both whereof
The cloud hath need to forge its lightning bolts,
That so there doth prevail an angry strife
Among the elements, as with loud roar
The air doth rage and heave with fires and winds.
For birth of warmth and death of cold are one,
And mark the springtime's advent; hence 'twere meet
That jarring elements, when mingled each
With each, make war and turmoil. And again,
When doth return the time of waning heat
And first chill touch of cold, that season marked
With name of autumn, then the wintry frosts

Once more do battle with the summer's warmth.
And hence it is these seasons may be termed
The narrows of the year, nor is it strange
If in these days are lightnings multiplied
And raging tempests gather in the sky,
Since from both camps at once is roused the clash
Of deadly strife, on this side armed with flames,
On that with mingled storms of wind and rain.

Thus were it meet to scan the nature true
Of heaven's thunderbolt,[1] and view the force
Whereby each several deed it compasseth,
Nor vainly turn Tyrrhenian riddles o'er,
Seeking some sign of gods' dark purposes,
Nor ask whence came this wingéd flash, or which
The quarter whither it hath sped, or how
E'en walled enclosures it hath breached, and thence,
Its reign of outrage o'er, hath gone its way,
Or what to us the lesson of the bolt
From heaven's own realms. But haply if it be
That Jove or other gods besides do shake
With shuddering crash the shining dome of heaven
And hurl their wrathful fires each where he will,

---

[1] Etruscan soothsayers claimed to be able to interpret the divine will from the entrails of sacrificial victims, to propitiate the anger of the gods as indicated by lightning or other marvels, and to interpret their significance according to Etruscan formulae. This art, which was referred to a divine origin, had long been practiced in Etruria. From about the time of the Punic wars, soothsayers from Etruria began to settle in Rome, and were employed both by private individuals and state officials, by whom their science was held in high esteem.

Why, pray, make they not sure that whosoe'er
Hath kept not from his heart some loathsome deed
Of conscious guilt, felled by the fiery dart,
Should breathe from out his shattered breast the flame
Of heaven's avenging bolt, a lesson sharp
For men to heed? Why, rather, oft will he
Who hath not known foul guilt be wrapt and snared,
All innocent, in tangled tongues of flame,
Caught on the instant in the whirling fires
Of heaven? Or wherefore do they aim their darts
At desert wastes, and spend their toil for naught?
Or haply are they practising their arms
And strengthening their sinews? Or again,
Why suffer they the Father's dart to blunt
Its edge upon the earth? Why doth himself
Its ruin brook, nor keep it for his foes?
Or why, forsooth, when skies on every side
Are calm and clear, doth Jove ne'er hurl his bolt
Upon the earth, and belch his rumblings forth?
Doth he then tarry till the clouds be risen,
And then himself descend thereto, that so
From close at hand he thence may calculate
His weapon's cast? Or to what end, I pray,
Doth he send down his shaft upon the sea?
What spite hath he against the waves, the mass
Of briny waters, and the brimming plains?
And why most often doth he cast his darts
At lofty spots, that so on mountain tops
We see most frequent traces of his fire?
Or, doth he haply wish us to beware
His lightning's onslaught, wherefore is he loth

To let us see its cast? But doth he wish
To whelm us all unwitting with his fire,
Why from that very quarter doth he send
His thunders forth, that we the stroke may shun?
Why doth he gather in advance his gloom,
His rumblings and his threats? And how, I ask,
Canst thou believe that he can hurl at once
His bolts to many sides? Or darest thou claim
It ne'er hath come to pass that several strokes
Are in an instant made? Nay, oft hath chanced,
And needs must chance, that e'en as rains and showers
In many a region fall, so at one time
Are fashioned many bolts. And, last of all,
Wherefore with hostile dart doth he make wreck
Of holy shrines of gods, and e'en o'erthrow
His own proud dwelling-places? Why destroy
The fair-wrought statues of the gods, and rob
Of all their ancient pride at one fell stroke
E'en images of his own form divine?

And next, 'tis no hard task herefrom to learn
How loosed from heaven above upon the sea
There fall those whirling horrors which the Greeks,
In keeping with their nature, marked with name
Of presters.[2] For at times 'twill come to pass
That as it were a twisting column lowered
From out the sky will drop upon the sea,
And round its midst, deep stirred by howling blasts,

[2] Lucretius seems to include in the term "presters" both whirlwinds and
waterspouts.

The waters seethe and boil, till every craft
In that wild maelstrom caught is sore bestead
And cometh into jeopardy. And this
At times befalleth when the violent force
Of rising wind cannot avail to burst
The cloud it fain would rend, but from above
Doth press it downward, till from sky to sea
'Tis lowered like a column, ell by ell,
As though somewhat by thrust of giant fist
And arm above were flung upon the waves
In one long eddying mass. And when at length
Its force hath rent the cloud, straightway the wind
Will burst upon the sea and rouse forthwith
A strange confusion in the deep. For down
Doth drop a whirling eddy, in its train
Dragging the yielding cloud-mass, and when once
Down to the ocean's level it hath flung
The storm cloud, big with dread, straightway itself
Doth plunge amain into the deep, and there
With mighty roar of rage stir all the sea
To seething fury. And ofttimes 'twill chance
An eddying wind, all else apart, will wrap
Itself in clouds, as many seeds thereof
It gathereth from the air, and as it were
Will counterfeit the whirling prester dropt
From out the sky. And when upon the earth
This eddy hath descended, and hath burst
Its bonds asunder, so it speweth forth
A furious rush of whirlwind and of storm.
But since but rarely doth it thus befall,
And since on land its course must needs be barred

By mountain heights, so is it viewed more oft
On some wide sweep of sea, and in the expanse
Of open skies that spread their realms afar.

   Now clouds will gather when, as on they fly
Through these high realms of heaven, in numbers vast
Bodies of rougher mold will meet, so formed
That though in slender wise linked each on each,
Yet can they cling in union. And 'tis these
That first make tiny clouds to form, which straight
Lay hold one on another, and unite
As in a flock; and as they gather, so
They grow in bulk and drift before the winds,
Until at last a furious storm hath risen.
Then too it will befall that mountain tops,
The more their towering heights are raised aloft
Toward the sky, the more with gathering gloom
Of murky cloud they smoke; for that when first
The clouds take shape, ere yet our eyes can mark
Their slender texture, winds will waft them on
And herd them round the topmost mountain peaks;
And there at length 'twill come to pass that massed
In greater throng and denser grown, their forms
Can be discerned, till all at once they seem
E'en from the very mountain tops to rise
Into the sky. For fact and sense alike,
Whenas we scale a mountain height, proclaim
That windy regions stretch above. Again,
That nature doth upraise from all the sea
Great store of bodies will a garment prove,

As hung upon the shore it gathereth
A clinging moisture. Wherefore all the more
'Tis clear that many bodies too can rise
To swell the clouds from out the restless surge
Of the salt sea. For kindred natures mark
These moistures twain. And oft besides we see
From every stream, and e'en from earth itself
Thick mists and vapors rise, which like a breath
Breathed forth and borne aloft shroud all the sky
In their dark mystery, and as they meet
Build slowly one by one the towering clouds.
And from above as well the surging tides
Of starry ether, pressing down thereon,
Weave as it were a tapestry of cloud
Beneath the blue. And oft it will befall
That hither to these realms of sky will come
Those bodies from without which fashion clouds
And wingéd storms. For I have shown ere now
That countless is their number, and the sum
Of the vast deep doth know no measure; aye,
And I have taught thee with what wondrous speed
These bodies fly, and how in one brief breath
It is their wont to course through realms of space
That none can mark. Hence 'tis not strange if oft
In but a moment, brooding high above,
Darkness and storm will smother sea and lands
In gathering clouds, for that on every hand
Through all the ether-ways, and as it were
Through breathing-holes of all the great world round
Is given unto the flying particles
Issue and entry wheresoe'er they will.

Now list, while I unfold the wise wherein
Deep in the high-piled clouds there gathereth
The rainy moisture, and the unprisoned shower
Descendeth on the earth. First thou wilt grant
That with the clouds from out all things doth rise
Great store of seeds of moisture, and that thus
Will grow alike both clouds and whatsoe'er
Of moisture is contained therein, as e'en
Our bodies grow, together with their blood,
And sweat likewise, and all the humors held
Within the limbs. And oft besides they take
Much moisture from the sea, e'en as the wool
Of hanging fleeces, whensoe'er the winds
Will waft their masses o'er the vasty deep;
And in like wise from every stream doth rise
Its dole of moisture to the clouds. And so,
When many seeds of waters, risen in ways
Diverse, and finding increase here and yon
From many a source, have duly gathered there,
'Tis then from double cause the dense packed clouds
Would fain discharge their showers; for furious winds
Do crowd them close, and e'en their very mass,
When great their gathered throng, doth weigh them down
And crush them from above, till forth doth burst
The streaming rain. Or once again, when clouds
Grow rare before the winds, or neath the lash
Of burning rays flung from the sun above
Their texture is unknit, so will they send
Their rainy moisture forth, till all doth drip
With copious drops, e'en as a mass of wax
Over a flaming fire will melt and flow.

And heavy rain will come to pass when clouds
By either force are sore beset, by weight
Of their own mass, and thrust of harrying wind.
'Tis then the rains are wont to linger, aye,
Long is their dreary stay, when many seeds
Of waters meet, as cloud piled high with cloud
And streaming storm in one vast surge is borne
From every side, and earth in steaming mist
Doth breathe her vapors forth. And when perchance
Amid the lowering storm the sun hath flamed
With his bright beams athwart the storm-cloud's spray,
Then in a sudden glory mid the murk
Of leaden cloud doth burst the rainbow's gleam.

And all things else that come to birth above
And find their growth on high, yea, whatsoe'er
Doth gather in the storm-clouds, one and all,
Snow, winds and hail, chill frost, the mighty strength
Of ice, whose iron hand doth turn to stone
The waters, and as with a curb doth halt
The eager streams on every hand—all these
'Tis but an easy task to scan withal,
And in thy mind to mark the mode wherein
Each one doth come to be, and what the cause
Wherefrom 'tis born, when thou hast learned aright
The powers vouchsafed unto the elements.

List now, and learn what law hath been ordained
For tremblings of the earth. But first hold fast
Within thy mind that earth deep down no less
Than here above is filled on every hand

With windy caverns, and doth bear besides
Within its bosom many a lake and pool,
With many a cliff and beetling crag between;
And ample store of streams besides, deep hid
Beneath the crust of earth, roll on amain
Their surging tides and mighty boulders plunged
Beneath their waters. For plain truth, I ween,
Doth warrant that our earth in every part
Must stand like to itself. Since, then, all these
Are set beneath linked each on each, the earth
Above will tremble, stirred by mighty shock
Of falling masses, when deep down below
Slow time hath laid in ruin some cavern vast;
Yea, e'en whole mountains sink, and far and wide,
Roused by the sudden shock, doth creep abroad
An answering tremor. And with right, since oft
Will houses by a paven street, deep jarred
By passing wains of no great weight, no less
Quiver and quake whenas some rut deep worn
Within the road doth jolt the iron-shod wheels
On either side. So too it will befall
When loosed by years from earth a mighty mass
Of soil will plunge far down into the depths
Of some vast pool of water, and the earth
Beneath the heavy flood will toss and sway,
E'en as at times a vessel scarce can bide
At peace save when the liquid pent within
Hath ceased to surge and toss with shifting tide.

So, too, when winds, swift mustering through the deeps
Of earth's dim caverns, from this side or that

Leap to the assault, and gathering all their strength
Into a mighty onslaught fall amain
Upon the lofty caves, then doth the earth
Give way and lean unto that side whereto
The wind's wild surge hath swept it. And anon
High builded houses on the earth above,
The more they upward tower, will rock and sway,
And toward the selfsame side will lean, the while
Their loosened timbers hang upon the verge
Of crashing ruin. Yet mankind is loth
To trust the tale that somewhere doth await
Our mighty world a day of death and doom,
E'en though they oft behold so great a mass
Of earth sink down in ruin. Nay, were it not
That winds must pause for breath, no force, I ween,
Could set a curb on things, or rein them back
Once bent on ruin. But now, since turn by turn
They rage and pause, and as it were once more
Will rally to the charge, then yielding ground
Are beaten back again, 'tis therefore earth
More oft will havoc threaten than in truth
Make wreck of all; for backward doth it sway
E'en as it hath leaned forward, and anon
Its wayward tottering righteth and once more
Doth stand in steady poise. Thus, then, it is
That builded structures throughout all their height
Will rock, top more than midmost part, mid-zone
More than the base, and base the merest jot.

This too doth stand as cause wherefrom will rise
The mighty shock, when on a sudden wind

And some strong force of air, gathered from realms
Without, or e'en in earth itself, have swept
In mighty turmoil through her vasty caves
And swirl in whirling eddies, till anon
Their gathered force hath rent its prison, and forth
They burst upon the instant, and the earth
Deep riven apart doth yawn with gaping jaws.
E'en so in Syrian Sidon once of old
It did befall; and thus was spelled the doom
Of Peloponnesian Aegium, cities each
In ruins laid by this outrush of air
And shaking of the earth that rose therefrom.
And many a high-walled inland town besides
Hath crumbled neath some mighty shock, and oft
Have cities by the sea sunk to a grave
Deep down beneath the watery waves, with all
Who dwelt therein. And haply should it fail
To issue forth, yet will that very shock
Of air, and all the wind's wild violence,
As in a sudden fit of shivering, spread
Through all the devious ways of earth, and thus
Will set all things a-tremble; e'en as cold,
When deep into our limbs hath stolen its chill,
Doth shake them all unwilling, and provoke
A shivering movement. So throughout the ways
Of their great cities, numbed with anxious dread,
Men stand a-tremble, fearing instant doom
From houses o'er their heads, or hollowed caves
Beneath their feet, lest with a sudden blast
The power of earth should rend their walls, and ope
Wide gaping jaws whose void she fain would fill

With her own tottering ruins. Thus as they will
Let men believe that heaven and earth are dowered
With form imperishable, warded for aye
Neath some eternal safeguard; yet will oft
On this side or on that the very force
Of present peril wield its torturing goad
Of fear, lest haply, snatched from neath their feet
With sudden shock the stricken earth be hurled
Into the abyss, and all the sum of things
Go ruining after, till this world of worlds
Be left once more a formless wilderness.

    And more than all, the minds of men are prone
To marvel that no increase to the sea
Doth nature bring, since there doth come thereto
So great a flood of waters, yea, so vast
The store of streams from every clime. Add, too,
The shifting showers and scudding storms that drench
With flooding moisture every sea and land,
And add its springs as well; yet scarce will all
Beside the sea's vast sum be counted more
Than increase of a single drop. Wherefore
'Tis less of wonder if the vast sea-plains
Know naught of growth. Then doth the sun besides
By his fierce heat great part thereof withdraw;
(For oft his burning rays do we behold
To dry our dripping garments). Yet no less
Beneath our eyes the boundless seas spread wide
Their many waters. Wherefore, though he draw
From out each several place but scant supply
Of moisture from the watery plains, yet spread

O'er space so vast, great harvest doth he reap
From all the seas. Again, the winds that sweep
The watery wastes avail as well to lift
Much store of moisture, as ofttimes we see
In but a single night our roads blown dry,
Their soft mud caked in hardened crusts. Then too
I have disclosed that clouds as well will lift
Abundant moisture, drawn from out the expanse
Of ocean's plains, and far o'er all the lands
Cast it abroad what time the rains descend
Upon the earth, and swift winds drive the clouds.
And last, since earth is framed with texture rare
And bordereth on the seas, hemming their shores
On every hand, so must it needs befall
That e'en as from the lands the waters flow
Into the sea, so from the salt sea-plains
In selfsame wise back through the soil will creep
The oozing moisture drop by drop. For thus,
Its bitter brine strained through, it floweth back
And gathereth to each spring and river head,
Whence forth o'er all the lands its fresh sweet streams
It poureth, wheresoe'er its tinkling feet
Have wandered down their winding watery way.

Now what the cause that from the gaping maw
Of Aetna oft in seething turmoil breathe
His blazing fires, I shall unfold. For bent
On no small stroke of ruin hath arisen
His flaming tempest, as with tyrant hand
Stretched o'er the broad Sicilian fields he drew
Unto himself the gaze of all that dwelt

In neighboring lands, till every breast was filled
With shuddering dread at what might be the guise
Of this new horror framed by nature's hand.

Herein 'twill serve thee well to hold a view
Both wide and deep, and with appraising eye
To scan each quarter, that thou mayst recall
To mind how fathomless doth stand the sum
Of things, and so mayst mark how small a part,
Yea, infinitely small, of all that sum
Is our own heaven—a lesser part, I ween,
Than is a single man of all the earth.
And shouldst thou hold this truth set clear and plain
Before thine eyes and scan it well, so then
Would many a thing thy wonder cease to wake.
For which of us doth marvel if a man
Hath caught within his limbs a fever, risen
With burning heat, or some distemper else
Hath seized upon his members? For a foot
May swell upon a sudden, or a twinge
Of pain lay hold upon the teeth or dart
Into the eyeballs; or the holy fire [3]
May break out on the body, and anon
May spread and burn, and creeping here and there
Sear as with flame what part soe'er its fire
Hath seized upon, and spread throughout the limbs;
Because, we may be sure, the seeds of things
Are many, and this earth and heaven do hold

wwwwwwwwwwwwwwwwwwwwwwww

[3] The Romans called by the name of the Holy Fire the disease which we
know as erysipelas, or, colloquially, St. Anthony's Fire.

Large stores of taint and malady wherefrom
A force of ill unmeasured may avail
To spread abroad. So then we must suppose
That from the infinite in store so vast
All things may be supplied through all the realms
Of heaven and earth, that, stirred with sudden shock,
Earth may be moved, and over sea and land
May sweep the rapid whirlwind, and the fire
Of Aetna burst its bounds, till all the heavens
Are bright with flame. (Thus, too, it doth befall,
And all the dome of heaven doth blaze, and storms
Of rain arise in greater mass, whene'er
The seeds of waters thus have chanced to throng.)
'But,' thou wilt say, 'exceeding great doth rise
The seething fury of this blaze!' So be;
And thus likewise that stream which mightiest
Doth seem to him who ne'er before hath viewed
A greater; so a tree, a man, will seem
Exceeding huge, and whatsoe'er each one
Hath seen the mightiest in its kind, all these
He fain would hold gigantic; yet if all
Were set together, yea, with heaven and earth
And sea besides, still would they stand as naught
Before the vast eternal sum of sums.

But now what are the ways whereby that flame,
Roused on a sudden from the vasty deeps
Of Aetna's furnaces, doth breathe abroad,
I shall unfold. First, then, through all the height
Of this vast mountain doth his nature stand
Deep hollowed out beneath, and everywhere

On flinty vaults doth rest. Then every cave
Is filled with wind and air; for wind doth rise
When air is stirred to movement; and anon
As it hath gathered heat, and by its rage
Hath kindled rocks and earth on every hand
Where'er its force hath fallen, and struck therefrom
Fires hot with leaping flames, straightway itself
Will swiftly rise aloft, and high above
Cleave through the midst the mountain's very jaws.
So doth it fling its heat afar, and far
Doth waft its ash and roll a thick black murk
Of smoke abroad, the while it hurleth forth
Great stones of wondrous weight; lest thou be prone
To doubt this untamed force may be of air.
And in great part the sea doth dash its waves
And draw into itself its flooding tides
E'en at his very roots. Yea, from its deeps
Great caverns spread beneath, their hollows joined
With his deep yawning mouth. So by this path
We must confess the waters pass within;
And clear fact, too, doth urge belief that wind
Is mixt therewith, and from the sea doth find
An entry deep within; then forth will breathe
Its mighty blast, lifting therewith a mass
Of flame, yea, casting up great rocks withal,
And clouds of dust. For at the topmost peak
Lie craters, as the folk who dwell hard by
Do name them, while we term them jaws or mouths

Some things there are as well whereof to tell
One cause sufficeth not, but we must name

Yet others in whose ranks the one true cause
May well be numbered; as, wert thou to see
Lying apart the body of a man
Whence life had fled, so were it meet to name
Each several cause of death, that one thereof
Might sort with truth. For neither couldst thou prove
He met his death by steel, or cold, or seized
By some distemper, or mayhap from draught
Of poison. But we know somewhat akin
To these hath sealed his fate. And so likewise
In many a case we well may hold the same.

    The Nile alone of all the streams of earth
Doth rise at summer's advent and o'erflow
The plains of all the land of Egypt, yea,
Oft e'en in summer's midmost heat his floods
Will drench the fields with moisture, since 'tis then,
In summer's prime, those northern gales, which now
Men name etesian winds pursue their course
Set dead against his mouths, and with their blasts
Breasting his tides they check and stem his flow,
Till all his channel, choked with high-heaped floods,
Doth halt its current. For beyond all doubt
Those blasts that rise amid the frosty signs
That gird the pole sweep full against his stream,
While he doth journey from the southern climes
Where heat doth reign, rising amidst the tribes
Of black-skinned men burnt by the sun, a realm
Far inland in the region of midday.
Or haply it may be that heaps of sand
May choke his mouths and bar his surging waves,

Whenas the sea, deep churned by harrying winds,
Doth drive the sand within; and thus 'twill chance
His stream hath less free issue, and his floods
Likewise are hampered in their downward flow.
Or it may be perchance that at his source
Rains more abundant in this season fall,
Since toward those regions then the etesian blasts
Of northwinds herd the scudding clouds. And there,
When they have gathered, banished unto realms
Of midday, so at length the clouds, packed close
About the towering mountain tops, are chafed
And sore beset. Or haply, too, his floods
May swell from deep amidst the lofty heights
Of Ethiopia, where with melting rays
The all-beholding sun doth make the fields
Of glittering snow run down unto the plains.

Now list, while I unfold to thee the tale
Of all those regions and those pools we term
Avernian, and with what nature dowered
They have their being. First, the very name
Avernian is assigned them from their deeds
And wonted ways,[4] since deadly bane they prove
To birds of every kind; for when in flight

wwwwwwwwwwwwwwwwwwwwwwwwww

[4] Avernian districts, so called from the Greek *aornos,* birdless, are regions
which exhale vapors that are fatal to any bird which flies over them. The
best known is the region of Lake Avernus, near Cumae, in the vicinity
of Naples. Because of the mysterious nature of this district, Roman superstition placed near Lake Avernus the entrance to the lower world. In
ancient times there appeared to have been other localities of similar nature, notably on the Acropolis at Athens, and in Syria.

Full o'er these spots they soar, straightway forgot
Is all their sweep of wing; they slacken sail,
And, neck adroop, fall headlong to the earth,
If such the region's nature, or will plunge
Into the water's depths if so it be
Avernus' pool doth chance to spread beneath.
And hard by Cumae is that spot, where choked
With reeking sulphur and enriched with store
Of boiling springs the very mountains smoke.
Then too there is a place within the walls
Of Athens, yea, upon the very height
Loved of Tritonian Pallas, giver of life,
Where ne'er a harsh-voiced crow [5] will deign to reef
His full-spread wings, e'en when the altars smoke
With sumptuous offerings; so wide their flight
They wing, albeit not from bitter wrath
Of Pallas at their vigil, as have sung
The poets of the Greeks, but 'tis the place
By its own nature bringeth all to pass.
In Syria too, men say, there may be seen
A spot whose baneful breath, whene'er the breeds
Of fourfoot beasts have once set foot thereon,
Constraineth them to sink to earth, as felled
By sudden slaughtering stroke in votive rite

wwwwwwwwwwwwwwwwwwwww

[5] According to an early Greek tradition, Erechtheus, mythical king of
Athens, was born with the combined form of a human infant and a
serpent. Pallas (Athena) put the child in a chest, which she entrusted to
the care of the daughters of Cecrops, with express instructions that the
chest should not be opened. The two eldest disobeyed, and opened the
chest; whereupon a watchful crow flew off with the news to Pallas, who
in anger expelled it and all other crows forever from her Acropolis.

To gods below. Yet one and all of these
By natural laws are shaped, and clear doth stand
The birth and cause thereof; lest one perchance
Might deem the gate of Orcus hath been set
In these domains, and haply hold that hence
The gods of darkness lead men's souls below
To shores of Acheron; e'en as 'tis thought
That stags of wingéd feet by their own scent
Will oft drag forth from out their lairs the breeds
Of crawling serpents. Yet how far removed
From reasoning true all this doth stand, give ear
And learn; for now I shall essay to tell
The fact itself.

First, I assert once more
A truth which oft ere now I have proclaimed
As well, that in the earth lie shapes of things
Of every kind, many whereof are meet
For food and vital needs, while many hold
Seeds of disease, and speed the wings of death.
And how for breeds diverse things all unlike
Are fit for needs of life, I have ere this
Disclosed, for that their natures each from each
At variance stand, their textures varied, aye,
And e'en the shapes of their first elements.
And so into our ears doth many a thing
Enter with hurt, and many harsh to touch
Pass e'en into our nostrils; others still
There are, not few in number, which should best
Be shunned by touch, or by the sight of eye
Avoided, or will bitter prove to taste.

Next we may see how many things are fraught
With hurtful influence to man, and prove
Both foul and noxious. First, to certain trees
Is given a shade so baneful that ofttimes
'Twill bring an aching to the head if one
Hath lain beneath stretched out upon the sward.
A tree there is besides upon the heights
Of Helicon which by the noxious scent
Its blossoms breathe is wont to kill a man.
All these, we may be sure, in this wise spring
From out the ground, because the earth doth hold
Within itself abundant store of seeds
Of many things, mingled in many a wise,
And one by one doth bring them to the light.
Then too, a lamp at night, when newly quenched,
Meeting the nostrils with its pungent reek
Will straightway lull to sleep one who is prone
To fall and foam with dread distemper's stroke.
So too a woman from the heavy scent
Of musky castor oftentimes will sink
Into a drowse, the while her gay-hued work
Doth slip unheeded from her slender hands,
If so be she hath smelt it in the time
Her monthly flow is on her. Many a thing
Besides there is, the which throughout our frame
Will loose the drooping members, and constrain
The very soul to totter on its throne
Within our body. So, if filled with food
Beyond thy wont thou tarry in a bath
Of heated water, with what ease thou'lt chance
To faint and fall amid the steaming reek!

And smell of charcoal will an entry find
Into the brain, unless with careful heed
We quaff large draughts of water. And whene'er
A burning fever, mastering all our limbs,
Hath seized upon us, then the smell of wine
Is as a slaughtering blow. And seest not too
E'en in the earth how sulphur is begot
And pitch doth cake in crusts of noisome stench?
Or, once again, when probing with the pick
Deep in the hidden ways of earth, men trace
The veins of gold or silver, what foul reek
From deep beneath Scaptensula [6] doth breathe!
And what rank breath the mines of gold exhale!
How strange they make men's faces, yea, e'en change
Their very color! Hast not seen and heard
How they are wont in but brief time to die,
And how life's powers will fail in those whom force
Of dire necessity imprisoneth there
In toil so grievous? All these vapors then
Doth earth send steaming forth, and breathe abroad
Into the clear wide spaces of the sky.

So these Avernian regions too must needs
Waft up to birds some deadly fumes, which rise
From out the earth into the air, and thus
They taint the expanse of heaven in this domain
Or that; and soon as e'er on speeding wing
A bird is thither borne, 'tis halted there
Seized by the secret bane, and straight doth fall

[6] A town in Thrace, celebrated for its silver mines.

E'en toward the very spot wherefrom arise
The deadly vapors. And once fallen thereon
The selfsame force of that envenomed air
Doth wrest from all its limbs the dole of life
That still remaineth. For at first 'twill bring
A surge of faintness; then 'twill come to pass,
When it hath plunged into the very source
Of deadly taint, that there it must perforce
Breathe forth its life as well, since all about
Doth lie a plenteous store of bitter bane.

Or it may be at times the violent force
Of this Avernian breath may thrust aside
The air that hath its place betwixt the birds
And earth below, till in its room is left
A well-nigh empty space. And when in flight
They soar full o'er this spot, straightway the lift
Of their strong pinions faltereth, shorn of use,
And all the effort of their beating wings
On either side doth fail; and when no more
Can they avail to struggle or to rest
Upon their wings, then nature, as is meet,
By their own weight constraineth them to sink
Upon the ground; and, lying helpless there
In all but empty space, they cast abroad
Their dying souls through all the body's pores.

Again, in summer colder doth become
The water in our wells, since all the earth
Groweth more rare with heat, and if mayhap
Itself hath seeds of warmth, 'twill cast them forth

Into the air. Thus then, the more the earth
Is robbed of heat, the colder will become
The moisture it doth hold concealed within.
And in its turn when all the earth is gripped
By cold, and doth contract, and as it were
More solid grow, then as 'twere meet 'twill chance
That as it shrinketh, so into the wells
Will it exude the heat itself doth hold.

'Tis said there floweth hard by Ammon's shrine
A spring in daylight cold, but in the hours
Of darkness it doth warmer grow. Whereat
Men marvel greatly, and would fain believe
That by the sun's fierce heat beneath the earth
'Tis made to boil in haste, when night hath wrapt
The earth in darkness dread. But this, I ween,
Is banished far from truth and reasoning sound.
For surely, when the sun with warm caress
Touching the spring's uncovered body, scarce
Could heat it on its outward side, though blest
With warmth so great his light in air above,
How, pray, beneath the earth, whose frame doth stand
So densely massed, could he contrive to make
The water seethe and boil, and fill it full
Of furious heat? And all the more when scarce,
For all his blazing rays, can he avail
E'en through the walls of houses to diffuse
His piercing heat? What then doth stand as cause?
'Tis this, we may be sure: that all the soil
About the spring is warmer and more rare
Than elsewhere in the earth, and many seeds

Of fire there be which lie dispersed about
The body of the water. Hence, when night
With dewy shadows veileth all the earth,
Straightway her soil is chilled deep down within
And doth contract; whereby it doth befall
As pressed by some strong hand, 'twill cause to flow
Into the fount whatever store it hath
Of seeds of heat, the which in turn bring touch
Of warmth unto its streams. But when the sun
New rising with his genial rays doth part
The earth asunder, and with mounting heat
Hath made it grow more rare, then back once more
Into their old abodes anon will creep
The particles of fire, and to the earth
Retireth all the water's heat. And thus
The spring will colder grow in light of day.
Then too, the water's moisture by the rays
The sun doth cast is troubled, and by day
Doth rarer grow beneath his shimmering heat;
And hence it is that it doth lose forthwith
Whatever seeds of fire it hath; as oft
'Twill yield its deep-hid store of frost, and melt
Its ice, and loose the bonds that held it fast.

There is besides an icy spring whereon
If tow be laid, straightway it catcheth fire
And casteth forth a flame; yea, e'en a torch
Is likewise kindled and doth shed a gleam
Across the waters as it floateth, driven
Before the breezes; since, no doubt, there lie
Within the water many seeds of heat,

And from the very earth beneath there needs
Must rise aloft through all the spring a store
Of fiery bodies which at once are breathed
Abroad and issue forth into the air,
Yet not in throngs so vast that all the spring
Doth seethe with heat; wherefore they are constrained
As by some force within to issue forth
In thinly scattered ranks with sudden bursts
From out the water's depths, and, risen above,
Join there in union. E'en as there is found
Within the sea at Aradus a spring
That gusheth forth with waters sweet, and wide
On every hand doth part the ocean's brine;
And so, in many a spot besides, the main
To thirsting seamen doth vouchsafe the boon
Of sweet relief, since mid its salty pools
It poureth water fresh. So too, those seeds
Of heat in this cold spring of ours are wont
To burst their way and flow abroad; and when
They gather in the tow, or haply cling
Unto the substance of the torch, straightway
With readiness they kindle to a blaze,
Since tow and torch alike hold many seeds
Of fire well hid within. And seest not too
When thou dost hold a fresh-snuffed taper close
To some bright burning night-lamp, ere it touch
The flame 'tis all ablaze? And so it is
With any torch as well. And many things
Besides, when touched by heat alone, will burst
Into a blaze ere yet the flame itself

Hath reached them close at hand. This then as well
We must suppose doth in our spring befall.

And next I shall essay to tell withal
The law of nature whence doth come to pass
That strength of iron availeth to be drawn
Unto that stone the Greeks are wont to name
The magnet,[7] from the land that gave it birth,
Since first 'twas found, they say, within the realms
Of the Magnetes. And upon this stone
Men gaze with wonder; for it oft will forge
A chain of rings suspended from itself;
Yea, five or even more may one discern
At times, hung down in order, and asway
With every breath of air, as one doth hang
Upon another, clinging from beneath,
As through its fellow each doth come to feel
The stone's firm fettering force; so armed with power
Of penetration doth its might prevail.

In matters of this sort full many a truth
Must needs be firmly stablished ere thou come
To spell the secret of the thing itself,
And long must be the winding path whereby
Thou must approach thereto. Wherefore the more
Do I bespeak attentive ear and mind.

---

[7] The lodestone, or natural magnet, was well known to both the Greeks
and the Romans, who, because it occurred plentifully in the district of
Magnesia near the Aegean coast, gave it the name of *magnes*, or the
Magnesian stone. In English-speaking countries the ore is commonly
known as magnetite.

First, from all things of whatsoever kind
We can behold, it needs must be that e'er
Do flow and fly abroad to every side
Bodies that strike the eye and stir our sight,
The while from others ebb unceasing streams
Of scent, e'en as from rivers cold will flow,
Or heat from out the sun, or briny spray
Upriseth from the billows of the main
To gnaw the walls that line some rockbound shore.
So too do voices diverse in their sound
Fly ever through the air; or now the tang
Of salty moisture lingereth on our lips
As by the sea we wander; or 'twill chance
That quite in other wise, as we behold
A draught of wormwood mixt with water, straight
There riseth in the mouth a bitter taste.
With flow so unremitting from each thing
Is borne its flux appropriate, shed abroad
To every quarter from each side; nor aught
Of pause or respite to this flow is given,
Since constant is our feeling, and 'tis ours
To grasp alway sight, scent, and sound of things.

Now would I venture to recall once more
How all things stand with body rare; a truth
Which in my earlier verses shineth clear.
For while 'twill serve thee well to write this word
Upon thine heart for many a cause besides,
'Twere meet above all else in this whereof
I now essay to speak, to hold assured
That naught doth stand in view save it be framed

Of mingled void and body. First, we see
That oft in caves the rocks that hang above
Will teem with moisture till the trickling drops
Drip down from every side. So too, doth sweat
Ooze forth from out our body; beard and hair
Will grow on all our limbs and members; food
Is spread through all the veins, yea, and doth bring
Increase and nurture to our inmost parts,
E'en to the very nails. Cold, too, and genial heat
We feel to pass through bronze, aye, feel it creep
Through gold and silver, as we duly hold
A well-filled cup. Voices will likewise fly
Through walls of stone-built houses, smell and cold
Find entry, and the heat of fire, which oft
Is wont to pierce e'en through the strength of iron.
And last, e'en where the breastplate of the sky
Doth gird the earth about, there enter in
Bodies of cloud and seeds of raging storms,
And force of ills withal that from without
An entrance find; and tempests mustering
From earth and heaven will hasten, as is meet,
To distant realms of sky and earth, since naught
There is but hath within a texture rare.

　　Add this as well, that not all bodies cast
From off each several thing are dowered with sense
Of like effect, nor in the selfsame wise
To all things suited. First of all, the sun
Doth bake and parch the ground, but winter's ice
He melteth, and doth make the drifted snows
Upon the mountain heights run down in streams

Beneath his rays. And wax will liquefy
In his fierce heat. So too, will fire constrain
Cold bronze to yield its hardness, and will loose
The bonds of gold; but hides and flesh 'twill make
To shrink and draw together. Yet the touch
Of water's moisture hardeneth iron fresh drawn
From flaming fire, while skins and flesh, made hard
By heat, 'twill render soft. Wild olive's taste
Doth bring to bearded goats as keen delight
As though 'twere rich with soothing savor steeped
In rare ambrosia, or the very balm
Of nectar; yet for man no plant doth spring
To swelling leaf a bitterer meat than this.
Again, a sow is wont to shun the taste
Of marjoram, and look with dread on oil
Of any kind; for these to bristling swine
Are deadly bane, whereas to us they seem
Ofttimes to bring refreshment. But in wise
Quite opposite, while mud to us doth seem
The foulest filth, this very thing is seen
To be to swine a pleasure, that therein
They wallow without stint, nor e'er are filled.

This still remaineth, which I hold 'twere well
To call to mind ere I essay to touch
The theme itself. Since many pores there be
To various things assigned, 'twere meet that these
Be dowered with natures differing each from each,
And keeping each its own peculiar mold
And its appropriate paths. For verily
In living creatures there doth dwell a range

Of varied senses, each whereof in wise
Its own admitteth to itself whate'er
Will prove its proper object. For we see
That through this door will enter sounds, through that
The taste from savors, while a third will ope
The gate to scent of odors. And again,
One thing is seen to pierce through rocks, through wood
Another; this will pass through gold, while that
Will find an outward path through glass, or this
Through silver. For 'tis clear that by one road
Stream images, while by another heat
Doth pass upon its way; and one will prove
To speed along the selfsame course at pace
More swift than others. This, we make no doubt,
The nature of the paths doth bring to pass,
For that in many ways it varieth,
As we have shown but now, since all unlike
The nature and the texture of all things.

  Wherefore, when all these things have once been set
Upon foundation sure, designed with care
And fashioned to our use, an easy task
'Twill be to build thereon our theme, and bring
Into the light the cause which doth attract
The strength of iron. First, it needs must be
That from the stone doth stream an ample store
Of seeds, or haply it may be a draft,
Which by its thrust doth part the tract of air
Which hath its wonted place betwixt the stone
And ring of iron. And when this space between
Is emptied, and much room midway is changed

To void, straightway will forward leap a throng
Of first beginnings of the iron, and fall
Still joined in one within the void, whereon
The ring itself will follow, moving thus
With all its body. Nor is aught, I ween,
More closely linked in its first elements
All woven in one than is the natural strength
Of sturdy iron, and its cold roughness. Hence
'Tis less of marvel, since its elements
Are such as I have shown, if no great store
Of bodies springing from the iron can sweep
Into the void, save that the ring itself
Must follow after; yea, and thus it doth,
And followeth on till it hath reached at length
The stone itself whereto with fastenings
Unseen it clingeth. And on every hand
The same befalleth: on which side soe'er,
Athwart, above, room changeth into void,
So are the neighboring bodies borne forthwith
Into the vacant space. For driven by blows
From source without they move, nor e'er, 'tis clear,
Can of themselves rise upward through the air.
And this likewise we mark, which hath its part
In furtherance hereof, yea, doth promote
This very movement, since when once the air
Before the ring doth rarer grow, and more
And more its erstwhile room is left unfilled
And tenantless, straightway 'twill come to pass
That all the air which hath its place behind
Will drive as 'twere the ring before, and thrust
Its body forward. For the air set round

On every side doth never cease to smite
Upon all things; but in such case 'twill chance
To thrust the iron before it, since beyond
There lieth empty space which doth receive
The ring into itself. Then doth this air
Whereof I speak, threading its tenuous way
Amongst the iron's close latticed pores, attain
At last its tiny particles, and thrust
And drive it forward, e'en as wind will waft
A vessel under sail. Again, all things
Must needs hold air within their frame, since rare
They are of body, and the air is set
Close round them each and all. 'Tis then this air
Deep hid within the iron that e'er is tossed
With restless motion, and 'tis thus, no doubt,
'Twill smite the ring and stir it deep within;
Whereat, e'en as 'twere meet, the ring is borne
Toward that same side whereto it first did move
In headlong haste, striving with might and main
To reach its goal within that empty spot.

Then too, from time to time it will befall
That iron's nature from the stone will move
In quick retreat, yea, e'en is prone to flee
And follow turn by turn. Nay, I have seen
Rings forged of Samothracian iron leap up,
And iron filings in a brazen bowl
Move in a frenzy when a magnet stone
Was held beneath. So eagerly they seemed
To strive to flee the stone. But when the brass
Is set between, straightway there doth arise

A mighty discord, since, we may be sure,
When once the effluence from the brass hath seized
With sudden force the open passageways
Within the iron and entered in, thereon
There followeth the effluence from the stone,
And findeth all the iron choked, nor path
Is left wherethrough it might find way to stream
As in aforetime. Hence it is constrained
To beat and buffet with its surging tide
The very texture of the iron; and thus
'Twill banish from itself, and through the brass
Will drive afar that very thing which else
It commonly will draw into its frame.

Herein forbear to marvel that the tide
That streameth from this stone can not avail
To move yet other things in selfsame wise;
For armed with solid weight will some things stand
Unmoved, as gold, while some, since they are framed
Of body rare wherethrough the streaming tides
Pass all untouched, can ne'er to any side
Be driven; amongst which kind are seen to stand
All things of woody substance. But betwixt
These twain doth lie the frame of iron; and so,
When it hath drawn into itself a store
Of particles of brass, 'tis then at length
It doth befall that with their streaming tides
The magnet stones will drive it on before.

And yet these powers to other things besides
Are not so alien that but scanty store

Is mine to tell of things of selfsame kind,
Each singly meet for each. First thou dost see
That stones by mortar's strength alone are held
In union; wood is firmly joined by naught
Save neat's glue; in such wise that e'en the grain
Of boards will yawn in cracks, ere yet the bonds
Of glue will loose their hold. So too the juice
Born of the grape with ease will deign to mix
With water's flowing streams, while heavy pitch
And swimming olive oil refuse. So too
To wool alone will cling the purple dye
Of Tyrian shell, and in such wise that ne'er
Can it be quenched, e'en though thou be at pains
With Neptune's wave its whiteness to restore,
Nay, should the sea entire, with all its floods
Essay to wash it clean. Or, once again,
Hath not one thing alone the power to bind
Gold unto gold? And brass to brass is fused
By use of tin. And many a case besides
Might we discover; but of what avail?
No need hast thou of long and devious ways,
Nor were it meet that I my toil should spend
In such endeavors, but 'twere best, I ween,
In brief and scanty words to sum the whole.
For 'tis those things whose textures each on each
So aptly fall that voids and solids meet,
This unto that and that to this, that link
In closest union. And at times 'twill chance
That fettered each to each they may be held
As 'twere knit fast by rings and hooks; and thus
It doth appear in this our stone and iron.

Next, what may be the law of plagues, and whence
Doth on a sudden rise the fatal force
Of fell disease, to breathe its deadly bane
Upon the race of men and on the herds
Of kine, I shall unfold. First, I have shown
Ere now that seeds of many things abide
Meet for our life, and many too that fly
On every hand which breed disease and death.
And when perchance they meet in random throngs
And taint the sky, then all the air is filled
With dread distemper. So doth all this force
Of bane and pestilence arise from source
Without the earth, and through the skies descend,
As clouds and mists; or haply gathereth
Ofttimes and riseth from the earth itself
When, filled with moisture, lashed with flooding rains
And burning suns, it hath assumed therefrom
Unwonted foulness. Seest not too how they
Who journey far from home and native skies
Are oft assailed by strangeness of the airs
And untried waters, for no reason else
Than that all things are unaccustomed? Aye,
For how at variance may we deem the clime
The Britons know and that which broodeth o'er
The plains of Egypt, where in crippled wise
Doth slant the axis of the earth; how wide
A difference doth lie betwixt the skies
Of Pontus and of Gades, and beyond
E'en to the tribes of black-skinned men deep burned
By scorching suns. And even as we see
These fourfold climes that lie apart, spread wide

Neath the four winds and quarters of the sky,
At variance each with each, so will be seen
Men's color and their faces to be marked
With aspects widely varied; so will ills
Diverse lay hold upon their races, each
According to its kind. For thus doth rage
The elephant disease,[8] which hath its rise
Along the waters of the Nile, deep hid
In midmost Egypt, nor doth e'er prevail
In any region else. In Attic realms
Men's feet will ail, but in Achaean lands
'Tis eyes that are assailed. And so each place
Will bring to various parts and limbs its meed
Of bane, whereof the diverse airs are cause.
Thus when an atmosphere that may be prone
To work us harm doth set itself astir,
And its distempered air hath once begun
To creep, as fog or mist doth slowly drag
Its crawling length, blighting with taint and change
All things where'er it goeth, then at last,
When it hath gained our sky it doth thereto
Corruption bring, and make it all at one
With its own nature, and a bane to us.
And so with sudden stroke the deadly force
Of this unwonted pestilence doth fall
Upon the crops or other food besides
Of human kind, or forage of the flocks;

wwwwwwwwwwwwwwwwwwwwwww

8 The "elephant disease", known as elephantiasis, is a lymphatic disease
characterized by extreme roughness and wartiness of the skin, and often
by excessive swelling of one or both legs.

Or haply its pollution will remain
Poised in the very air, and when we draw
With every breath these mingled airs, perforce
We take into our frame the taint as well.
And in like wise the pestilence will fall
Upon the herds, and mid the laggard flocks
Of bleating sheep will spread the fateful scourge
Of the distemper. And it mattereth not
Whether we fare to regions fraught with ill
Unto our bodies, and perchance may change
The mantle of the heavens, or if so be
Nature of her own will doth haply bring
On us a tainted sky, or aught besides
Unwonted to our use, the which by force
Of very suddenness may bring us low.

Such was the manner of that fateful breath
Of pestilence [9] that once in Cecrops' realms
Spread death o'er all the fields, made streets a waste,
And drained the city of its folk. For risen
Far down in Egypt's borders, sweeping o'er
A vast expanse of air and brimming plains
Of ocean, did it come at last to brood

~~~~~~~~~~~~~~~~~~~~~~~~~~~~~~~~

[9] This masterly description of the plague at Athens (430 B.C.) is borrowed from Thucydides. As in Lucretius' time, so in our day, the medical
profession is still unable to identify this and other visitations of such
"plagues" that have ravaged various sections of Europe and Asia. The
disease has been identified with measles, scarlet fever, smallpox, bubonic
plague, typhus fever, malignant scarlatina, yellow fever, and others; yet,
despite Lucretius' detailed description of symptoms, there can be no
certainty.

O'er all Pandion's race, whence horde on horde
Were yielded up to sickness and to death.
And at the first they felt the head to burn
With fever, both the eyes grew red, and glazed
With an unwonted brightness; now the throat
Was black within and oozed with blood, while choked
And sore beset was all the voice's path
With burning ulcers; yea, the tongue itself,
The spokesman of the mind, would drip with blood,
Weakened with pain, heavy in movement, rough
To touch. And thereupon, when through the throat
The bitter seizure's strength had filled the breast
And gathered e'en into the anguished heart
Of the afflicted, then in truth were loosed
The very fastenings of life. The breath
Rolled forth from out the mouth a noisome stench,
E'en as doth rise from rotting carcasses
Cast out unburied. Yea, and faint would grow
Forthwith the strength of all the mind and force
Of the whole body, as e'en now it lay
Before death's very threshold. And withal
Upon their torturing pains would e'er attend
An anxious anguish and the mingled sound
Of moans and sobbing. And through night and day
A constant retching ever and again
Would rack their limbs unceasingly, till, all
Their feeble forces shattered, they would lie
Outworn, whose slender strength was spent before.
And yet in none thereof couldst thou discern
The outer skin upon the frame to burn
With feverish heat, but rather 'twould present

Unto the hand a general touch of mild
And gentle warmth, the while in every part
'Twas flushed with redness, as with cankered sores
Of deep-burned ulcers, e'en as is its wont
When o'er the limbs is spread the holy fire.
But to their very bones the inmost parts
Of men would burn, and in the stomach raged
A flame as in a furnace. Nor could aught,
However thin and light, upon their limbs
Afford relief to any, but 'twas wind
And cold they craved alway. And some would cast
Their fevered limbs into the icy streams,
Hurling their naked bodies with a leap
Into the waters. Many a one would plunge
Headlong into the cooling watery depths
Of some chance well, seeking to meet its flood
With mouth agape. And still their quenchless thirst,
E'en though it drowned their bodies, yet could make
An ample deluge of no more avail
Than tiny trickling drops. Nor aught of rest
Was there from ill; men laid their bodies down
In utter weariness. The healer's art
Muttered in dread despair, as o'er and o'er
They turned on them wide fevered eyes that knew
No balm of sleep. And many a sign of death
Besides would meet their view: the mind's estate
Distraught with pain and fear, the gloomy brow,
The strained and frenzied mien, the ears beset
And plagued with ringing sounds, the breath quick
    drawn
Or rare and sluggish, drops of glistening sweat

Upon the neck, the spittle thin and scant,
Infused with saffron tinge and salt to taste,
Brought up with torture through the throat by dint
Of hollow coughing. In the hands as well
The sinews ceased not to contract, the limbs
To tremble, and a numbing chill to creep
Up from the feet at slow relentless pace.
Likewise, as drew the final moment near,
The nostrils were compressed, and pinched and thin
The nose along its tip, deep sunk the eyes,
The temples hollow, skin grown hard and cold,
The lips drawn in a grin, the forehead tense
And swollen. And at no long interval
Therefrom their limbs would lie stretched stiff in death.
For with the eighth bright splendor of the sun,
Or neath his ninth clear torch would they give o'er
The light of life. And if so be that one
Thereof had 'scaped the stroke of doom, no less
In after days would languishing and death
Await him still, beset with noisome sores
And black and fetid purging; or ofttimes
With aching head a flow of tainted blood
Would pour from out his nostrils; for thereto
Would stream amain his very strength, yea, all
His body's life. Or haply when a man
Had 'scaped this cruel flow of poisoned blood,
Yet would the sore affliction find its way
Into his sinews and his limbs, and e'en
Invade his generative parts. And some
In crushing fear of death's approach would choose
To live shorn by the knife of manhood's signs,

While some would cling to life bereft of hands
Or feet, and others wanting eyes, so sharp
A fear of death had seized them in its grasp.
And some there were on whom forgetfulness
Of all things laid its hold, till e'en themselves
They could not know. And though in countless heaps
Bodies on bodies lay upon the ground
Unburied, yet the tribes of birds and beasts
Would range afar, that so they might escape
The bitter stench, or haply drawing near
To taste thereof, would forthwith droop and fall
In instant death. And yet not oft, forsooth,
In those dread days would any bird appear,
Or would the sullen breeds of beasts come forth
From out their forest lairs. For many a one
Would droop with pain and die. And more than all
The faithful breed of dogs in agony
Would yield their lives, strewn wide through every street;
For from their limbs the seizure's violence
Would wrest the very life. And everywhere
In furtive haste, as if in rivalry,
Deserted biers were hurried by, with none
To mourn. Nor aught was found to bring relief
To all alike; for what to one had given
The strength to draw within his lips the breath
Of sweet life-giving air, and lift his gaze
To regions of the sky, to others oft
Would prove a bane, and brought them low in death.

And this one thing besides, mid all this grief,
Was pitiful and fraught with deepest woe,

That each man as he saw himself entrapped
In toils of the contagion, knowing well
That he was doomed to death, all courage lost,
Would lie with hopeless heart, and bent on death
Would then and there yield up his soul to doom.
Nor e'er for one brief moment would the stroke
Of ravening pestilence forbear to seize
On one upon another, as on flocks
Of woolly sheep or horned herds. And this
Beyond all else heaped death on death: for all
Who shunned to tend their own afflicted, moved
By greed for life and fear of death, themselves
In after days their cruel carelessness
Would punish with a death of shame and fraught
With deep disgrace, outcast and reft of help.
But those who had stood by would yield their lives
To the corruption and the grinding toil
They were constrained for honor's sake to bear
By pleading voices of the weary, joined
With murmur of complaining. Thus it was
That all the worthier ones would meet their death.
And as men vied in laying in the grave
Their host of dead, piled one on other, so
Worn out with weeping and with woe they took
Their homeward way, whereat the greater part
Would seek their beds from grief. Nor yet could one
Be found in this dread time who had been left
Untouched by pain, or death, or sorrow's blight.

    And so by now each keeper of the flock,
And every herdsman, and all they who drove

The curving plow, had fallen a helpless prey
To weary languor, and their bodies thrust
Within some rude hut's walls would lie unmarked,
Consigned to death by want and taint of ill.
Oft on their lifeless offspring thou mightst see
The lifeless forms of parents, and again
Young children yielding up the breath of life
Upon their very mothers and their sires.
In no small measure, too, this grievous blight
Streamed from the fields into the town, conveyed
By all the sickly hordes of peasant folk
That thronged from every side, touched with the taint
Of the distemper, filling all the ways
And all the houses; wherefore all the more,
Packed close within the town, death piled them high
In huddling heaps. And many a body, too,
Dragged forth by thirst, and tumbled heels o'er head
Along the streets, lay strewn beside the marge
Of water-fountains, reft of life's sweet breath
By water's fatal sweetness; many a one
Full plain to view throughout the open squares
And once thronged streets thou mightst have seen, with
    limbs
Drooping upon their half-dead bodies, foul
With filth and rags, doomed to a living death
Through squalor of the body, seeming naught
Save skin and bones, and all but buried now
In dirt and sores. And now grim death had filled
E'en all the holy shrines of gods with heaps
Of lifeless bodies, all the temples blest
With heavenly presences on every side

Were choked with carcasses, for every place
The temple guardians had filled with guests.
So little now the worship of the gods
Could profit, or their presence; for the sense
Of present sorrow had o'ertopped it all.
No more within the city did prevail
That ancient burial rite wherewith till now
This pious folk had e'er been wont to lay
Their dead away; for all the folk abode
Disordered and dismayed, and every man
In sorrow laid his own away as best
His present need might urge; and many a shift
The sudden crisis prompted, and the curse
Of pinching want; for oft with outcries loud
They laid their kin on pyres built high by hands
Of others, and would set the torch thereto,
Wrangling with fierce and bloody strife, or e'er
They should desert the bodies of their own.[10]

[10] It seems hardly credible that Lucretius should have closed his great
work abruptly with the description of the plague at Athens. See Introduction for further evidence as to the unfinished state of the poem.

CRITICAL APPENDIX

BOOK ONE

599. I have incorporated here Munro's suggested verses to fill an obvious gap:
corporibus, quod iam nobis minimum esse videtur
debet item ratione pari minimum esse cacumen

860. One or more verses are lost here, of which the sense is given, following the stop-gap suggested by Lambinus:
et nervos alienigenis ex partibus esse

873. Munro's interpolation here again seems to be the best available:
ex alienigenis quae tellure exoriuntur.
sic itidem quae ligna emittunt corpora aluntur,

998. I prefer to keep, as the least of a number of evils, the MS. order of verses 998-1001, rather than transferring them, with Munro and Bailey, to follow 983, or with Giussani, to follow 1007.

1013. Again I have followed Munro's interpolation:
sed spatium supra docui sine fine patere,
si finita igitur summa esset materiai,

1068. None of the suggested stop-gaps is completely satisfactory for the missing verses following 1093 and corresponding with the mutilated verses 1068-1075. I have therefore filled in the sense of the passage as a makeshift.

BOOK TWO

164. Missing verse supplied by Marullus, whom I have followed:

nam neque consilio debent tardata morari

461. I have followed the sense of Brieger's interpolation, adopted also by Giussani, for the missing verse or verses:

ventis differri rapidis nostrisque veneno

465. Munro's emendation of *habeto* for *debet* has been adopted for this verse. If this is the correct reading, no lacuna need be assumed.

601. For want of a more satisfactory emendation, I have adopted Lachmann's conjecture of *sublime* for *sedibus.*

681. A verse is lost here, of which I have given what appears to be the sense.

748. Munro's interpolation is here followed:

corpora quae constant nullo coniuncta colore

903. For the lost verse I have followed Munro's astute interpolation:

ipsi sensilibus, mortalia semina reddunt

BOOK THREE

84. *Suadet* has been suspected by many commentators. Certainly the abrupt shift in meaning from *hunc* in verse 82 to the repeated *hunc* of 83 is most infelicitous. I suggest reading *suavem* for *suadet,* and punctuating with

comma instead of full stop after 82. Thus all three infinitives will depend on *obliti*, and all difficulties disappear.

97. The sense of a missing verse following 97 has been supplied.

591-614. The translation here follows Guissani's arrangement.

823. The suggestion of Marullus and Lambinus has been adopted for the verse which has been lost:

scilicet a vera longe ratione remotum est

1011. A verse is needed here to complete the sense.

BOOK FOUR

126. A number of verses are lost at this point, the probable sense of which I have given.

144. No satisfactory conjecture has been made to supply the verse missing after 144. It evidently contained some such word as *expediam*.

216. A number of verses have been lost after 216. I have filled in the gap as the argument seems to demand.

289. Goebel's conjecture for the missing verse after 289 seems to be the sanest:

quasque foris res tam simili ratione videri

686. Careful study of the whole argument of this passage seems to warrant the transposition, following Susemihl and Giussani, of verses 706-721 to follow 686.

990. No conjecture for the last two feet of this verse has been satisfactory. *Saepe quiete* is of course impossible, and is an obvious repeat from 999 (991). I suggest *prodere flatum* as a way out of the difficulty. In the arrangement

of verses 990-999 I follow the generally accepted order in modern editions.

BOOK FIVE

28. Gap closed to make sense.

273. I suspect that we should read here

aera linquitur ut dicam

Cf. II 914 and V 795. *Igitur* looks suspicious.

384. It seems evident that a verse has dropped out here, as there is no correlative of *vel* in 383. It is too far a cry to verse 410, more particularly as Lucretius all through this passage is describing the two-sided battle between heat and moisture. I suggest for the missing verse:

ardorem vel cum solis restinxerit umor.

704. Munro, followed by Brieger and Bailey, interpolates here:

qui faciunt solis nova semper lumina gigni,

which is possibly the best that can be done with the passage.

1012. A verse is lost, the sense of which is clear.

1207. I should certainly uphold *pectora,* the reading of the MS. Surely there is no reason to cavil at *in pectora oppressa,* which the interlocked order clearly indicates. The obvious meaning is: 'this anxiety which (heretofore) has been crushed deep into our hearts by other ills.' Brieger's comment: 'in pectore nihil caput erigere possit nisi infra pectus sit, i.e. in ventre,' is mere flippant smartness. He has missed the point altogether. Even Giussani has created unnecessary difficulties over the passage, and the same is true of Munro. Merrill's makeshift in taking *in* as 'against' is gratuitous.

BOOK SIX

45ff. This passage is incomplete as it stands, a number of single verses having been lost. In the interest of consecutive interpretation I have attempted to give it a meaning.

403. I follow Giussani in transferring here verses 421-422, which are apparently out of place. The rest of the passage 400-420 follows the traditional order, as Giussani's arguments for wholesale transposition seem to lack cogency.

550. I suggest for this admittedly cryptic verse:
nec minus exultant ut sulcus cumque viai
as closer to the garbled MS. reading:
nec minus exultantes dupuis cumque viam
Sulcus is a rut in a paved street. (Note that the poet speaks of houses *propter viam,* which would suggest town houses.)

697. I have adopted Munro's interpolation for the missing verse:
fluctibus, admixtam vim venti, intrareque ab isto

839. A considerable number of verses appear to have fallen out here, possibly, as Lachmann attempts to prove, owing to the loss of a complete page of the archetype.

954. Giussani's suggestion for the sense of the missing verse seems reasonable.

1246. I do not agree with Munro, and later editions

which follow him, in the statement that 1247-49 appear to be out of place and unconnected with what precedes and follows. Neither is it necessary to assume the loss of verses after 1246. Revise the punctuation, and the passage becomes clear:

inque aliis alium populum sepelire suorum
certantes lacrimis lassi luctuque redibant;

Here *inque aliis alium* is to be taken with *sepelire*. Thus the passage gains immeasurably in consistency and forceful realism.

1262. I have adopted Lachmann's inspired emendation of *astu* for the *aestus* of the MS.